"WHY DO RULING CLASSES FEAR HISTORY?"

and Other Questions

"WHY DO RULING CLASSES FEAR HISTORY?"

and Other Questions

Harvey J. Kaye

With a Foreword by Daniel Singer

St. Martin's Press
New York

E
169.12
.K34
1996

ISBN 0-312-12691-3

Library of Congress Cataloging-in-Publication Data
Kaye, Harvey J.
    Why do ruling classes fear history? : and other questions / Harvey
J. Kaye.
        p.   cm.
    Includes bibliographical references and index.
    ISBN 0-312-12691-3
    1. United States—Intellectual life—20th century. 2. History-
-Study and teaching—United States. 3. Education—Political
aspects—United States. 4. Democracy—United States.
5. Radicalism—United States. 6. History, Modern—20th century-
-Philosophy. I. Title.
E169.12.K34 1995
306'.0973—dc20
                                                    95-36783
                                                    CIP

Book Design by Acme Art, Inc.

First Edition: January 1996
10 9 8 7 6 5 4 3 2 1

CONTENTS

FOREWORD

WE DON'T KNOW YET, said a Polish wit, what our past is going to be, and Walter Benjamin, quoted in this book, elaborates on the same theme in his "Theses on the Philosophy of History": "Only that historian will have the gift of fanning the spark of hope in the past who is firmly convinced that even the dead will not be safe from the enemy if he wins. And the enemy (the ruling class) has not ceased to be victorious." Mastery of the past is a powerful weapon in current political struggle. Amnesia paralyzes nations, not just individuals. Stalin may have been a champion of falsification, but he did not have a monopoly on the rewriting of history. The process goes on.

But has not History come to a full stop? The recently fashionable variations on this topic were themselves part and parcel of the manipulation. Francis Fukuyama and his pseudo-Hegelian predictions may now be discarded: From Bosnia to Chechnya, far from standing still, history is quickening pace. But the propaganda campaign about "the end of history" had a deeper purpose. Its main message was that capitalism is eternal.

You will notice the agility of our official pundits. A few years ago they were preaching that the "evil empire" was a hell with no exit (and this is why it was worse than Pinochet's Chile or the Greece of the colonels). As their argument naturally collapsed together with the Berlin Wall, they simply reversed it. Cleverly identifying the fall of the neo-Stalinist empire with the funeral of socialism, they now preach that it is our own system—call it paradise, hell, or purgatory—from which there is no possible escape. And, for the time being, they are successful in spreading this conviction or, rather, this mood of resignation.

Indeed, this is probably the major ideological conflict, the kulturkampf, of the period. On one side stands the establishment, using the full might of its propaganda machine to proclaim that the disintegration of Stalin's heritage is a final proof not only that there is no alternative to capitalism, but also that there can be none. To rebel individually may be just, yet any attempt to alter society radically through collective action is absurd and actually criminal, since it inevitably leads to the gulag. We are no longer to be attracted by the vision of an "American dream." We are to be repelled by a past nightmare and discouraged by the current void, the nothingness.

On the other side stands the still small band of resisters that, without promising inevitable success, tries to revive the basic belief that society, and therefore life, can be changed by collective political action. Obviously, the world is not moved by ideas alone. The future of our system will, ultimately, be determined by its own contradictions, its discontents, and by the irruption of the people onto the political stage. The timing and the very nature of that entry, however, will have much to do with the people's grasp of the issues involved and the presence of a project, the glimpse of a solution, and it is here that the intellectuals do have their important part to play.

This collection of essays shows that Harvey Kaye has been an active participant in this crucial ideological confrontation. As a historian he addresses his fellows, urging them to teach their students and the general public that "the present is history and nothing is gained without struggle"; in other words, that the current power relations or institutions have been forged in the past and can be reshaped today and tomorrow. He does not limit himself, however, to his professional colleagues. He urges intellectuals in general not to perform another *trahison des clercs*. He does not have in mind so much the custodians of the conservative consensus, who did sell their intellectual birthright, admittedly for more than a fistful of dollars. He thinks more of the disappointed members of the once rebel generation who now seek shelter in academic ivory towers. He calls on them to return as "public intellectuals" helping the people to probe below the glittering surface in search for reasons why.

This line of thought leads him to examine the broader role of education, to seek ways in which the school could be an instrument for the preparation of critical citizens. Its function should not be to produce graduates simply able to assess the consistency of an argument, like in formal logic, but to produce thinking individuals ready to question the premises on which the argument is based, future citizens capable of pondering over the nature of their society, over its vested interests, and even over solutions leading beyond the confines of that society. He dreams of a school that would help in turning the ordinary working people from objects into subjects of their history or, as he might put it, of an extension of democracy until "we the people" shall rule.

"It is by the goodness of God that we have in our country three unspeakably precious things: freedom of speech, freedom of conscience, and the prudence never to practice either." Mark Twain must have penned those lines with a twinkle in his eye, knowing that not all his fellow citizens shared such caution. Written with wit, elegance, and passion, drawing on the author's personal and professional experience, Harvey Kaye's book provides food for thought for that other constituency, for the "imprudent" Americans. At this stage, when the forces of Unreason spread, alas, not only in the United States or, to use the words of his favorite, Tom Paine, in the "times that try men's souls," this antidote, this counterpoison is a most valuable contribution.

—Daniel Singer
Paris
March 1995

INTRODUCTION

It is not enough to know the ensemble of relations as they exist at any given time as a given system. They must be known genetically, in the movement of their formation. For each individual is the synthesis not only of existing relations, but of the history of these relations. He is a précis of all the past.

—Antonio Gramsci

WRITTEN IN THE SPACE afforded between full-time teaching and work on larger literary projects, the chapters that follow were originally composed as lectures, articles, and reviews. They register the questions I have felt compelled to ask, the arguments I have been eager to engage, the judgements I have felt obliged to render, the angers I have been unable to suppress, and the memories I have been driven to record during the past several years in response both to the dramatic and often confusing events and developments of the day *and* to the interpretations rendered of them by political spin-doctors, corporate public-relations teams, media pundits, and academic critics (who, too often, have been indistinguishable from each other).

Though appearing far less coherent than the other admittedly varied works of history and politics that I have authored and edited, this collection is not merely accidental for, while it is easier to impose order on what has transpired than on what is yet to come, there are definite historical and biographical lines and cables that connect these many pieces. However diverse and far-reaching its contents appear, this is a book about history and memory, education and democracy, intellectuals and politics.

These themes have always been problematic, but for some time after the Second World War, at least in the United States, their problematic character was obfuscated by the pressures and politics of the Cold War and by the benefits (however unequally shared) of the truly remarkable economic growth and development of the postwar decades. Nevertheless, the many struggles of the 1960s and the ensuing political and economic crises of the 1970s made the divisions and antagonisms of American life all the more evident and contested. The grand–governing narrative of America that had prevailed for so long, in which the United States was understood as the embodiment of progress and justice in a single nation-state, was challenged from below by those hoping to realize it, and more seriously undermined by other events and developments national and international. Even more crucial, what had commenced in the 1960s as progressive demands for the extension and deepening of liberty, equality, and democracy—and were just beginning to be realized by decade's end—were ever more intensively responded to in the 1970s by conservative mobilizations and, in time, concerted class war from above entailing wide-ranging political, industrial, and ideological campaigns.

The majority of the essays collected here represent attempts both to respond to those "New Right" campaigns and the forces of reaction orchestrating them *and* to look beyond them. In order that the respective pieces continue to reflect the political moment at which each was written, I have not significantly revised or updated them. The essays in Part One address history and memory. Following "A Note in Memory of Isaac Deutscher," the next four chapters were written especially to call attention to and offer serious warning of the many efforts on the part of conservative and neoconservative intellectuals in the wake of the Cold War to promote the view that the struggle for democracy is finished and to reconstruct public discourse in terms of the monstrous idea that we are at the "end of history," the notion, as Daniel Singer has scornfully put it, that the "age of capital is eternal."

Even in the face of the triumph of capital and a profound crisis of the left and radical-democratic politics, I remain confident that we will witness resurgent struggles against the powers that be—as the closing arguments of chapter 2, my 1994 Deutscher Memorial Lecture, "Why Do Ruling Classes Fear History?," attest. However, the inevitability of such struggles does not absolve us of the responsibility of answering lies with truths, repulsing ideological campaigns, and continuing to cultivate and educate the popular desire for justice, freedom, equality, and democracy. If anything, it makes our historical and intellectual agencies all the more imperative—a proposition to which I am sure the great socialist writer and dissident intellectual, Isaac Deutscher, would have subscribed.

The remaining chapters of Part One also treat history and memory, considering such varied subjects as photography and historical consciousness, the historical meaning of the establishment of an international Memory Prize, the formation and re-formation of American public memory, the culture wars, and the impact, personal and public, of the continuing capitalist transformation of our national pastime, baseball.

Though the theme of history and memory remains evident, the essays in Part Two are concerned specifically with education and democracy. If, as I have come to believe, one of the real tests of a democracy is the education it affords its citizens-to-be—in terms of resources provided, values celebrated, and practices cultivated—we are clearly failing our young people and ourselves. Unfortunately, aside from those directly involved in "ed schools" and teacher training programs, my colleagues on the academic left for a variety of (inadequate) reasons have generally ignored issues of schooling, curriculum, and pedagogy, other than those related to their own domain of "higher education."

However, where too many of us have refused to tread, New Right politicos and intellectuals have not hesitated to go and, eager to refashion notions of the public good and thereby create a new conservative ruling consensus, they have made public education a prime target of their campaigns. Here, as elsewhere, however deep and complex the crisis was at the outset of the Age of Reagan, it has since been compounded by budgetary threats and constraints and the right's varied and seemingly contradictory initiatives, ranging from the populist-sounding schemes of "school choice" and "education vouchers" to the more elitist ones involving "defense of the literary canon" and "national standards." In these chapters, I critically examine several of the central debates and positions and try to offer alternatives to the arguments advanced both right and left.

Finally, the chapters in Part Three deal with intellectuals and politics. The first three, including the biographical portrait of my lifelong political hero, Tom Paine, speak of American radicalism as the *prophetic memory* of American history and the struggle to create an ever more free, equal, and democratic society. These are followed by chapters on the American sociologist and critic C. Wright Mills and the English historian and activist E. P. Thompson (who, notably, were themselves good friends). These two late-twentieth-century figures had a tremendous influence on their own generation and, most especially, on the younger cohorts of radical intellectuals. The last four pieces proffer critical reflections on my own generation's aspirations and endeavors to reinvigorate the American radical tradition, to redeem the prophetic memory of American possibilities in the face of what must be recognized—all the more so, when viewed historically—as a new American Crisis.

◆

I have dedicated this book, first of all, to my late grandparents, whose presence and influence, along with that of my parents, I continue to feel, not in some mystical or spiritual fashion, but *materially,* in my very sensibilities, thoughts, and actions. Indeed, those who read through the ensuing chapters will find many a reference to both of my grandfathers.

Those references to my father's father—who, following the Russian Revolution of 1905, came to New York's Lower East Side as a young boy and worked his way up and through law school to become a trial attorney—acknowledge the influence of his persuasive storytelling, his historical interests and reflections, particularly his practice of challenging the present with the experience and aspirations of the past, *and* his political inclinations.

I think it was also from him that I acquired a love of books which entailed not simply acquiring them but, beyond that, working through them. I distinctly recall being fascinated by certain of the titles that sat on the low shelves in the back of the dining room of his and my grandmother's apartment. Along with the writings of Tom Paine, which my grandfather passed on to me (an act that is noted at various points in this work), there was H. G. Wells's hefty *Outline of History* (1920). My grandparents lived across the street from the Brooklyn Museum; I allowed Wells to be my guide through its many and diverse rooms of art and archaeology (where, to my boyish delight, they actually had an unwrapped "mummy" on display). I devoured the *Outline* in chunks and, while I didn't follow its every chapter, the book served as my first introduction to "humankind." Moreover, it further convinced me that history is large and universal, and that in spite of catastrophes, humanity has been making something of itself.

My grandfather died in 1979, just before the New Right's ascendance to political power. But had he been around to hear Francis Fukuyama's proclamation ten years later that we had arrived at the "end of history," Grandpa Lou would have been amused and, likely, would have referred us either to Wells's words in the *Outline*— "Let the reader but refer to the earlier time charts we have given in this history, and he will see the true measure and transitoriness of all the conflicts, deprivations, and miseries of this present period of painful and yet hopeful change"—or, even better, to Paine's rousing line in *Common Sense* that "We have it in our power to begin the world over again."

The references to my mother's father—an insurance salesman and the only one of my grandparents born in America—recognize his love of place, that is, New York City; and of sports, especially baseball—in fact, one New York team in particular, the Brooklyn Dodgers. Though no radical, my grandfather fully appreciated and celebrated the politics of bringing Jackie Robinson onto the Dodgers, making Robinson the first African American ballplayer in the major leagues. He also understood the power of capital and mourned its capacity to subordinate other values to those of the market.

At the same time, there is no denying the strength of my grandmothers' influences. My father's mother I knew least. Having suffered a stroke and a heart attack, her speech was impeded but she was a fighter and, by all accounts, was not to be deterred. She was a beautiful and passionate woman who enjoyed horse races and card games, regularly disobeying her doctors' orders in favor of getting herself trackside or a seat at the poker table. Gaming aside, my daughters would do well to inherit her enthusiasm and perseverance.

Even more powerful an influence was my mother's mother, and since I was the firstborn grandchild—a grandson, in a world structured by gender—she could not do enough for me. Fortunately, my pleasures have always been relatively simple (at least I think so), and I fully remember that among my greatest thrills as a child were those times when she allowed me to eat my lunch sitting out on the fire escape of her Brooklyn apartment overlooking the street with all its variety of peoples and entertainments. Though she was not "educated," my grandmother, who effectively suppressed all recollection or, at least, discussion of her East European childhood, was smart. She knew what was right and what was indecent. Cruelty, poverty, and neglect were indecent. She could not understand them anywhere, but especially not in America.

My grandparents themselves had long been friends, and my parents had been childhood sweethearts. Thus, holiday occasions— Rosh Hashanah, Thanksgiving, Passover, July 4th, Labor Day— brought our relatively small family together over big and splendid dinners. The table was extended and covered with food, and the air was filled with voices speaking of theater and television, baseball and football, politics and fashion. Discussions were loud and disagreements were plentiful. Not every heated discussion was creative, but I grew up believing that arguments are dialectically charged opportunities for testing or, in some cases, actually finding one's own ideas and words. At the beginning of each semester, I strain to explain that Talmudic truth to my students, who have in most cases been raised quite differently.

♦

There are many people to acknowledge and, quite possibly, their numbers are greater than usual since this is a collection of essays written over several years. First, I must thank Daniel Singer for providing the Foreword. It has been several years since I first wrote to him to let him know how much I admired his writing and depended on his regular installments on European politics in the *Nation*. Since I knew of his long personal relationship to the late Isaac and Tamara Deutscher, Daniel was one of the first people I called to tell of my having been awarded the Deutscher Memorial Prize and, thus, it seemed to me most appropriate to invite him to contribute the Foreword to this volume. These paragraphs also allow me the opportunity to publicly thank him and his wife, Jeanne, for visiting my family and me in the fall of 1990 in order to speak to my students and colleagues on the politics and political economies of post-Communist Eastern Europe. I remain hopeful that I can persuade him to write a book on post–Cold War Europe and the prospects for a truly democratic socialism.

In addition to the publishers and editors of the writings collected herein (identified on the title pages of the respective chapters), I want to thank my editor at St. Martin's Press, Michael Flamini, for his immediate interest in and commitment to my bringing these essays together in a single volume. Also, I want to thank Suzanne Oshinsky for her editorial labors.

Colleagues, comrades, and cousins who have helped me think through the many arguments presented—though they are not responsible for them—include Victor Kiernan, Elliott Gorn, Ellen Wood, Henry Giroux, Paul Buhle, Mari Jo Buhle, Doreen Rudé, Dorothy Thompson, Ron Baba, Tony Galt, Craig Lockard, Alison Kibler, Hugh Miller, Lynn Walter, Carol Emmons, Ray Hutchison, Jerry Lembcke, Steve Paulson, Doris Meadows, Greg Ruggiero,

Stuart Sahulka, Dave Jowett, Jerry Rodesch, Mark Perkins, Joe Kincheloe, Yvette Cohen, Ron Sexton, Carl Chinn, Maura Burnett, Cecelia Cancellaro, and Arthur Shapiro.

Naturally, my students have helped me by listening and welcoming or resisting—and who should be remembered more in a book concerned in part with education? Most notable among those who have put up with me during the years in which these chapters were taking shape and, hopefully, learned a thing or two at the same time have been Sue Jackson, Greg Widen, Melissa Friese, Stephanie Cataldo, Eve Mueller, Kristel Hawley, Paula Schroeder, Joe Lannoye, Jody Krejcarek, Todd Dobesch, Cindy Karman, Craig Coenen, Connie Pemrich, Scott Hoffman, Jorge Tirado, Kirstin Hellwig, Tracy-Lee La Tour, Tim Casper, Jennifer Bloom, Thai Yang, Sarah Koneazny, and Roger Ohr.

No work is ever accomplished until it has passed the review of my in-house critics, to two of whom, Rhiannon and Fiona Kaye—along with their new cousin, Michael—this book is also dedicated. They have heard me read all of these chapters aloud and, now, as they grow older, they even occasionally sit themselves down before the word processor and consider my words on their own. Luckily for me, they are always willing to give me their observations, reservations, recommendations, and smiles. I just hope that as they grow even older, they'll continue to allow me to do the same with their work *and* that I'll have as much to offer. Lastly, there is my chief editor and companion, Lorna. Even if she knows it well already, I want to record again my appreciation and my love.

—Harvey J. Kaye
Green Bay, Wisconsin
July 1995

*In memory of my grandparents, Louis & Pearl Kaye
and Nathan & Jeannette Sehres, and, as they would
have insisted, in honor of their great-grandchildren,
my daughters, Rhiannon and Fiona,
and my nephew, Michael.*

PART ONE

HISTORY AND MEMORY

1 A Note in Memory of Isaac Deutscher, Historian and Socialist Intellectual (1907–1967)[*]

The role of the intellectuals—Jews and non-Jews alike—of those who are aware of the depth of the Jewish tragedy and of the menace of its recurrence, is to remain eternal protestors: to maintain the opposition to the powers that be, to militate against the taboos and conventions, to struggle for a society in which nationalism and racialism will at last lose their hold on the human mind. I know that this is no easy way out; it may be distressing and hurtful; and for those who take it there can be no precise formulation of a set of precepts for action. But if we do not remain eternal protestors, we shall be moving within a vicious and pernicious circle, a suicidal circle.

—Isaac Deutscher,
The Non-Jewish Jew and Other Essays

AGAINST VOICES OF PESSIMISM and resignation, Isaac Deutscher always insisted on the persistence of hope and the significance and possibility of human agency. Suffering exile from Poland and the loss of his family in the Holocaust, he did not surrender. As his dear friend Daniel Singer wrote just a few years after Deutscher's untimely death in 1967 at the age of 60: "Circumstances may have been harsh, yet

[*] This chapter originated as my opening remarks on the occasion of delivering the 1994 Deutscher Memorial Lecture (see chapter 2).

Deutscher refused to yield. He rejected at once the philosophy of despair and the comfort of self deception. . . . He would always scan the planet for new lessons and new hopes."[1] Or, as the former British diplomat and scholar of Soviet Russia E. H. Carr observed in his Introduction to a posthumous edition of Deutscher's *Heretics and Renegades*: "Deutscher was heir to both the Enlightenment and Marxism. . . . And in the running battle . . . between principle and expediency, Utopianism and realism, faith and cynicism, optimism and despair, he stood unwaveringly on the side of the first."[2]

Moreover, expelled from the Polish Communist Party in 1932 for his opposition to Stalinist orthodoxy, Deutscher based his hopes not upon lies and fictions but upon truths, for truth is revolutionary, and a democratic socialism can be built on nothing less.

In all of his writings—but most brilliantly in what is arguably the greatest biography ever composed, the trilogy of Trotsky's life, *The Prophet Armed, The Prophet Unarmed, The Prophet Outcast*[3]—Deutscher articulated the dialectic of structure and agency and the tragic and ironic character of revolutionary struggle. And yet, even as he chronicles the experience of defeat after so remarkable a triumph, he engages our thinking about what was accomplished, what might have been and, in circumstances to come, what might yet be.

Scholarly and political testimonials abound: There is the recollection by an ex-communist mineworker in Britain that "to those of us who were groping in the 1950s for an explanation of the brutally irrational distortions which had cramped the life of the socialist movement, the almost lone voice of Deutscher came as a blinding revelation. . . . For so many of us, he was a regenerator of hope. In him we found the link between humanism and socialism which allowed us to rediscover Marx and our own history."[4]

The godfather of the American New Left, C. Wright Mills, accorded Deutscher his highest praise by including him in the ranks of the "plain Marxists"—those who truly work in the Grand Old Man's intellectual and historical tradition. And Lee Baxandall reports that all the editors of *Studies on the Left*, the first significant intellectual forum of the movement in the United States, read Deutscher and recommended him to newcomers.[5]

Of course, Deutscher came to be very well known in North America, but not only for his writings. He had originally traveled in the early 1950s from London (his and his wife Tamara's home after his departure from Poland on the eve of the Second World War) to the United States in order to work in the Trotsky archives, later returning not only to do further research but also, with the resurgence of American activism, to respond to invitations to speak before student and broader political audiences about the Cold War and Vietnam. According to contemporary accounts, he was inspiring and never patronizing. He expressed admiration for both student and minority mobilizations, yet he urged New Leftists to recognize their own political limitations and appreciate the radical heritage, imperatives, and potentialities of working-class organization and struggle.[6]

Given the vibrancy of British socialist culture (at least at the time), the impact of Deutscher's work was probably even greater on that side of the Atlantic. The writer Mervyn Jones, whose novel *Joseph* (as in Joseph Stalin) drew directly from Deutscher's studies, thankfully recalls the historian's "great generosity, powerful intellect, probing curiosity, and extraordinary literary gifts." And, speaking for a generation of British, European, and American New Leftists, Perry Anderson writes in "The Legacy of Isaac Deutscher" that "he was one of the great socialist writers of this century."[7]

There are so many others, but most of all I like Tariq Ali's memoir in *Street-Fighting Years*. Terribly dispirited for having been severely stricken with the mumps, he was given the Trotsky biography to read. "[They are] the kinds of books that can change one's life," he says, "[and] they certainly did mine. I was entranced. Friends who shared the house with me at the time will testify that I was incapable of paying attention to anything else. I stayed in bed until I finished all three volumes. It took me a week, during which time my disease mysteriously disappeared."[8]

I recall Isaac Deutscher and his contributions not simply because this book bears the title of my 1994 lecture honoring his memory. Nor is it just because so much of my own work has been as a student of Marxist historiography. Even more, it is because my own re-encounter with his life and work actually led me to pose the question, *"Why do ruling classes fear history?"*

In Poland in the mid-1930s under the Pilsudski dictatorship, Deutscher, the young journalist and editor, experienced first-hand the censorship of an authoritarian state; and he would be far worse threatened if they should discover his first book-length project, a social history of the nation encompassing the making of the Pilsudski regime. Daniel Singer recounts:

> As things stood, just to keep the book at home was to invite a prison sentence the next time his room was raided by the police. Thus, the manuscript was hidden in the house of a sympathizer, whose parents were sufficiently "respectable" to defy suspicion. One day, however, as there were rumours that the police were extending their range, the alarmed sympathizer contacted Isaac to ask him what to do with the manuscript. On the spur of the moment . . . Isaac told him to burn it, and so his first major work ended as ashes in one of those big Polish stoves.[9]

Furthermore, in reading Deutscher's biographies of Stalin and Trotsky, I was necessarily reminded of Stalin's compulsion to dictate not only lives and deaths but, also, "the past," *and* of Deutscher's own commitment to not allow Stalin's "histories" to go critically unanswered.

In words that should serve to remind many of us of the commitments that first motivated us to the discipline, Singer goes on to write of how, following his wartime service, "Deutscher donned the mantle of the historian—to remain true to himself and his revolutionary past. . . . His ambition was to clear the ground for new revolutionary generations, to salvage for them the message of October. The militant could only do it by becoming a committed historian."

2 Why Do Ruling Classes Fear History? The 1994 Deutscher Memorial Lecture*

1989 WAS THE TWO-HUNDREDTH anniversary of the French Revolution, and—contrary to the schemes of governing classes both West and East—developments of that year seemed to provide dramatic living proof that the grand ideals of 1789 were not just remembered but still inspiring and informing action.

Across Eurasia and beyond, people struggled anew for liberty, equality, and democracy. Rebellions claimed control of public spaces and toppled rulers and regimes. There were triumphs, like the tearing down of the Berlin Wall, and there were tragedies, like the Tiananmen Square massacre. But, together, these events reminded people globally of the popular desire for freedom and the demand for "power to the people!" There was reason to celebrate and to believe more was yet to come.

And yet, within just a few years the hope and sense of possibility engendered by those events and the end of the Cold War have been overtaken by other, darker developments, and the spiritual order of the day has become one of despair and cynicism. Emulating the most brutal traditions of our century, the politics of the new world order are apparently dominated by greed, hatred, and mass murder—sadly, I need merely mention Somalia, Bosnia, Rwanda. European life itself is marked by resurgent nationalisms, xenophobia,

---

* Originally presented as the Isaac and Tamara Deutscher Memorial Lecture at the London School of Economics on November 8, 1994, a shorter version of this chapter was first published in the international human rights magazine *Index on Censorship*, vol. 24, May 1995.

and, most bizarrely, in view of the tragic successes of the Nazis in their attempts to rid the continent of Jews, anti-Semitism.

At the same time—and surely contributing in massive proportion to the reinvigoration of these brutalities—the market now rules globally, North and South, subsuming everything and everyone to the command of capital, intensifying already gross inequalities as the rich grow richer and working people poorer, and ever threatening to completely destroy the Western labor movement and its finest twentieth-century achievement, social-democratic government.

It becomes more and more difficult to gain a hearing for the "public good" or "commonweal." Public discourse and private thoughts across the political spectrum seem to accept—as the American neoconservative Francis Fukuyama put it—that we are at "the end of history."[1] With the global triumph of capitalism we are believed to have arrived at the terminus of world-historical development, the culmination of universal history, entailing not only the collapse of the Soviet Union but the consignment of *all* varieties of socialism to the graveyard of history. Fundamentalisms and particularisms may arise to challenge liberal capitalism, but there is no universal alternative to it now or in the future. In fact, Edward Lutwak's recent survey of the world makes Fukuyama's own thesis seem downright optimistic. In place of liberalism, Lutwak sees "Fascism As the Wave of Future."[2]

In any case, radical-democratic possibilities are finished; the further progress and development of liberty and equality is foreclosed, forever. To think otherwise is declared, and widely perceived to be, not just utopian, but dangerous.

I do not accept that assumption, and I will not defer to it. We are not fulfilled and our requirements and satisfactions are not simply material. History and its progressive political possibilities are not resolved.

Still, I take the "end of history" most seriously. I do so not merely because the appearance of Fukuyama's brash work was a smartly timed literary and commercial coup, orchestrated with the financial support of a corporately endowed New Right foundation, but because—however illusory a notion it really is—this idea has articulated anew the perennial ambitions and dreams of the powers that be to make their regimes and social orders not just omnipotent and universal, but immortal. And, at least for now, it does seem to capture in a single phrase the dominant historical vision.

To those of us who still aspire to advance the critical and democratic ideals of the Enlightenment and the Age of Revolution, the old question—*What is to be done?*—continues to present itself. And yet, there would seem to be an even prior and more urgent question: From where can we draw sustenance, hope, and a sense of possibility when, admittedly, there are substantial reasons to be pessimistic?

Most immediately, I can do no better than to quote Deutscher himself: "Awareness of historical perspective seems to me," he wrote, "to provide the best antidote to extravagant pessimism as well as extravagant optimism over the great problems of our time."[3]

Beyond that, what I have in mind may strike you as rather perverse. I want us to stare fully and deeply into the eyes of the ruling and governing classes. I want us to appreciate what they see. Victor Kiernan, the phenomenal British historian of empires, nation-states, and so many other subjects, has never ceased to remind me that our rulers have been able to secure their rule over and over again because they are more united, more class conscious and, politically, more intelligent. *They* are regularly in the driver's seat, we are not; thus, however eager to deceive themselves they may be—and it is imperative that they try to do so—they are also better positioned to spy the road ahead and behind.

It is my contention that however imposing the ruling classes' power may be, and however acquiescent may seem the people over whom they exercise it, the eyes of the ruling classes reflect not surety and confidence, but apprehension and anxiety. *What* is it that they see? *What* is it that they recognize? *What* is it that they know? The American radical historian Howard Zinn points us toward an answer:

When we become depressed at the thought of the enormous power that governments, multinational corporations, armies and police have to control minds, crush dissents, and destroy rebellions, we should consider a phenomenon that I have always found interesting: Those who possess enormous power are surprisingly nervous about their ability to hold on to their power. They react almost hysterically to what seem to be puny and unthreatening signs of opposition. . . . Is it possible that the people in authority know something that we don't know?[4]

In the looks and actions of the powerful, we may discover what exercises them so and, at the same time, be reminded of what we appear to be on the verge of forgetting. Ultimately, we will have to ask: *Why do ruling classes fear history?*

◆

I have a story to tell, one that I have been carrying around with me for several years. It is not long, nor grand, nor epic in its proportions. And, to be sure, there are many other, more powerful ones. Nevertheless, I think it can serve as a place to begin.

Early in the fall of 1986, one of my colleagues, Craig Lockard, deposited on my desk an article from the *Far Eastern Economic Review* relating the trials and tribulations of a young dissident, Yu Si Min, before the powers and authorities of the South Korean state.[5] Craig correctly figured that my students and I would find it intriguing, for it made reference to a text we had been reading and discussing in class.

The story begins in 1978 with Yu setting out for the capital from his southern provincial city, having been accepted to study economics at the most prestigious of the country's academic institutions, Seoul National University.

This was a tremendous moment for him and his family. Yu was the fifth of six children; his parents had scrimped and saved for many years to make sure that he could further his education. As he told it, on leaving his family's home he could actually feel his "mother's proud gaze falling on [his] shoulders"; and, en route, he swore that he would pursue a lucrative career in order to reimburse his parents for everything they had gone through.

However, life in Seoul was not as he had expected. Yu was shocked by the low wages and terrible laboring conditions suffered by workers, especially by women and teenage girls, and before the end of his first year at college he had become involved in running night-school classes in a factory district, an activity that quickly brought him to the attention of the authorities.

Eventually, the police picked him up. They interrogated him for three days, trying to find out if he was encouraging strikes and union organizing, both of which were banned by the government.

When martial law was declared in May 1980, Yu was one of thousands of demonstrators hauled in for demanding the restoration of democratic rights such as freedom of the press, freedom of assembly, and the legalization of independent labor unions. His first prison term lasted three months, during which time he was beaten regularly. Then, on his release, he was immediately drafted into the army. As a known student protester Yu was guaranteed harsh treatment and, like others in his straits, he was posted to a unit patrolling the demilitarized zone separating the two Koreas. This practice was supposedly intended to heighten one's awareness of the North's threat to the South's security because, along with the sub-zero temperatures and frequent harassment, there was the constant "danger of sudden firefights."

Released from service in the spring of 1983, Yu was readmitted to university. However, within weeks of his return he was joining in demonstrations and was soon under arrest once again, this time charged with assault, after he and other students detained several police agents "discovered spying at the university."

Sentenced to a year in jail, Yu was placed in "solitary confinement . . . cut off from the rest of the world." His cell was

> 1.8 meters long and 1.2 wide, with nine coin-sized ventilation holes. The walls and floor were covered with plastic foam to

prevent any noise filtering in and a double door blocked any view of the corridor beyond. "The first thing that occurred to me," he said, "was that I had better learn to get along with the silence."

Yu kept himself occupied with needlework. But—ever the student—he laid out for himself a rigorous syllabus and worked his way through 150 volumes of world literature, including "everything by Dostoevsky and Tolstoy." There were, however, two works which were forbidden to him because they were considered "subversive": Nehru's *Glimpses of World History* and E. H. Carr's *What is History?*[6]

My own students wondered why these two books in particular were considered "subversive." What made them "special"? Most immediately, my students figured it was because Nehru had been a triumphant rebel against empire and a prominent leader of the non-aligned movement, and Carr had been the author of a monumental, and not unsympathetic, *History of the Soviet Union*. But some of my students went on to examine their respective chapters, assuming that censors actually read the works they keep from others. In doing so, they discovered that *Glimpses of World History* had originated in the 1930s as letters written by Nehru from British colonial jails to his young daughter, Indira. Informed by universalism, humanism, and Marxism, and acknowledging social forces high and low, the letters narrate a global history of empire and independence, reaction and revolution, destruction and creative innovation.

Next, in the book they all were supposed to be reading, *What is History?*, they heard Carr arguing forcefully against the prevailing pessimism of his peers. Even with its disasters, modern history is still progressive, he contends, for we continue to see the mutual expansion and deepening of reason and freedom. And, in those terms, Carr calls upon his fellow historians to acknowledge their intellectual and political responsibilities and "present fundamental challenges in the name of reason to the current way of doing things. . . ."[7]

Viewing these books from the perspective of the powerful, that is, from the office of the prison censors, my students agreed that they were unquestionably "subversive." *But,* they then asked—and I loved them when they did—wouldn't that be true, at least to some extent, of critical history in all regimes of unequal power and wealth?

◆

I have told Yu Si Min's story because I believe it renders in microcosm the universal compulsion of ruling classes to control not only polity and economy, but also culture and thought, most especially historical memory, consciousness, and imagination. There, in his jail cell, his self-made reading room, physically isolated and alone, Yu was completely under the command of the state. Seemingly with confidence, his warders allowed him access to a great many literary works; but, in truth, they were ever anxious and ever watchful, and driven to prevent him from reading the two requested books, the works specifically addressing history.[8]

Yu's prison experience summons up a long, long record of ruling-class suppressions, occultations, mystifications, corruptions, and falsifications of history. Standing before us is the arch-antidemocrat Plato, dialogically laying out in his *Republic* a blueprint for a class-ordered society—one in which poets and protohistorians are to be carefully regulated, and consensus is to be founded upon a grand historical fabrication:

> "Now," I said, "can we devise one of those lies—the kind which crop up as occasion demands . . . so that with a single noble lie we can indoctrinate the rulers themselves preferably, but, at the least, the rest of the community?"
>
> "What sort of lie?" he asked.
>
> "Nothing too outlandish," I replied, "just a tall story about something which happened all over the place in times past, . . .

but which hasn't happened in our lifetimes and I'm not sure it could and people would need a great deal of convincing about."[9]

(Strangely enough, Plato's *Republic* might well have been one of the "great works" allowed on Yu's prison syllabus.)

Clearly distinguishing between "the past" as ideological construct and "history" as critical knowledge, in *The Death of the Past* J. H. Plumb succinctly summarizes the parade of ruling class elaborations and uses of the former from ancient to recent times: "The past was constantly involved in the present, and all that enshrined the past—monuments, inscriptions, records—were essential weapons in government, in securing the authority, not only of the king, but also of those whose power he symbolized and sanctified. . . . "

Plumb may have underestimated the persistence of the past today, and the continuing efforts of elites to compose and direct it, but he appreciated its essential significance: "Myths and legends, king-lists and genealogies . . . Whig-interpretations and Manifest Destinies. . . . All rulers needed an interpretation of the past to justify the authority of their government. . . . The past has always been the handmaid of authority."[10]

Our own century is hardly free of such practices. Subscribing to the Party's slogan in Orwell's *1984*—"Who controls the past controls the future; who controls the present controls the past"— totalitarian and authoritarian regimes have ceaselessly sought to dominate and manipulate public and private memory. It was true of Nazism and Fascism, it has been true of Communism, and it has been true of a great host of pettier, though not necessarily meeker, dictatorships.

Compared to the devastations of blitzkrieg and conquest and the organized murder of six million Jews, book burnings and perversions of the past seem minor crimes, but they should never be discounted, for the Nazis' criminal treatment of history served to rationalize and justify to the German people their later crimes against humanity. Those who deny that the Holocaust ever happened may be exercising their right of free speech (and demonstrating that ruling classes do not have an absolute monopoly on trying to suppress the past), but they are also committing atrocities against memory and history. The presence in Europe's streets of neo-Nazis, along with the reascendance of Fascist politicians, is chilling.[11]

Censorship in the Soviet Union began under Lenin as a "temporary measure." However, as David Remnick writes in *Lenin's Tomb:* "The Kremlin took history so seriously that it created a massive bureaucracy to control it, to fabricate its language and content, so that murderous and arbitrary purges became a 'triumph over enemies and spies,' and the reigning tyrant, a 'Friend to All Children.'"[12]

Isaac Deutscher gives accounts of how, early on in Stalin's campaigns against his rivals, he "started the prodigious falsification of history which was to descend like an avalanche upon Russia's intellectual horizons" and of how, by the onset of the 1930s, he was requiring falsehoods and cover-ups ever more massive. Show trials, purges, famines, deportations, prison camps, murders in the millions. Stalin and the Party imposed a grand "conspiracy of silence."

After more than a quarter century, the horrors and the lies, and the suppression of any reference to them, were bound together so tightly that Stalin's successors could not afford to loosen the controls too much. How could they when they had all been his "accomplices"?[13] Khrushchev himself fully appreciated the powers of the past and, ironically, offered one of the finest—though hardly universally deserved—tributes to my profession that I have ever come upon: "Historians are dangerous people, capable of turning everything topsy-turvy. They have to be watched."

While the darkest days did not return, history remained under close supervision and regulation—with occasional "thaws," followed regularly by "purges"—until glasnost and perestroika in the mid-1980s. Yet, Gorbachev was no fool. Even he would have preferred, at least at the outset, not to extend opening and restructuring to questions of the past. Indeed, it was not until Gorbachev imagined that allowing public reexamination and revision of the historical record would help to undermine his opposition that he called for the filling in of the all-too-many "blank spots."[14]

Having been so well supervised, professional scholars were themselves at first hesitant about undertaking the now licensed reexamination of Soviet experience. But others were not, and very quickly the historical past was asserting itself everywhere. I distinctly remember the Soviet government's announcement in May 1988 that, in view of the great changes under way, school history examinations were being cancelled. In time, more was to be canceled than that.

Gorbachev's miscalculations—assuming he never actually intended the breakup of the Soviet Union—also invited the renewal and redemption of politics and history in Eastern Europe. In 1988, on the twentieth anniversary of Prague Spring and the crushing of the Czechoslovak experiment in socialist democracy, the dissident group Charter 77 issued a statement which concluded with the following:

> We call only for truth. The truth about the past and the truth about the present are indivisible. Without accepting the truth about what happened it is impossible to address correctly what is happening now; without the truth about what is happening now it is impossible to substantially improve the existing state of affairs.

In the Baltic Republics, too, political insurgency was accompanied by calls for the complete disclosure of the "secret protocols" of the 1939 Hitler-Stalin Pact that had sealed their fates. Similarly, changes under way in Poland—so long striven for by the workers and intellectuals of Solidarity—generated a series of historical "revelations" regarding Soviet actions before, during, and after the Second World War. And in Hungary, along with popular demands for political reform, a "Committee for Historical Justice" was organized to pursue the recovery of the buried past of the Revolution of 1956.[15]

Submerged since 1945, extreme nationalist and reactionary forces reasserted themselves in each of these instances, threatening in their respective fashions to replace the Communist suppression of memory and history with nationalist repressions. Nevertheless, the importance of history to the liberation movements of 1989 authenticated the words of the Czech novelist Kundera, that "The struggle of man against power, is the struggle of man against forgetting."[16]

Further east, the Communist Chinese leadership, in spite of all their revolutionary designs, actually renewed their imperial forerunners' management of the past and those who studied it. In fact, Mao and his cadres, in the words of Jonathan Unger, were: "Even more determined to control the messages imparted in works of history—to bend those messages in ways favourable to official policy lines and to extirpate any manifestation of dissent or opposition that might be hidden in historical allegory. . . . In short, historians were to serve as handmaidens to the Party propagandists."[17]

The degree of control exercised since 1949 has varied—though obviously not as much as the historiographical directions dictated by the government's changing political and economic policies. For their part, Chinese historians and other producers of "the past" have themselves occasionally, though unsuccessfully, spoken up for the "right to remember"—as in 1989, when, in a petition supporting the students and workers mobilizing in Tiananmen Square, a group of writers in Shanghai called for "free historical enquiry." However, following the massacre on the night of June 4 there came the predictable ideological backlash, commencing with the government's propaganda machine describing the army's violent suppression of the democracy movement as actions taken against "counter-revolutionaries."

◆

It is difficult to treat the governing classes of contemporary liberal states in the same pages as those relating the experiences of Fascism and Communism. But our ruling elites are not innocents, and we must make every effort not to forget that the institutions, laws, and customs that constrain them are the results of long and continuing struggles from below.

In the years leading up to the Second World War, Japanese education was a blatant instrument of indoctrination, intended to cultivate in children the belief that the nation's overseas expansion was a sacred campaign to bring the "whole world under one roof," and, to guarantee that they promoted "loyalty to the emperor and love of country," all schoolbooks were subject to review and certification by the Ministry of Education. However, with Japan's defeat and the ensuing American Occupation, educational practices were reformed and, within certain guidelines, teachers were permitted to choose their own texts. But this did not last long.

By the 1950s, the conservative, Liberal-Democratic Party government had succeeded—against the opposition of the Teachers Union—in reinstituting state controls over education and the authorization of textbooks. This meant that, in spite of the growing scholarly historiography, the government was able to have removed from the books specific references to the atrocities committed by the Imperial Japanese military during the Second World War—the most infamous of these being the 1937 "Rape of Nanking." Recently—due to persistent legal campaigns by liberals and leftists and, maybe even more significant, diplomatic wrangles with the governments of those countries that had suffered Japanese depredations—prohibitions have been reduced or withdrawn. However, state control and censorship of textbooks continues.[18]

To varying degrees, the distortion and occlusion of the historical past by governing elites has characterized public history and historical education in all of the former Axis countries—regularly with the acquiescence, if not the encouragement, of their former opponents eagerly pursuing Cold-War and anti-left ends. Consider the politics of amnesia inherent in Austrians' adherence to an image of themselves as having been merely "the victims" of German expansionism; or the "historical" initiatives of German Chancellor Helmut Kohl, ranging from the Bitburg ceremonies in 1985 to his recent plans to commemorate the fiftieth anniversary of the plot to assassinate Hitler that deliberately excluded representatives of the socialist and Communist resistance movements. We might also register here the half-century's worth of political prevarications and equivocations in France engendered by the nation's "Vichy Syndrome."[19]

◆

Whereas the archives have been opened in Berlin and Moscow, American and other Western secrets about state and corporate crimes committed under license of the Cold War are only beginning to seep out. Secret deals with Nazis and Fascists, domestic spying and red-baiting, atomic-radiation tests on military personnel and civilians, assassinations and the overthrow of governments, plans for a first-strike nuclear attack—I will stop before I start sounding like Oliver Stone, producer of the film *JFK.*

And yet, there remains the comment by a former U.S. official that "possibly, one-third of American history is classified." (I won't even begin to guess at all the Official Secrets squirreled away somewhere in Britain.)

Moreover, in the United States, perhaps no less so than in Japan, history textbooks in the postwar decades have excluded or limited reference to the darker events and persistent social struggles that shaped the nation's history and continue to do so. In favor of a Cold-War consensus and the pursuit of anti-communism at home and abroad, high school history books unanimously represented America's westward expansion and overseas interventions in terms of Manifest Destiny, the defense of the hemisphere, and/or support of anti-colonial struggles.[20] Naturally, democracy was a central theme of these books' narratives of progress; however, ignoring the persistent limitations, exclusions, and oppressions, these texts articulated—well before Fukuyama was old enough to think about it—a vision of postwar America as the culmination of Western and world history.

Not only the schoolbooks, the most official of public histories, but also all of American mass culture, from Madison Avenue to Hollywood, projected this assumption. As the 1950s gave way to the 1960s, liberals and conservatives alike seemed to share in the historical belief that in America we were witness to the "end of ideology."[21] Those who resisted were effectively marginalized and had no credibility. Or so it seemed for a brief while.

Fomented in part by the very contradiction between the history portrayed and the history lived, American radicalism was renewed in the 1960s. And the struggles for the civil rights of racial and ethnic minorities, the social rights of the poor, the equal rights of women, *and* the cessation of imperial wars—along with the much less celebrated but no less remarkable working-class insurgency for industrial rights and workplace democracy[22]—together instigated serious reforms of the American polity and economy.

These struggles also inspired dramatic revisions in historical study and thought, including the socialization and democratization of the past—that is, the recovery and incorporation into the historical record of previously ignored class, race and gender experiences and agencies.

Unfortunately, though predictably, these democratic campaigns and accomplishments also provoked profound reactions on the part of the power elite, who grew increasingly worried that the several struggles of the day were on the verge of coalescing into a broad radical-democratic movement and thus promising reforms on an even grander scale. In public statements and manifestos such as the Trilateral Commission's 1975 report, *The Crisis of Democracy,* the voices of the corporate class declaimed that the Western polities were facing "governmental overload," more specifically, a "crisis" in which the problems of "governance" stemmed from "an excess of democracy." The threat was clearly acknowledged as coming from below—from minorities, women, public interest groups, and labor unions—but the real culprits were made out to be university and other "value-oriented intellectuals" (for which, read historians and their kin).[23]

Thus, for the past 20 years we have been subjected, both in the United States and, for very much the same reasons, in Britain, to what Ralph Miliband identified as "class war from above" against the achievements of liberalism and social democracy and the progressive changes wrought by the diverse struggles of the 1960s. And a pronounced feature of these "revolutions from above" has been vigorous and concerted campaigning to reshape historical memory, consciousness, and imagination—the climax of which was to be the pronouncement that we had actually arrived at the "end of history."[24] Strongly encouraged and lucratively bankrolled by the business elites, Ronald Reagan and Margaret Thatcher, along with their Republican and Conservative minions, brilliantly articulated mythical renditions of their respective nations' histories. Gross distortions and occlusions of the past were incessant but, in particular, we might recall Reagan's harking back to a supposedly happier, safer, and more economically robust America, existing some time—depending on the occasion—before the upheavals and Great Society programs of the 1960s *or,* in some cases, before the New Deal of the 1930s. For Thatcher the good old days were those when "Victorian Values" were supposed to have prevailed and the British people had somehow been both more self-reliant and kinder *and* more entrepreneurial and philanthropic (which combination applied was determined, presumably, by one's class circumstances).

Reagan and Thatcher spoke of the past as a time of "shared values" and insisted on the necessity of reinstating them. These were not flashes of nostalgia, but weapons directed against liberals, trade unionists, socialists, feminists, the poor, and racial and ethnic minorities. Both Reagan and Thatcher offered a rhetoric of consensus actually intended to bolster a politics of social division and a political economy of capital accumulation and class inequality.

Furthermore, the New Right leaders' ambitions for "the past" were not merely rhetorical. In neo-McCarthyite language, they declared their hostility for the scholarly and pedagogical labors of the new historians, and proceeded to initiate "culture wars" by translating the media-touted "crises of historical education" into major civic, if not defense, issues. Then, under the guise of responding to student ignorance and spreading historical amnesia, Republican and Tory secretaries of education introduced unprecedented schemes for "national standards" and "national curricula" in which History was to be a central subject. And they made every effort to determine that the narratives rendered in those syllabi and curricula would contribute to the development of their aspired-to conservative orders.

In this age of spectacle and entertainment, New Right efforts to subordinate historical education have been enhanced, if not overshadowed (at least in America), by corporate reconstructions of the past. Thinking specifically of Madison Avenue's renderings of the 1960s, an older colleague warned me some years ago that "You can spit at the capitalist system in protest. Some company will harvest it, refine it, and package it. And your mother will buy it for you for Christmas." In film, television, and advertising, past and present are sanitized and commodified; and now we have the proposal by the Disney Corporation to develop a new theme park to be called "Disney's America," which promises—and here the mind boggles, not knowing whether to laugh or to cry—to create "realistic renderings of the nation's past," including slavery and the Civil War. In a truly Orwellian fashion, we are to be provided History for the "End of History."

Consider again the varied, but universal and unremitting drive of ruling and governing classes to subordinate not only the present but the past. Surely, you don't have to be a Marxist to recognize the hegemonic ambitions entailed when a hired hand of the powers that be proclaims that the present order of things is eternal. Comprehended politically and historically, the handsomely subsidized intellectuals of the New Right with their end-of-history project stand in the very same queue as the schemers in Plato's *Republic* with their "tall story"—all of them intent upon deterring democracy, not enhancing it.

♦

Just what is it about history that so distresses the ruling and governing classes that they are driven to control and command it? Inverting Orwell, Kundera writes:

> The past is full of life, eager to irritate us, provoke and insult us, tempt us to destroy or repaint it. The only reason people want to be masters of the future is to change the past. They

are fighting for access to the laboratories where photographs are retouched and biographies and histories rewritten.[25]

It is not confidence that authorizes such actions, but trepidation; it is not conviction about the course of history that leads the ruling class to declare it finished, but anxiety induced by what they see there.

I began by proposing that we look directly into the eyes of the powerful, to discover what they see, what they recognize, what they know. I should have asked: What do they see, but try to obscure? What do they recognize, but attempt to deny? What do they know, but endeavor to conceal? Boris Kagarlitsky refers us to Marx's own assessment of censorship: "The law against a frame of mind is not a law of the state promulgated for its citizens, but the law of *one party against another party.* . . . Laws against frame of mind are the involuntary cry of a bad conscience." Absolutely. But it is not only guilt which obliges proscriptions. Knowing this, Kagarlitsky adds the following, with the effect, intended or not, of directing our thinking well beyond the experiences of fascism and communism: "Censorship is introduced by those who fear public opinion, the very existence of censorship is a sign that oppositional thought is alive and cannot be eradicated—that alongside the ruling bureaucratic 'party' there is also a *de facto* democratic party."[26]

Why do ruling classes fear history? Because, beyond their crimes, and beyond the tragedies and ironies that are so demanding of hope and spirit, *they see and they know*—as did their forerunners— that history has been, and remains, a process of struggle for freedom and for justice—and, increasingly, at least since the late eighteenth century, it has been, as the late Raymond Williams once put it, a *Long Revolution,*[27] at the political heart of which is the fight for liberty, equality, and democracy.

Moreover, they realize that however many times history has entailed the "experience of defeat" for the peoples and classes who have sought to make it otherwise, the Long Revolution has also afforded great victories. In search of a reason to hope, Ronald Aronson ventures this:

The real historical advances in human social morality have occurred through such struggles. Slavery has been abolished, democratic rights have been won, certain elements of dignity and equality promised and achieved, wars ended, other wars forestalled—only because we have acted. Projected, now desperately, now with confidence, in collective visions by movement after movement, sacrificed for, agitated for, partially achieved, then legitimized by law and custom, social progress has been *made true* every step of the way.[28]

Indeed—whether in resistance, rebellion, or revolution—it is not only the victories that weigh in; the defeats, as well, have contributed to the making of democracy. The Levellers and Diggers of seventeenth-century Albion and later generations of Radical, Luddite, and Chartist artisans and proletarians; the Parisian sansculottes and communards; the rebellious black slaves of the Americas; the radical mechanics, Populist farmers, Socialist workers, and Wobbly laborers, native and immigrant, of the United States; the revolutionary campesinos, vaqueros, and *obreros* of Mexico; the workers defending Republican Spain and their comrades in the International Brigades; the partisans of Occupied Europe and Jewish fighters in the Warsaw Ghetto; the anti-apartheid demonstrators at Sharpeville in South Africa; and the Chinese students and workers of 1919 and 1989, have all, in their respective ways, endowed the struggle.

My Russian-Jewish grandfather, who came to America after the 1905 Russian Revolution and campaigned as a socialist youth on New York's Lower East Side, passed on to me while I was still a boy his copies of the writings of Tom Paine. Among them was the revolutionary pamphlet *Common Sense,* wherein Paine boldly wrote: "We have it in our power to begin the world over again." 1776, 1789, 1810, 1848, 1871, 1910, 1917, 1945, 1949, 1959, 1968, 1989, 1993, and so many other radical-democratic moments large and small have renewed that possibility.

Whatever they say, the powerful have not forgotten. Nor have they forgotten the defiance expressed in the lines of Rosa

Luxemburg, while still evading the arrest by the proto-Nazi Freikorps that would lead to her murder: "'Order reigns in Berlin.' You stupid lackeys! Your 'order' is built on sand. Tomorrow the revolution will rear ahead once more and announce to your horror amid the brass of trumpets: 'I was, I am, I always will be!'"

The democratic narrative has long haunted the imaginations of the ruling classes, and it must do so all the more today because it is the very foundation upon which contemporary political legitimacy stands. However insincere, hypocritical, or blasphemous their words, for much of this century, and for far longer in America, rulers and governors have been obliged to speak within, and to, a discourse of democracy—often, a discourse rooted in a revolutionary moment. However limited, debased, or eviscerated the institutions, the idea of "rule by the people" has become the ideological cornerstone of modern government. As John Dunn observes: "Nothing else in the history of the world . . . enjoys the same untrammeled authority for human beings today, and does so virtually across the globe."[29]

Ironically, the very content of the hegemonic ideology serves to remind us of our democratic ideals and holds out to us the possibility of further realizing them. Sometimes it is obvious; but, again, sometimes—especially, in our liberal end-of-history polities— you have to listen closely, very closely, to appreciate the apprehensiveness of the governing elites.

Consider the ascension in 1992 of the Democrat William Jefferson Clinton to the presidency of the United States, after a dozen years of conservative Republican government. In his Inaugural Address, the new president urged Americans "to be bold, embrace change and share the sacrifices needed for the nation to progress."

It is necessary to recall that Clinton sought to connect his own pretended "political vision" to that of the revolutionary author of the Declaration of Independence, Thomas Jefferson. Following his pilgrimage to Jefferson's home at Monticello and, then, a journey to the District of Columbia along the route traveled by the third president in 1801, Clinton's inaugural speech was laden with Jeffersonian references. I have in mind one remark in particular: his statement that "Thomas Jefferson believed that to preserve the very foundations of our nation, we would need dramatic change from time to time."

But, of course, as every child of the 1960s (such as Clinton) knows, that is not exactly what the Founding Father said. The words Jefferson himself proffered were: "I hold that a little *rebellion* now and then is a good thing, and as necessary in the political world as storms in the physical."

How should we read Clinton's "revision" of the radical Jefferson? As an innocent act? As an act in favor of national, political reconciliation? Or, as I did (though hoping to be proven wrong): as an act in favor of the existing order by yet another representative of the governing class, who—having campaigned in the name of "change"—had no intention of actually rousing American historical memory and imagination for fear the people might really pursue it?

◆

From the Fascist prison cell that was supposed to break him and that, physically, eventually did, Antonio Gramsci penned these words to his young son, reminding us, from the bottom up, of where we might draw sustenance, hope, and a sense of possibility:

> My Darling Delio, I am feeling tired and cannot write a lot. But write to me always and tell me about everything that interests you in school. I think you must like history, as I did when I was your age, because it deals with men, as many men as possible, all the men in the world in so far as they unite together in society, and work and struggle and make a bid for a better life. All that can't fail to please you more than anything else. Isn't that right?[30]

In the same spirit, Howard Zinn modestly explains his own "Failure to Quit":

> I can understand pessimism, but I don't believe in it. It's not simply a matter of faith, but of historical evidence. Not over-

whelming evidence, just enough to give hope, because for hope we don't need certainty, only possibility. Despite all those confident statements that "history shows . . ." and "history proves. . . ," hope is all the past can offer us. . . . When I hear so often that there is little hope for change in the '90s, I think back to the despair that accompanied the onset of the '60s.[31]

Tormented by what they see in and know about the past and the making of the present, the powerful recognize, as Khrushchev did, that, to the extent that they pursue their scholarly and pedagogical labors critically, historians can be "dangerous people." We are not only capable of wielding the powers of the past against the powerful themselves, but—by offering *historical* challenges to despair and cynicism—of making radical contributions to popular memory, consciousness, and imagination.

What is to be done? Deutscher himself once wrote that the role of intellectuals "is to remain eternal protestors." I like that. However, in acknowledgement and appreciation of the very fears of the powers that be, I would take this idea further—in a way I am sure he would have approved.

Poaching a term from my mentor, Victor Kiernan, I would argue that our responsibility and task is to secure, bear witness to, and critically advance the *prophetic memory* of the struggle for democracy.[32] Thus, for Marxist and other radical historians the fundamental project remains: the recovery of the past, the education of desire, *and* the cultivation, as Gramsci himself urged, of "an historical, dialectical conception of the world . . . one which understands movement and change . . . which appreciates the sum of effort and sacrifice which the present has cost the past and which the future is costing the present . . . and which conceives the contemporary world as a synthesis of the past, of all past generations, which projects itself into the future."[33]

Why do ruling classes fear history? Because they know that however ancient the democratic idea, the modern democratic narrative has really only just begun. As Joel Kovel reflects in his recent study of McCarthyism: "Yes, the dead-end variant of socialism that went under the name of Soviet Communism ultimately failed badly. But the capitalist order, with all its brilliant achievements, has not succeeded; it has only won."[34]

It would make things easier if it could be otherwise, but the future growth and development of capitalism and of democracy cannot be mutual; extending the reaches of the former necessarily requires that democracy be constrained or even further constricted. The ongoing globalization of capitalist relations of exploitation and oppression means, as it has before, that previously secured democratic victories will be severely challenged and fresh democratic aspirations will continue to be harshly confronted. But, as Deutscher said in *The Unfinished Revolution,* "[failing nuclear annihilation] nowhere will history come to a close."[35]

The point is that working-class and other struggles from below will continue to assert themselves. Indeed, in ways we have yet to make out, global capital also makes possible its dialectical opposition on a global scale. On the good possibility that our own agencies do matter, we must work hard to make sure, whether they are national or international, that these struggles too are informed by the prophetic memory of liberty, equality, and democracy.

We cannot know what will transpire; but be assured that our governors fully expect the historic and perennial demand for power to the people to be renewed. It's reflected in their eyes.

3 The Revolutionary Overthrow of Socialism?[*]

IRVING KRISTOL, THE GODFATHER of neoconservatism, has declared that "The major political event of the twentieth century is the death of socialism." This is not merely the observation of a former leftist and now right-wing American who has to search hard to find a socialist political presence in his country; Conservative Prime Minister Margaret Thatcher confidently announced not too long ago that she would erase socialism from the British political map.

Socialism, indeed, is in crisis. Western European socialist parties are regularly defeated in elections; their cousins in southern Europe win elections (or dictate terms of coalition) but cannot define socialism as an alternative social order or, even, political economy. The Soviet Union and its Eastern (or is it Central?) European satellites ceased to inspire years ago; recent developments under Gorbachev are most welcome, but it will take a miracle—or a revolution—to reform those regimes such that they would represent societies to be admired in the West. So-called Third World socialisms are regularly as tragic in character as the colonialisms they have replaced.

A question which presents itself is: Should those of us committed to the making of truly democratic, free, and equal social orders stop deluding ourselves that our project—a project historically called socialism—is at all feasible? The answer that Peter Berger, an American sociologist, provides in his new book, *The Capitalist Revolution,* is that the goals of democracy, equality, liberty, and

* This chapter originally appeared in *The Times Higher Education Supplement,* July 24, 1987, as a review of Peter Berger, *The Capitalist Revolution: Fifty Propositions about Prosperity, Equality, and Liberty* (New York, 1987).

prosperity are worth pursuing, but that we are terribly mistaken to see these as associated with the making of socialism; for, he contends, if they are associated with a particular mode of socioeconomic organization, it is capitalism, not socialism.

The author of a variety of works on social theory, the sociology of knowledge and religion, and social change and "modernization," Berger is perhaps best known for his little book *Invitation to Sociology* (1963), that is still widely used and read in introductory courses. Though I was not a student of sociology, I remember as an undergraduate in the late 1960s at Rutgers University—where Berger was teaching in the women's college, Douglass—that he was extremely well liked and respected by students for being a sincere humanist concerned about both the historical world and his students' personal development. In fact, he was on the left in those years, and at least one of his articles from that period can be found in the socialist journal *New Left Review*. However, as he states in the Preface to *The Capitalist Revolution*: "Perhaps it is one of the ironies of my professional career that, very largely because of my perception of capitalism, I moved to the 'right' while a sizable segment of my colleagues in the social sciences moved to the 'left.'" Berger is now a university professor and director of the Institute for the Study of Economic Culture at Boston University where, from 1981 to 1984, he chaired the Seminar on Modern Capitalism, the papers of which he refers to regularly as sources for the new volume. His own articles now usually appear in neoconservative publications and periodicals.

In *The Capitalist Revolution*, Berger surveys the "evidence" regarding capitalism's connections with economic growth and prosperity, class and inequality, democracy and freedom, and development in the Third World. He does so comparatively, counterposing capitalism to feudalism, East Asian capitalism to Third World socialisms, and industrial capitalism to industrial socialism. Based on his findings, he offers fifty "propositions about prosperity, equality, and liberty." These would lead us to conclude that, however many social problems and structural faults there are in capitalism as a mode of production, it is the one system that can provide affluence, maximize individualism, and allow for freedom and democracy. He presents his arguments clearly, and one does not have to be an academic sociologist or economist to understand his points.

Though not entirely a throwback to the 1950s and early 1960s, Berger's book does resurrect certain theoretical currents that dominated American social thought at that time, such as Weberian approaches to capitalism and class and modernization theory; though I should add that he is not at all alone among contemporary sociologists in doing so. His principal intellectual target is Marx and Marxisms—I use the singular "target" because although he acknowledges that differences exist among Marxists today, he still lumps them/us together as a single "paradigm." He (mistakenly) says that a basic problem with the Marxist paradigm is that, proffering capitalism as the primary and central determinant of modern history, it fails to distinguish between the forces specific to capitalism as a form of socioeconomic organization and the generic forces of modernization that are necessarily characteristic of *both* capitalist and socialist development. At the same time, though he approaches his subject from the modernization paradigm, he warns against this paradigm's own tendency to technological determinism and its failure to distinguish adequately the differences between capitalism and socialism.

Following his theoretical introduction, Berger proceeds to "examine" the evidence and lay out his propositions as to why we have never had it so good and, moreover, why we should be extremely wary about giving up capitalism (understood as a market economy) for socialism (a command economy). Given the limits of a review, I can attend only to his central propositions.

First: Industrial capitalism has developed the "greatest productive capacity" and provided the "highest standards of living for large masses of people in human history." Rejecting the romantic view held by some historians about premodern ages, Berger does, however, accept the "pessimists' view" of the early Industrial Revolution; nevertheless, he says, the costs of industrialization experienced by peasants and artisans in the West in the nineteenth century should not be read as inevitable for developing countries today. Regarding the issues of the relative distribution of wealth and income and social mobility, he contends that the evidence (which is never properly displayed) indicates that evolving patterns of inequality are more closely related to the generic processes of modernization than the particular forms of socioeconomic organization in which they occur (a truly contentious proposition).

Second: "Capitalism is a necessary but not sufficient condition of democracy under modern conditions"; indeed, he proffers that "If capitalist development is successful in generating economic growth from which a sizable proportion of the population benefits, pressures toward democracy are likely to appear."

Third: Western individualism antedated the development of capitalism, but "At least in Western societies, if not elsewhere as well, capitalism is the necessary but not sufficient condition of the continuing reality of individual autonomy." It should be noted that in a characteristically Weberian fashion he argues that certain ingredients of "Western bourgeois culture (activism, rational innovativeness, and self-discipline)" are essential to "successful capitalist development anywhere"; and in a Durkheimian fashion he observes that capitalism requires certain "communal solidarities (like family and religion)" to balance off individualism.

Recognizing that the prosperity and freedoms of the West have been seen by some critics as developing at the expense of Third World countries, Berger turns to consider capitalism and Third World development. He rejects Marxist and neo-Marxist theories of imperialism from Lenin to Andre Gunder Frank, referring to dependency theory as "Third-Worldist ideology." He then offers two sets of propositions, one dealing with the Third World, the other with East Asian capitalism. He suggests that "The inclusion of a Third World economy within the international capitalist system tends to favor its economic development" and that "Capitalist development is more likely than socialist development to improve the material standard of life of people in the contemporary Third World, including the poorest groups." His best evidence for this is the East Asian capitalisms of South Korea, Taiwan, Hong Kong, and Singapore (together known as the Four Little Dragons). These, he states, attest to the "superior productive power of industrial capitalism" and disprove the "development of underdevelopment thesis" that a country cannot successfully develop in a state of dependence on international capitalism. Moreover, although East Asian capitalisms provide only "weak support" for the proposition that "successful capitalist development generates pressures towards democracy," he contends that "movements toward democracy and individuation have been greatly strengthened by their [these East Asian countries'] adherence to an international capitalist system centered in the West."

Regarding industrial socialism we encounter the standard criticisms. Socialism is linked with "pervasive bureaucratization and inefficiency of the economy" and is found inevitably to involve "authoritarian governance" and to be inclined towards "totalitarianism." The introduction of a market economy—which is currently being tried out—will inevitably run up against both political and economic limits and, anyhow, he insists, an effective market economy cannot operate without "private ownership of the means of production." Finally, he declares, whereas capitalism is incapable of generating legitimations and is itself mythically impotent, "socialism is one of the most powerful myths of the modern era."

Berger's propositions confirm most of Margaret Thatcher's and Ronald Reagan's suspicions about the value and benefits of capitalism and the dangers and evils of socialism; for all of his assertions that the work is an objective social scientific study, it remains a celebration of bourgeois culture and the market economy. Yet, the crisis of socialism has reached such proportions that even socialists and Communists have begun reassessing capitalism and socialism along the lines proposed by Berger. It would be a worthwhile exercise for the left to confront Berger's book head-on, not merely to reject his propositions, but also to sharpen its own thinking on the issues.

Having said this, I nevertheless have very serious reservations about the work both as a social historian and as a democratic socialist. I will offer just a few of these. First, Berger's modernization approach suffers from the same problem as does classical modernization theory. That is, however much he stresses historical perspective, his own thinking is insufficiently historical. For example, he outlines the process of industrialization as if it has always been fundamentally the same process throughout different historical circumstances, but it is *not* just the circumstances that have changed, the very process of "modernization" has changed regarding its level of technologies, capital and labor requirements, and so on.

Second, his narrative of the making of liberal capitalism fails to attend to the ways in which Western democracy and freedoms are themselves the products of persistent struggles from below of peasants, artisans, and workers motivated by anti-feudal and, later, *anti-capitalist* sentiments, values, and ideas. Thus, Western societies may evidence historical relations between capitalism and democracy, and capitalism and individualism, but the relations are arguably those of antagonism, contradiction, and conflict as much as anything else.

Third, to follow on the previous point, Berger almost completely ignores the historic connection between capitalism and fascism (another "totalitarianism"). In fact, revising his proposition that "Capitalism is a necessary but not sufficient condition of democracy," might we not propose that "Capitalism is a necessary but not sufficient condition of *fascism* under modern conditions"? This highlights a more general problem with *The Capitalist Revolution,* which is that it tends to ignore or gloss over the darker and uglier sides of capitalism. Thus, a fourth reservation I have relates to his treatment of capitalism and the Third World. Along with his discussions of past and present "successful" capitalisms, he might wish to consider such "unsuccessful" capitalisms as the Philippines and pre-revolutionary Nicaragua. We might well ask him to rethink in a more detailed and critical fashion the relationship between capitalism and dictatorship in the recent brutal and tragic histories of Chile and Argentina. His reliance on Jeane Kirkpatrick's model of totalitarian and authoritarian regimes—apparently intended to rationalize U.S. support for murderous pro-capitalist Third World governments and right-wing terrorism—is crudely inadequate.

Admittedly, none of these criticisms speaks to the tragedies of Soviet or Chinese-style communism or the possibilities for socialist democracies in the West, East, or Third World. If all Berger is really saying is that it is better to be middle or working class in successful liberal-democratic capitalism than it is to be a peasant in feudalism or a worker in the Soviet Union, then he has no dissent from me, though this is a pretty tired and banal proposition. (As my wife has observed, it's about as meaningful as the smile-inducing sign that hangs in my parents' basement: "I'd rather be rich and healthy than poor and sick.")

Finally, it is funny that his claim that capitalism generates no great myths is followed by a statement that only one of my fellow—and well-off—twentieth-century Americans could say with a straight face: "The benefits of capitalism *are* attainable."

4 The Age of Revolution Past and Present: A Note on Democracy and Capitalism in the Spring of 1989*

I HAVE JUST COMPLETED teaching "The Age of Revolution, 1776-1848," a seminar organized to commemorate the bicentennials of the U.S. Constitution and the French Revolution. During the past 16 weeks, my students and I attended not only to the world-historical developments of the American and French Revolutions, abolitionism and slave rebellions, and the Industrial Revolution and emergence of working-class politics, but also to the articles and stories in the current media assessing those events in light of the past 200 years, in particular pieces considering the legacy of 1789 in France and beyond. What we have observed is that such retrospection and commemoration has generally reflected the conservative tenor of contemporary politics in the Western liberal democracies. Even in France, where the Socialists are in power, it appears that the Revolution is no longer perceived as relevant, that the words of the Revolution—"Liberty, Equality, and Fraternity"—no longer inspire the nation's citizenry, other than for the commercial purpose of local festivities and tourism. Moreover, this state of affairs is being celebrated as evidence of the country's "political maturation."

Yet, as the semester unfolded, we became increasingly aware of and sensitive to the continuities from the late eighteenth to the late twentieth century. Indeed, regardless of the eagerness of political pundits and postmodern philosophers to tell us otherwise, it became

---

* This chapter was written in May 1989.

ever more apparent that we are still living within the narrative and experience of, as Eric Hobsbawm captured it, the Age of Revolution.

This has been most evident, of course, in the events under way in China (unfolding even as I write). It is arguable that the million and more students and workers who have thronged into the streets of Beijing and occupied Tiananmen Square represent the persistence and renewal of the struggles first undertaken two centuries ago by middle- and working-class people in their confrontations with monarchical and aristocratic authority.

It is not that history is simply repeating itself, for much has changed, but that the aspirations and visions advanced for independence and democratic rights in the Atlantic world of the late 1700s, so marvelously articulated in the writings of Tom Paine, continue today to reverberate in and engage the hopes and imaginations of people worldwide. Obviously, the Chinese have their own long history of rebellion and revolution upon which to draw, testified to by the students' sense that they are honoring the seventieth anniversary of the May 4th Movement of 1919, in which three thousand students stormed Beijing's Gates of Heavenly Peace, and, also, as the front-page headline story in the *New York Times* on Sunday, May 20, reports it, in the "Army's Cry: 'We Are People's Soldiers.'"

At the same time, however, those campaigning for reforms also seem to believe that their struggle connects with an international tradition of democratic struggle. The appearance of English-language banners in Tiananmen Square was clearly directed at Western, especially American, television cameras; and, arguably, there is an active sense of history registered in the making and display of a replica of the Statue of Liberty (France's mutually commemorative gift to America) in the streets of the Chinese capital.

But, of course, history is not one-dimensional. Along with the dramatic reports from China, the front page of the May 20 *New York Times* provided my students with a reminder of another, equally dramatic, way in which we continue to live within the evolving terms of the Age of Revolution. In an article titled "U.S. Businesses Loosen Link to Mother Country," the *Times* reporter wrote: "With a new surge of investment abroad, many American companies are shedding the banner of a national identity and proclaiming themselves to be global enterprises whose fortunes are no longer so dependent on the economy of the United States." He then quoted the words of the chief financial officer of Colgate-Palmolive: "The United States does not have an automatic call on our resources. . . . There is no mindset that puts this country first."

Whereas it was Tom Paine in the 1770s and 1790s who most enthusiastically championed the spirit of the democratic revolution, it was a couple of other radicals, Karl Marx and Frederick Engels, who in 1848 best captured the momentum of the Industrial Revolution. In their paean to the power of capital, *The Communist Manifesto*, they may have been wrong about the inevitability of the working class turning to socialism and the immediacy of such a revolution, but Marx and Engels were remarkably prescient in their view of capitalist progress: "The bourgeoisie has played a most revolutionary role in history. . . . The need of a constantly expanding market for its products chases the bourgeoisie over the whole surface of the globe. It must nestle everywhere, settle everywhere, establish connections everywhere." Indeed, the two seem to have comprehended that the global dynamic of capital would eventually lead it to challenge the very national politics and cultures of the European nation-states with which its development was originally bound up: "All fixed, fast-frozen relations, with their train of ancient and venerable prejudices and opinions, are swept away, all new-formed ones become antiquated before they can ossify. All that is solid melts into air, all that is holy is profaned. . . ."

Currently the clearest battles for democratic rights are being waged in Communist and Third World countries. My students wondered if the decoupling of corporate and national identities—that is, capitalism and nationalism—will instigate renewed democratic struggles in the West. One politically precocious fellow walked out of class muttering something about "Workers of the world unite. . . ."

5 The End of History? . . . Not![*]

THE CONCLUDING CHAPTER OF Walter Sellar and Robert Yeatman's classic send up of English school history texts and exams, *1066 And All That* (1931), is short and blunt:

Chapter LXII

- A BAD THING -

America was thus clearly top nation, and history came to a .

Francis Fukuyama's *The End of History and the Last Man* is no *1066 And All That;* it may seem foolish, but it is not funny, comic, or—contrary to the inclinations of a number of my colleagues—to be taken lightly.

To be clear about it—for, according to the reviews, quite a few of both his comrades and his critics continue to misconstrue his argument—Fukuyama's thesis is not simply about the end of the Cold War and national ascendance, that is, Soviet defeat and collapse and American victory (though given his relations with the powers that be, his current appointment at the Rand Corporation *and* his recent tenure in the Bush State Department as deputy director of the policy planning staff, I have wondered and worried that Fukuyama, à la Sellar and Yeatman, might be trying to tell us something about the USA vs. Japan and Germany). Rather, as he proclaimed in his

* This chapter was first published in the *Radical Historians Newsletter,* no. 67, November 1992, as a review of Francis Fukuyama's, *The End of History and the Last Man* (New York, 1992). I want to thank Jim O'Brien for his editorial assistance.

globally touted article in the *National Interest* (Summer 1989), what we are witnessing is the "unabashed victory of economic and political liberalism." Indeed, Fukuyama contends, we are witness to nothing less than the ultimate triumph of capitalist democracy: "the end point of mankind's ideological evolution and the universalization of Western liberal democracy as the final form of government."

The purpose of "Fukuyama, the book" is not only the unstated one of cashing in on the portentousness of the original piece and to respond to (a very few of) his critics, but to render, in the nineteenth-century fashion, a Universal History able to account for his astounding—though, as the *Nation* European editor Daniel Singer foresaw in *Is Socialism Doomed?* (1988), not unexpected—claim that we have truly arrived at the "end of history."

Of course, as Fukuyama realizes, a universal history worthy of the name requires a direction and dynamic. The grand narrative he offers is two-dimensional, economic, and political. Drawing on Plato's tripartite conception of the human soul to explain what motivates men *[sic]*, Fukuyama outlines an economic history that originates in and is driven forward by the "desiring" and "reasoning" parts of human nature, a history finding its greatest and finest historical expression in the cumulative, directional, and, he insists, irreversible process and products of modern science and technology, culminating today in global capitalism. But this is only half the story.

Alongside and tangled up with this tale of economic modernization is that of the progress of political life, supposedly powered onward by the third part of the Platonic soul, *thymos* or "spiritedness," which Fukuyama translates into historical terms as the Hegelian "struggle for recognition." It is the desire for self-esteem that originally drove "men" to seek to dominate others (men *and* women?) and to create aristocratic orders based on master-slave relations; and, thereafter, it was the inherently unsatisfying character of the recognition bondage afforded to all parties that further compelled men (*and* women?) to seek to overturn these social orders in such world-historic struggles as the American and French Revolutions.

Fukuyama declares that with the abolition of slavery and servitude and the establishment of the reciprocal and universal recognition of the liberal-democratic polity (that is, rights and representative government) the "contradiction" that engendered historical change and development is now effectively resolved. From 1776 and 1789 to the restoration of democratic regimes in southern Europe and Latin America in the 1970s and 1980s, and the spectacular events in Eastern Europe of 1989-91, the triumph and spread of capitalist democracy—however persistently problematic—is being realized.

Fukuyama is no simple propagandist. Admitting to the historical record the twentieth-century experiences of Central European fascism and East Asian authoritarianisms past and present, he grants that the development of capitalism does not necessarily entail the development of democracy and, moreover, that the chances for economic modernization may even be enhanced by efficient authoritarian rule (at least in the short run). He also grants that the triumph of capitalist democracy is still not a *global* reality. Currently the world remains divided between "post-historical" and "historical" nation-states and even in the former much remains to be done—though, he adds, the problems faced are "not obviously insoluble on the basis of liberal principles."

History may not be replete, but, according to Fukuyama, it is essentially complete. There are no *world*-historical alternatives to the post-historical world of capitalist democracy; no social order has ever or could ever address so effectively the needs of the human soul, none could ever measure up to its material and civic benefits. Swiftly depositing Soviet communism in the garbage pail of History, at the same time swallowing up social democracy as a mere variant of liberalism (I presume he gagged a bit on this one), in a very few words Fukuyama denies the viability of a democratic-socialist project and the possibility of a socialist democracy incorporating the best of liberalism. As Daniel Singer has warned, when it comes, the message will be straightforward and direct: "There was history but it has no future. The age of capital is eternal."

Worrying Fukuyama far more than the left's "egalitarian" critique of capitalist life, he says, is the prognosis of the right. Articulated most brutishly but poetically by Nietzsche, it declaims that liberal democracy produces "men [and women?] without chests," that is, "last men," men who are less than fully human, possessed of desire and reason but without *thymos*. And, thus, Fukuyama asks: "Is there not a side of the human personality that deliberately seeks out struggle, risk, and daring, and will this side not remain unfulfilled by the 'peace and prosperity' of contemporary liberal democracy?" Pondering this he remains somewhat anxious that the "fear of becoming 'last men' might lead men to assert themselves in new and unforeseen ways, even to the point of becoming once again bestial 'first men'. . . ." His hopeful answer to the threat of resurgent "megalothymia" is that the marketplace and activities such as sports (and the combination of the two—for example, the triumph of capital at the 1992 Barcelona Olympics) and presidential campaigns (so that's what they're really about?) will continue to provide outlets for troublesome "thymotic activity." I am tempted to add that we could always set up Aztec "flower wars" for insatiable megalothymiacs or, what the hell, give them spots on the McLaughlin Group and CNN's Capital Gang.

Fukuyama's history really is aggravating. It's not so much the errors of fact as it is the gross omissions. But should we really expect otherwise? Fukuyama is a philosopher, not a historian— leading me to recall the British Marxist historian V. G. Kiernan's reflection to me that "All that philosophers have discovered since the world began could be written on one sheet of paper." And in this vein it should be recognized that Fukuyama is not the only one who thinks we have reached the end of the line. Many a postmodern philosopher and critic (supposedly leftist) has also leapt from Hegel to Nietzsche, though more affirmatively so, and, having abandoned the Enlightenment and Marx along the way, has also contended that we've landed in "post-history" or, as the French would say, post-*histoire*. In short, the present is also our future. German social theorist and critic Jurgen Habermas was evidently onto something when he referred to an affinity between the New Right and the postmodernists.

Constructing his own neo-Hegelian and neo-Kojèvian version of past and present, Fukuyama ignores or glosses over significant aspects of modern political and social history. Crucially, he separates economics and politics and, even though he registers the fact that capitalism by no means secures a democratic polity, he fails to acknowledge, first, that the struggles to resist, reform and/or transcend the imperatives and rule of capital—engendered by (yes, I'll say it!) its inherently exploitative, oppressive, and antagonistic relations—have been a, if not *the*, primary dynamic of democratic development and, second, that the defense of capital and its prerogatives has been and remains a foremost obstacle and threat to freedom and democratic politics and possibilities.

Friends have suggested that I make too much of Fukuyama's book. Arguably, enough is being made of it by his publicists. (Like the original article, the book is being marketed globally, and on a recent trip to Britain I was astounded by the number of people right, left and center who were familiar with and admiring of Fukuyama's work.) However, it is not just a question of challenging his scholarship or, for that matter, his 15 minutes of fame (which, given his now regular appearances in the pages of such periodicals as the *New Republic* and the *New York Times*, seems to be stretching to a whole half hour!). Fukuyama is smart, very smart; but he is no less an ideologue for that, and his thesis that we are at the "end of history," that at best our present is our future, must be read as more than just a clever intellectual and commercial coup. Along with his neoconservative mentors and mates—such as Irving Kristol, Allan Bloom, William J. Bennett, Chester Finn, Hilton Kramer, Roger Kimball, and Dinesh D'Souza—Fukuyama is one of the retainers of Olin Foundation satrap William E. Simon, who in *A Time for Truth* (1978) declared cultural war on liberals and the intellectual and academic left in the name of free markets, free enterprise and, as Joseph Peschek put it, "Free the Fortune 500!" (It must be noted that one of the latest Olin-sponsored initiatives is the National Association of Scholars, which is leading the campaign "to reclaim the academy.")

The End of History and the Last Man, with its scholarly discourse, may seem remote from the political and cultural fray but it represents yet another neocon salvo in what they call "the battle for ideas." While the other Olinists have been working their bully-pulpits, Fukuyama has articulated the grand "historical" vision and legitimation of the ambitions and campaigns of the Reagan-Bush right and the powers they serve, to limit and, wherever possible, to reverse the struggles and accomplishments of recent generations for social democracy and gender and racial equality. Though the right failed to create the new ideological consensus that they sought, they have wrought devastation and hardship, anxiety and cynicism. Even the *New York Times* has dedicated front-page stories to the fact that under Reagan and Bush (though admittedly it may well have begun under Carter) the rich have grown dramatically richer while the rest of us have been made poorer in the class war from above that has been the past generation of American life.

Indeed, in a certain sense the New Right has effectively refurbished late-twentieth century capitalist hegemony—even if the Republicans face possible defeat and expulsion from government in the November 1992 elections. Not only Soviet communism, but also socialism, social democracy, and even New-Deal and Great-Society liberalism have been made seemingly archaic and outmoded.

Since 1989 we have heard a chorus of voices—of which Fukuyama's has been the "smartest" and most "elevated"—declaring "The collapse of communism. . . . The triumph of capitalism. . . . The death of socialism. . . . Capitalism: the wave of the future and forever. . . ." Renowned international management theorist Peter Drucker, in his book *The New Realities* (1989), writes that we have entered a new epoch in which "socialism [from American liberalism and European social democracy to Soviet communism] has become the anachronism. Instead of capitalism being a transition stage on the socialist road, it now increasingly appears that socialism is a detour on the capitalist road." Edward Yardeni, in-house intellectual for Prudential-Bache Securities, announced in a much-touted pamphlet *The Triumph of Capitalism* (1989): "The big picture shows that people around the world share a desire to prosper. And increasingly they believe that capitalism is the means to that end—not communism, socialism. . . ." American political economist and prominent intellectual figure of the left Robert Heilbroner, who had once predicted the demise of "business civilization," now offers a new view of capitalism's status. In an article in the *New Yorker* (January 31, 1989) titled "The Triumph of Capitalism," he said: ". . . the contest between capitalism and socialism is over: capitalism has won." And liberal sociologist and former West German parliamentarian (and Trilateralist) Ralf Dahrendorf, in *Reflections on the Revolution in Europe* (1990)—whose title plays on Edmund Burke's response to the French Revolution of 1789—commands that "the point has to be made that socialism is dead, and that *none of its variants* can be revived."

Nor is this the view of elite/ist intellectuals alone. Again, the New Right may not have secured (as of yet) a new ideological *consensus*. Nevertheless, after the long decade of the 1980s it appears they have succeeded in creating a political culture of lowered expectations and aspirations and, arguably, as some have asserted, a "cynical society." As Joyce Kolko accurately observes ". . . few people any longer even conceive of other than a capitalist future"; or, as Philip Mattera sadly notes in *Prosperity Lost* (1990): "These days there is not much collective dreaming in America."

And let us not forget that Fukuyama's book emanates from the very same camp that is bringing us Bush's America 2000, National Education Goals and, of all things, "National History Standards"—and potentially, following the lead of their British Thatcherite comrades, a national history curriculum. We should keep a close watch on the products emanating from such enterprises as the National Center for History in the Schools (a cooperative venture of UCLA and Lynne Cheney's radically neoconservative National Endowment for the Humanities), which has been charged with responsibility for developing our "National History Standards." Pursued under the guise of the crisis of history and historical education and the goal of improving student and citizen knowledge of "the past," the Bush administration's ambition to create a national history curriculum clearly has been intended to reverse the steadily growing presence and influence of critical historical scholarship and pedagogy in the academy by pushing schools to teach a conservative rendition of American, Western, and world history. I can see it now: "America was thus clearly top nation, and history came to a ."

But, of course, even if the grand narratives are dead, historical development does not come to a full stop (barring nuclear war . . .) and dramatic possibilities remain. The collapse of the Soviet Empire is most welcome—though let us hope reasonable agencies prevail. At the same time, ever caught up in the persistent crises and contradictions of capitalism, with deepening recession and the threat of depression, we must seek to confront and work to prevent the further deterioration and collapse of our own liberal-democratic polity. The class and social struggles from below for justice and equality whose histories we have been so eager to recover and recall may be subdued, fractured, and dispersed today, but they continue. The question is how popular grievances, anxieties and aspirations/frustrations will come to be expressed: in the development of broad popular movements for change, or in riots and risings Los Angeles–style and a turning to candidates such as Ross Perot? And how will the political elites attempt to control events at home and abroad?

There are no guarantees. As international historian Fred Halliday has recently written in *New Left Review* (May 1992), although socialism has been removed from the political agenda we should not blind ourselves to the alternative possibility, that is, "there is an alternative path which liberal democracy could take, namely a regression to various forms of barbarism, national and international, by way of some mixture prevailing of capitalist-authoritarian, nuclear, ecological, racist and recidivist trends."

Thus, there is much to be done if we are to respond to the end-of-history hucksters. Whether this response takes the name of socialism or radical democracy, our traditions demand renewal and refurbishment. All too often this imperative has been assumed to mean a "going back to the drawing boards" in which intellectuals, philosophers, and theorists retire to their rooms to perfect some new model for the masses. However, radical historians must pursue an alternative practice.

We must commence by recalling and reasserting the vision of historical study that originally drew us to the discipline: a vision of historians as citizen-scholars who by their labors of cultivating the dialogue between past and present contribute directly to public culture and debate, to the democratic formation and re-formation of political and social thought, to the struggles of working people and the oppressed.

We must continue to pursue—and all the more effectively communicate and cultivate—the powers of the past: perspective, critique, consciousness, remembrance, and imagination. Our project remains the *historical* education of desire. And in this fashion we might yet contribute to the development of a politics that, dialectically engaged with the past, reaches beyond the world as it is, beyond the "end of history," and provides for the extension and refinement of the values, relations, and practices of liberty, equality, and democracy.

6 Photography and Historical Consciousness: Nicaragua, 1978–1979*

CONTEMPORARY CONSCIOUSNESS IS APPARENTLY characterized by historical amnesia. Not only do we seem to know little about history, but too often we view what little we know in terms of either nostalgia—an uncritical celebration of the past—or progress—an uncritical celebration of the present and imminent future. And yet, the growing recognition of our amnesia has stimulated some to pursue the necessary task of recultivating historical consciousness, defined by the novelist John Berger as "the experience of seeking to give meaning to our lives, of trying to understand the history of which we can become the active agents." Also, it is increasingly recognized that the remaking of historical consciousness cannot be the burden of the historian alone, for, as Berger goes on to observe, the consequences of historical amnesia are not merely academic: "A people or class which is cut off from its own past is far less free to choose and to act as a people or class than one that has been able to situate itself in history."[1]

Furthermore, the effort to reconstruct historical consciousness requires more than merely the provision of *more* historical knowledge; it also requires a reexamination of the way(s) in which historical knowledge itself is constructed and presented. Such work has begun in historical and cultural studies and it has generated, among other things, renewed interest in the study of visual and oral

* This chapter originally appeared in *Studies in Visual Communication*, vol. 8, no. 2, summer 1982, as a review of Susan Meiselas's *Nicaragua, June 1978–July 1979,* edited with Claire Rosenberg (New York, 1981).

cultures, given rise to the literary analysis of historical texts, and raised the critical issue of perspective in historical studies, that is, the question: "from whose perspective has the history been written?"

Offering much to these reexaminations have been the rediscovered writings of the Frankfurt-School essayist and critic Walter Benjamin. I have in mind two of his articles in particular. First, speaking directly to historical consciousness, there is "The Storyteller," in which Benjamin contends that the traditional practice of storytelling has been displaced in the modern world both by the novel and, even more forcefully in terms of narrative as a form, by the daily newspaper and *information.*[2] And, second, addressing the question of historical perspective—that is, *whose* version of history will be remembered?—there are his "Theses on the Philosophy of History," in which he so beautifully writes: "Only that historian will have the gift of fanning the spark of hope in the past who is firmly convinced that even the dead will not be safe from the enemy [the ruling class] if he wins. And the enemy has not ceased to be victorious."[3]

Long concerned about the problem of historical consciousness, John Berger himself has been very much influenced by Benjamin's writings. And, increasingly, his work, both alone and in conjunction with the photographer Jean Mohr, has focused on the relationship among history, experience, memory, and storytelling in literature and photography. Specifically, with regard to visual communications, Berger has been anxious to contribute to the development of an alternative photography that does not merely reproduce the contemporary social order but, rather, by contributing to the reconstruction of historical consciousness, opposes it.[4]

By *alternative* photography, Berger is not referring merely to "photographs . . . used as a radical weapon in posters, newspapers, pamphlets, and so on" (of which, however, he does acknowledge the real value); nor does he mean simply "aiming [the camera] at different targets." Rather, he says, photography needs to change "its practice." The question is "how?"

Berger explains what he means by indicating the distinction between the private use of photography, in which "the context of the instant recorded is preserved so that the photograph lives in an ongoing continuity," and the public use, in which "torn from its context, [the photograph] becomes a dead object which, exactly because it is dead, lends itself to any arbitrary use." He argues that "the task of an alternative photography is to incorporate photography into social and political memory, instead of using it as a substitute which encourages the atrophy of any such memory." The first principle of such a practice is that "the photographer . . . think of her or himself not so much as a reporter to the rest of the world but, rather, as a recorder for those involved in the events photographed." In essence, what Berger goes on to urge is that the photographer understand herself as a storyteller contributing to memory and historical consciousness.[5]

I have raised the issue of historical consciousness and noted the arguments of Walter Benjamin and John Berger as part of this essay on Susan Meiselas's *Nicaragua, June 1978–July 1979* not only in order to indicate the concerns that inform the review but, more important, because this particular work of Meiselas is the best contemporary example I have seen of the alternative photography for which Berger is calling. On this point, it should be stated that when I first "read" *Nicaragua* I was not very enthusiastic. However, upon closer examination of the work *and* my own reading of it, I realized that it was not merely a photo-history, reporting on the Nicaraguan Revolution to me, a North American, but, far more, it was a visual record and narrative (story) of the revolution for those who fought it. Understanding that, I could better grasp and appreciate Meiselas's epigraph: "NICARAGUA /A year of news,/as if nothing had happened before,/as if the roots were not there,/and the victory not earned./This book was made so that we remember."

The struggle that culminated in the battles of 1978-1979 began more than 50 years ago. From 1912 to 1933 Nicaragua was virtually a protectorate of the United States. During these years, except for a brief period in the 1920s, the U.S. Marines occupied the country and U.S. financial agents directed Nicaragua's revenue system, national bank, and railways. This direct involvement was for the

announced purpose of maintaining the country's political and economic stability—and, thereby, it also served the purpose of protecting
U.S. commercial and military interests (which at the time included the
real possibility of constructing a second trans-isthmus canal).

Moreover, it was in the course of this 20-year period that the
Nicaraguan economy was tied to that of the United States in a
relationship that students of economic development have termed
"dependency." At the same time, to prevent the possibility of a socialist
or even Mexican-style revolution, the U.S. occupying forces reorganized
the Nicaraguan military into a National Guard to police the country.

In 1934, the American-organized Nicaraguan National
Guard murdered the popular and progressive rebel leader, Agusto
Cesar Sandino. Not long after, the chief of the Guard, General
Anastasio Somoza Garcia, made himself dictator (and sometime
president) of the country, and the regime he established was inherited
by his sons. In fact, the Somoza dynasty ruled Nicaragua right up
until the 1978-79 revolution, a struggle led by a political and military
force calling itself the Frente Sandinista de Liberación Nacional
(FSLN)—the "Sandinistas"—in memory of the slain rebel leader.

In their 45-year rule of Nicaragua, the Somoza family put
together a business empire worth almost $500 million, the activities
of which effectively controlled 60 percent of the nation's economy
and included approximately 25 percent of the country's arable land.[6]
At the same time, 50 percent of the population had an average annual
income of $90, unemployment was officially at 22 percent but
affected 60 percent of the population, illiteracy was 50 percent
nationwide (80 percent in many rural areas), and housing and health
conditions were horrible. According to Meiselas, whose figures are
derived from United States' and United Nations' statistics: "Of every
1,000 children born, 102 died. Of every 10 deaths, 6 were of
infectious diseases, which are curable."

The Sandinista forces were recruited from among the
peasants, the urban working class, and the semi-proletariat characteristic of Latin American cities. Additionally, there were significant
numbers of middle-class students and intellectuals who joined to

fight the Somoza regime. And by the final stages of the armed struggle the *anti-Somocistas* represented a broad coalition of classes and social groups, including notable elements from the upper class and the Catholic Church.[7] Thus, the overthrow of the Somoza regime was truly a *popular* revolution.

Meiselas's *Nicaragua* is a work of 71 color photographs, followed by 31 pages of text, including a map of the country, titles for the photos, personal statements, prose and poetry by those who made and experienced the revolution, and a chronology of Nicaragua's history. The photographs are presented in the form of a narrative of the revolution. Rather than breaking up the flow of the narrative into chapters, Meiselas, with her co-editor, Claire Rosenberg, indicates the temporality of what is to follow on a prefatory page (along with her note on the importance of remembering), dividing the photos into three sections: June 1978—The Somoza Regime; September 1978—Insurrection; and June-July 1979—The Final Offensive.

From the very outset of the narrative, Meiselas records the experience of the Nicaraguan people. Indeed, the photographs not only communicate the immediate experience but also effectively incorporate and indicate the history that is present in this experience. Thus, the first photograph is of a traditional Indian dance mask that the rebels wore during the fight against Somoza in order to conceal their identities. Two photos later (the numbers in brackets indicate the number of the photograph in the book), we see a woman washing clothes in an open sewer-creek in downtown Managua [3]. The partially demolished buildings in the background recall the devastation of the 1972 earthquake and the corruption of the Somoza regime, which treated the international aid given to Nicaragua as a source of quick profits. There follows a photo of a farmworker harvesting sugarcane with a machete, his arm raised to slash—reminding one of a painting by Millet—and in the background stands one of Nicaragua's many volcanoes [4]. (According to historical legend, a Nicaraguan postage stamp, showing picturesque volcanoes, scared off the U.S. government from constructing a second Central American canal there.)

The next picture is of a laborer carrying a sack of coffee or grain up a gangplank to a ship destined, one imagines, for North America [5]. Still another photo shows a young woman in a maid's uniform tending to two young children at a Managua country club [6]. Inequality in Latin America has been depicted visually in many ways (often such a photo, shot from a distance, shows us the shacks of the poor, standing next to a new "modern" luxury apartment building). But Meiselas is not merely indicating the material conditions of class stratification and the labors of the poor. More than that, she is recording the *lived* experience of the people. Her pictures are close and at eye level. The people are the subject and the other elements in the photos support the telling of their story. The narrative form is important, for individually the photos might be read quite differently—for example, the photo at the country club might have been taken by a relative of the children, except the maid's expression would have been different, perhaps, on the insistence of the photographer.

Thus, the photographs introduce the people of Nicaragua in relation to their past and present. However, the portrayal of the social and power structures is not yet complete. The pictures that immediately follow present the Somoza regime and its National Guard. One of the photos is a "graduation" picture at the Guards' elite infantry school [8]. The graduates are holding cans of Schlitz beer, cueing us both to the dependent relationship of the Nicaraguan economy upon the United States and to the fact that the U.S. Marines originally organized the Guard.

The pictures of the Guard [8, 9, 11, 12] are defined for us by a photo [10] of a group of children standing before a bonfire and harassing guardsmen (who stand outside the picture). The terror and the tragedy of the Somoza regime are presented in a picture of a dismembered body on a hillside outside Managua [14]. The place, we are told in the text, was known as a site where the Guard assassinated those it viewed as a threat. The very next photo is of a wall on which is spraypainted the words, "Where is Norman Gonzalez? The Dictatorship must answer" [15]. Such photos are not easily forgotten.

The 15 photos of the September insurrection show a people at war [23-37]. I recollect Berger's words: "Events force us now to admit the courage of a people or a class; not the courage of a people as represented by their professional armies, but made manifest in the actions of the entire population, men and women, young and old."[8]

In Matagalpa, where many of Meiselas's photos were taken, the rebellion began spontaneously and encouraged similar uprisings elsewhere. The spontaneity of the insurrection, and its rapid spread, caught even the Sandinistas by surprise. The photos Meiselas provides of the fighting shows "*los muchachos*" (youths) in baseball caps, faces covered with bandannas, armed with handguns and rifles, stationed by low piles of sandbags or moving through the streets. Other people stand in doorways, observing. *Los muchachos* have control of the town but they are awaiting the Guard's counterattack. In the photos that follow, the Guard is counterattacking with aerial bombardment and tanks. Buildings are destroyed and many are dead: "The strategy of total war recognizes that it is necessary to try to break the courage and resistance of a whole people."[9]

Looking through these photographs I am reminded of the novel *Reasons of State* by Alejo Carpentier, detailing the career of a Latin American dictator (such as Somoza). At one point, a longtime European acquaintance of the dictator makes excuses for being unable to have dinner with him on the dictator's return to Paris after brutally suppressing a rebellion back home; then, finally, referring to a report in the newspaper, the acquaintance says, "I know there's a lot of exaggeration in it all. . . . They do extraordinary things nowadays in the way of trick photography . . . of course, it's all false."[10]

The defeat of the September insurrection did not diminish the Sandinistas' struggle. In fact, the ranks of their forces grew even faster, enabling them to expand the guerrilla war and prepare for the final offensive that came the following summer.[11] Meiselas's visual narrative briefly shifts to the hills [38, 39, 40], showing young men and women living together and getting ready to return to fight for the towns. And in the photographs that follow [41-46], she records the intensifying repression: schoolbuses are stopped and the children and young people are frisked by soldiers [42]; pregnant women are questioned at gunpoint by paramilitary squads [44].

The photos of the final offensive [47-64] and victory [65-71] are also well done and the experience and excitement are strongly communicated. The photographs remain close to the experience, from behind the barricades to the liberation of town and city. In fact, even at those moments when you expect to view what is happening from a rooftop—for example, when the victory is being celebrated in the central plaza of Managua [68-69]—Meiselas continues to record the experience as it is being lived, that is, we see the celebration from the street and at *popular* eye level.

The struggle and victory over the Somoza regime, Meiselas records, "left 40,000 dead (1.5 percent of the population); 40,000 children orphaned; 200,000 families homeless. . . ." Somoza himself fled with his family to Miami, but a year and a half later he was killed in Paraguay (which is itself still—after 30 years—under the rule of the Stroessner dictatorship).

Reading Meiselas's *Nicaragua* I was led to recall another book of photographs that I acquired about 12 years ago, a collection of pictures from the Mexican Revolution, 1910-1917.[12] A variety of photos in the two works parallel, if not almost replicate, each other: the dictators taking part in ceremonies; the people in the streets carrying banners; cannons/tanks in the streets and the destruction wrought; young women rebels carrying rifles alongside the young men; a body being burned in the street to avoid epidemics; and so on. And there is a series of photographs in the Mexican collection that does not appear in the Nicaraguan book, and hopefully will never need to be added: that is, photos of U.S. troops landing in and occupying Vera Cruz (again, something that Nicaraguans themselves have already experienced this century).

In addition to its reminding us of the earlier Mexican Revolution, Meiselas's work, however much it is the telling of the Nicaraguan experience, draws our attention to contemporary struggles elsewhere in Central America, especially those in El Salvador and Guatemala. *¡La lucha continua!*

7 The Nobel Prize, the Memory Prize, and the Twentieth Century*

THE ANNOUNCEMENT OF THE Nobel prizes is always an exciting and inspiring occasion and, once again, it has stimulated discussion and reflection among my colleagues and students. The recent foundation of another international award, Le Prix de la Memoire (the Memory Prize), has gained less attention. Yet as we approach the end of this tumultuous century, this new prize may be more emblematic and expressive of all that our time has entailed and demands. Indeed, together, the Nobel and the Memory prizes might be viewed as boundary markers to the twentieth century.

The Nobel prizes were first awarded in 1901. They were established to recognize and reward those accomplishments in physics, chemistry, medicine, literature, economics (added in 1969), and peace deemed by the judges to have conferred "the greatest benefits on mankind." The endowment of the prizes well reflected the European world view of the long nineteenth century (1789-1914), whose historical consciousness was shaped by both the Enlightenment dream of the mutual advance of reason and freedom and the material experience of the Industrial Revolution with its technological progress and economic development. The Nobel prizes expressed the optimism, confidence, and belief in continued progress engendered by European modernity *and* supremacy.

* This chapter was first published in *The Times Higher Education Supplement,* November 30, 1990. I must thank Yvette Cohen for translating documents from the French and for her discussions with me about the Memory Prize.

At the same time, they revealed an anxiety about the future, shown by the inclusion of the Peace Prize. Alfred Nobel himself, the inventor of dynamite and other explosives whose accumulated fortune funded the prizes, lived the contradictions of the age most intensely. A lifelong pacifist who was committed to the peaceful application of his inventions, Nobel witnessed—unable to prevent it—their steady incorporation into the science of war. And, as we well know, Europeans and others proceeded to fulfill all of those anxious expectations and more in the course of two world wars, the Holocaust and other genocidal acts, and a parade of tyrannical and barbaric regimes.

As we approach the end of the century (and the millennium) we are chastened; we are less confident and less optimistic that the application of reason assures the advance of freedom or that the progress of technology necessarily promises social improvement. Naturally, we welcome the termination of the Cold War and celebrate the successful struggles for freedom and democratic rights in Central and Eastern Europe (and soon, we hope, elsewhere). Yet, we've come to understand the tenuousness of peace and democracy and to realize that, ironically and tragically, the finest ideals and aspirations can be perverted and rationalized to serve the crudest and cruelest of purposes and ends.

The most celebrated figures at the outset of this century were those of the scientist and the industrial innovator. Directing our attentions to the future, their initiatives promised the possibility of still further progress and even greater command over our natural and social environments. Today, however, following the horrors of the past several generations, the persons who should be accorded the greatest recognition are those who, taking up the task of bearing witness to the exterminations, the massacres, the tortures, direct our thoughts to the *past* and to the imperatives of remembrance, realizing that the final victories of the murderers and the torturers would be the suppression, deliberate or otherwise, of the knowledge of their criminal acts.

Awarded for the first time in 1989, the Memory Prize was instituted by the France-Libertes Foundation under the auspices of

Danielle Mitterand, the wife of the French president. Intended to recognize those who labor to secure our collective memory and to prevent the falsification of the historical record, the idea for the prize arose out of the growing awareness that "the expression, transmission, and preservation of Human Memory is the most effective means of struggling against the recurrence of barbarism." In 1989 the prize was presented to Serge Klarsfeld, the French historian and Nazi-hunter; the Matenadaran Museum of the Armenian People's Memory; and the Dalai Lama (who also received the Nobel Peace Prize in that year); and the 1990 recipients of the prize were the Memorial Association for the Remembrance of the Victims of Stalinism (USSR); the Kurdish Institute in Paris; and the House of the Slaves at Goree (Senegal).

The Nobel and Memory prizes reflect the different times in which they were created. The Nobel is grounded in imagination and the hope of progress, the Memory Prize in remembrance and the hope of justice. Together they articulate the paradox but, also, the promise of our century.

8 The Making of American Memory?*

POWERFUL TENDENCIES *OR* TENDENTIOUS POWER?

HOWEVER ANXIOUS WERE THE years following the Second World War, they were also the age of Pax Americana and the liberal consensus, and Americans' understanding of past, present, and future exuded confidence and optimism. As Frances Fitzgerald observed in the early 1970s: "The national myth is that of creativity and progress, of a steady climbing upward into power and prosperity, both for the individual and the country as a whole. Americans see history as a straight line and themselves standing at the cutting edge of it as representatives for all mankind."[1] The schooling in history we received in the 1950s and early 1960s reflected just such a vision of America.

In contrast to the postwar period, American historical memory, consciousness, and imagination have been subject to a pretty rough ride these past twenty years. In the wake of the struggles and shocks of the 1960s and, then, Vietnam, Watergate, and economic recession, the years since 1974 have been marked by anxiety and pessimism. By all accounts, we have been living through a series of "crises": of Democracy, of the Family, of the Welfare State,

* The first part of this chapter was first published in *American Quarterly,* vol. 46, no. 2, June 1994, as a review of Michael Kammen's *Mystic Chords of Memory: The Transformation of Tradition in American Culture* (New York, 1991). The latter part originally appeared in the *San Francisco Examiner,* July 7, 1993, as a review of Ronald Takaki's *A Different Mirror: A History of Multicultural America* (Boston, 1993).

of Education. In fact, Americans comprehend contemporary history as a "break" with the past; there is a pervasive sense of discontinuity and a growing belief that we are now suffering decline as did Greece, Rome, Spain, and Britain before us. What we have been experiencing is a crisis of what Fitzgerald called "the national myth" or what I would call a crisis of the grand–governing narrative of American experience.[2]

Historians themselves first became aware of the "crisis of history" in the mid-1970s, when they saw commitment to historical study collapse at all levels of schooling. It was a truly frustrating experience, for the very same developments that led to the enervation of the grand narrative and the devaluation of historical education engendered a tremendous popular demand for "the past" as people sought new ways of relating to history. Making the situation all the more exasperating was the fact that historical scholarship itself was flourishing with the development of the new social history and the refashioning of the past "from the bottom up" by way of class, race, and gender questions.[3] Unfortunately, however "radical" historians may have been in their research and writing, they regularly failed to appreciate the deeply *political* character of the crisis, and their "professional" responses to it were usually limited to concocting strategies and schemes to secure a larger share of the public-cultural "market."

Where historians feared to tread, pundits and politicos of the ascendant New Right rushed in to aggressively exploit anxieties *and* to articulate the crisis of history as a public issue. In pursuit of a new conservative consensus and governing narrative for late-twentieth-century corporate America, they placed the crisis directly on the political agenda via the agencies of the Reagan and Bush administrations. Encompassing such issues as the crisis of "the canon" and cultural literacy, and neo-McCarthyite rhetoric about "political correctness" ("PC"), by the close of the long decade of the 1980s the right had articulated the problem as an argument for the creation of "National History Standards." Whatever one's feelings about a national curriculum, it must not be forgotten that the demand for "standards" originated from the very same camp as the proclamation that we have reached "the end of history," that we have achieved the highest possible forms of liberty, equality, and democracy.[4]

Of course, even if historians have failed to recognize that the crisis has called for a decidedly more engaged cultural politics, their own scholarly endeavors have not failed to be shaped by the question. In addition to establishing programs to train applied and public historians, they have been actively exploring the social construction of American historical memory. Related to the development of "cultural studies," the most critical and also entertaining work has been produced by historians involved with MARHO (Mid-Atlantic Radical Historians Organization), but—as Michael Kammen's new book attests—such studies have not been limited to a single current.[5]

In both size and scope, *Mystic Chords of Memory* is the first "grand" volume on the subject of American memory. Attending to developments in the arts and literature, public rhetoric and sermonizing, associational activity and public pageantry, collecting and bequesting, restoration and re-creation, museum building and historiography, Kammen attempts nothing less than to tell the history of how American memory or "tradition" has been made and re-made through the course of two centuries.[6] The primary question he sets out to answer is: ". . . when and how did the United States become a land of the past, a culture with a discernible memory (or with a configuration of recognized pasts)?" He states that he has sought not only to capture the changing content of our national memory, but also the forces and conflicts shaping it, in particular, the changing roles of government and the private sector regarding custodianship *and* the varying effects of class, ethnicity, race, and regionalism. Although there are dry spots in the text, Kammen is a great storyteller and, even where his analysis is inadequate, I found his tales insightful.

A significant feature of the book is Kammen's commitment to comparing American experience with that of other countries, a commitment he pursues in three special coda chapters. He offers a variety of well-developed, though, in most instances, not exactly surprising observations, such as: "There has been a relentlessly dialogical relationship between the values of tradition and progress (or modernism) in American culture" such that we find a "tradition of progress" discourse; and, "It has been a dominant assumption for most of American history that the private sector rather than government ought to be the primary custodian of tradition." Far more problematic is his declaration that American experience has been characterized by a "quest for consensus and stability."[7] I shall return to this point.

Kammen divides the history of American memory into four periods: pre-1870, 1870-1915, 1915-1945, and 1945-1990. Reminding me of my own 1960s cohort's response to student social amnesia today, Kammen discusses how the Revolutionary generation's original eagerness to unburden themselves of "the past" later gave way to concern about younger generations' ignorance of history and indifference to tradition. Nevertheless, the formation of a national historical memory was inevitable (assuming the survival of a singular United States). New Englanders promoted the "Pilgrim Fathers" tradition, but it was not long before a more decidedly "national" tradition prevailed—the Revolution, July 4th and the Spirit of '76—providing the foundations for an American "civil religion." Kammen notes that history itself was a minor subject in schools, and historiography had to do more with teaching morality than teaching about the past.

The period 1870-1915 was characterized by a "new hunger for history and traditions" and in these decades, Kammen says, American memory began to "take form as a self-conscious phenomenon." In the face of Darwinism and the power of science, history and tradition became "surrogates" for religion and faith and inspired the further cultivation of a national*istic* American civil religion expressed in patriotic hymns, flag worship, and pilgrimages to sacred national sites. The hunger for "the past" was evident in a variety of ways, from the manifold efforts—North and South—to commemorate the Civil War, to the explosion of professional historical scholarship and publication. Civil War commemorations were not intended to resuscitate regional differences and hostilities but to promote White reconciliation; thus, the selective memory of the nation continued to exclude African American experience and participation. However, this did not keep Black Americans from securing their own historical memories and creating traditions such as "Juneteenth" in celebration of their emancipation from slavery.

Carried out predominantly through individual and private enterprise (enabling "malefactors" like Andrew Carnegie, and the Vanderbilt family to transform themselves into "benefactors" by endowing libraries, museums, and universities), fascination with and praise for the past actually had more to do with celebrating the present. Kammen does a splendid job of recounting competing efforts by factions of the elite to determine the national memory (for example, Franco- vs. Anglo-philes, and the subsequent victory of "Anglo-American Civilization"). But most intriguing is his discussion of how upper-class "historical" anxieties and ambitions were motivated by the cultural and political "challenges" posed by immigration. Noting that these practices revealed a broader racism than simple Negrophobia, he highlights the rise of "Anglo-Saxonism" and filiopiety (ancestor worship) evidenced by the new popularity of genealogy and the foundation of lineage-based associations such as the Daughters of the American Revolution.

Yet, however good it felt to elevate one's forebears, it didn't do anything to address the (new) immigrants who—assuredly—were energetically engaged in organizing unions *and* socialist and anarchist groups. In other words, the issue remained of what to do about the "millions of newcomers alien to our traditions." Reactions to the newcomers ranged from the xenophobic to the pedagogical, that is, from anti-democratic dreams of apartheid to instituting programs of "Americanization" including the enhancement of history curricula to more effectively inculcate American traditions in the children of Italians, Slavs, Jews, and so on. Indeed, the public discourse of the turn of the century bears a striking resemblance to that of today regarding the "crisis of history" and the question of cultural literacy.

As we would expect, immigrants' responses also varied (though these are relatively underdeveloped by Kammen).

The years 1915-1945 witnessed dramatic shifts in the making of American memory and tradition. Though Europeanism persisted, Americana and Americanism were clearly ascendant; there was the emergence of a uniquely American aesthetic in the arts, constituted by a symbiosis of modernism and nostalgia. As Kammen puts it: "Americans declared their cultural independence." The central question on the cultural agenda seems to have become that of the priority to be given to fomenting a "national culture" as opposed to regional "folk cultures." Private undertakings remained paramount in the 1920s and, Kammen stresses, the shape of Americana was heavily determined by very rich collectors and prestigious museums. Most notable and original were the respective creations of Henry Ford and John D. Rockefeller, Greenfield Village in Michigan and Colonial Williamsburg in Virginia. Yet, equally important in Kammen's narrative is Roosevelt's New Deal of the 1930s, for it involved government taking on a much greater role than hitherto as curator and custodian of America's past. Whether via public or private enterprise, a notable development of the period was the "democratization" of tradition in terms of both content and accessibility.

Kammen contends that American life since 1945 has been characterized by a "pronounced sense of discontinuity between past and present," engendering an unprecedented appetite for "the past" and an explosion in the number and variety of public and commercial activities and commodities seeking to satisfy or exploit it. History becomes a "cash crop." (I cannot help but note that the local newspaper has just arrived at our home and the special Memorial Day 1993 cover of the enclosed *USA Weekend Magazine* announces: "AMERICANA—For Summer, Fresh Looks at Old Favorites: The Alamo, Graceland and Many More.")

Kammen tells a few of his very best stories in this section, for example, those about the Freedom Train and the Civil War Centennial. Visited by 3.5 million people, the red, white, and blue–painted Freedom Train traveled America in 1947-49 carrying an exhibition of 127 historic documents. Accomplished through government and business cooperation, its creation was clearly intended to promote patriotism (but *not* commodities, as it certainly would today) and domestic Cold Warriorism. Yet, the story is not as one-dimensional as it seems. The Freedom Train's opponents included not just Communists, radicals, and pacifists but, especially at the outset, Republicans fearful of the benefits to be derived by Truman and the Democrats. Moreover, we are reminded of the liberal character of the postwar consensus by the fact that the Freedom Train carried more than one political message: The directors of the foundation responsible for its tour declared that they "would not tolerate any form of [racial] segregation during the scheduled visits" and, due to official unwillingness to comply, the Freedom Train bypassed Memphis and Birmingham.

However much Kammen's storytelling makes these chapters on the years 1945-90 interesting and enjoyable, in the end I found his treatment of the period disappointing. Although he grants that the nostalgia boom really didn't take off until the 1970s, Kammen insists that Americans' sense of "discontinuity" originated in the late 1940s. In so doing, he fails to appreciate the hegemonic character of the postwar liberal consensus and its governing narrative and, crucially, the depth and extent of the crisis that later shook American historical consciousness in the 1970s. Furthermore, like so many of his colleagues he also fails to recognize the deeply political character of the crisis of history and the significance of the concerted campaigns of the New Right and their corporate sponsors to shape American historical memory and imagination.

Mystic Chords of Memory is an impressive book, and all future work on the subject will have to touch base with it. However, as much as I learned from and was engaged by Kammen's storytelling, the work as a whole is not gripping. Kammen does a remarkable job of relating the aspirations and agencies of the upper classes and the conflicts and competitions *within* their ranks (his skill here can teach a great deal to radical historians); but, as his treatment of the 1970s and 1980s indicates, he fails to develop the kind of critical social and political history of American memory and tradition that his introductory remarks seemed to promise.

Kammen the storyteller is clearly sensitive to inequalities and injustices and, also, to the ironic character of history, but he doesn't take his analyses of power, hegemony, and conflict far enough. The narrative does not sufficiently portray the prevailing class and social struggles over the "selective tradition" and the dynamic interplay between those struggles and American political development. Occasionally a sense of history from the bottom up does reveal itself in the narrative—for example, in Kammen's one-paragraph discussion of John Steinbeck's *Grapes of Wrath* he says: "Among the statements which the widely read novel sought to make were two which are related: even poor people have histories, and in their own way they understand that perfectly well." Still, I am tempted to say that the work itself remains too genteel—that it could have used a good dose of "bottom-up" thinking.

In spite of Kammen's apparent recognition of the ideological ambitions of the elites, he ends up offering yet another version of "consensus history," succinctly summarized in his thesis statement that "Although there have been a great many political conflicts concerning American traditions, ultimately there is a *powerful tendency in the United States to depoliticize traditions for the sake of 'reconciliation.'* Consequently, the politics of culture in this country has everything to do with the process of contestation *and* with the subsequent quest for reconciliation" (my italics). Admittedly, popular rebellions have subsided since the 1960s, but, considering the class war from above to which we have been subjected these past twenty years, and the use and abuse of history pursued by the powers that be as part of it, such an assertion is rather surprising.

Where Kammen sees a "powerful tendency," I would ask us to look more closely for "powerful" human agencies. And, where he sees the "depoliticization of traditions for the sake of reconciliation," I would ask us to remember that what we actually may be witnessing is "the pursuit of hegemony" in which a governing class attempts to (re)secure the political and social order through "consensus-building."

As Antonio Gramsci observed: "[Within essential limits] hegemony presupposes that account be taken of the interests and tendencies of the groups over which hegemony is to be exercised, and that a certain compromise equilibrium be formed—in other words, that the leading group should make sacrifices."[8]

Again, in spite of his attention to elite ambitions and conflicts, Kammen seems incapable of asking to what extent American elites have constituted *governing*—or, dare I say it in this "post-Marxist" age, *ruling*—classes, with all that this entails, and thus to what extent such efforts at "reconciliation" actually have been efforts to "depoliticize" American life—with its ever-threatening social contradictions and persistent values of freedom, equality, and democracy—in favor of the status quo and the continued predominance of the elites of the day. What Kammen doesn't seem to realize is that a neutered politics is still a "politics."

TOWARD A MULTICULTURAL AMERICAN MEMORY

My great-grandparents were Russian Jewish artisans who came to America—to Ellis Island and the sweatshops of New York City's Lower East Side—to escape pogroms and poverty. Upon becoming a lawyer during the "Red Scare" of the early 1920s, my grandfather, a young socialist, changed our family name of Kaminetsky to Kaye because the former sounded too "foreign and Bolshevik." My best buddy, the grandson of Japanese immigrants to California, was born in an internment camp in Arkansas while both our fathers were fighting America's enemies in the Second World War. A professor of architecture and planning, my friend also works with the Oneida Indians of Wisconsin in their efforts to transcend the miseries of the past and create a better life on the reservation.

Anyone who tries to write a history of the United States today will have to find a way of expressing both the tragic contradictions and the great possibilities to be found in our multicultural national past and present and in the biographies of families like the

Jewish American Kayes, the Japanese American Babas, and the Native American Skenandores. But it's not just a matter of literary talent. In the words of the New Right pundits and politicos, there is a "culture war" under way over what it means to be an American. Thus, to write a new history of America is to become engaged in those battles.

Conservatives have sought to block the development of a multicultural approach to the nation's past. They argue that to teach such a history undermines our "national" identity and pride and foments ethnic tribalism. From a quite different vantage point, Afrocentrists also oppose it. They claim that even a *multi*cultural history suppresses the particular experiences and achievements of African Americans. At the same time, liberals who support multi-cultural education often want to turn it into a mere celebration of "differences and variety."

Following a more critical path, Ronald Takaki's *A Different Mirror* demonstrates that multiculturalism is essential not only to comprehending the diversity of experience that has been and remains America, but also to appreciating the long and continuing struggles to realize those very principles we proclaim to be so fundamental to American life—freedom, equality, and democratic citizenship.

The grandson of Japanese immigrant plantation workers in Hawaii, Takaki is a professor of ethnic studies at Berkeley and author of several works on race and ethnicity in America, including the award-winning volume *Strangers from a Different Shore: A History of Asian Americans* (1989). In his new book *A Different Mirror,* he offers a grander view of American history extending from the "age of encounter" through the latter half of the twentieth century and peopled respectively by Indians, Africans, Mexicans, Irish, Chinese, Japanese, and Jews.

Takaki has done his homework, and *A Different Mirror* deserves a very wide readership (though, unfortunately, Italian Americans, among others, will be disappointed that their immigrant forebears do not find a larger place in the volume). Drawing on the many studies of class, race and ethnicity, and gender published since the 1960s, and weaving into his story the words of memoir, poetry, and fiction, he provides a moving synthesis of the making of America.

Contrary to the accusations that multiculturalists reduce American experience to "victimology," Takaki's subjects are not victims. Conquest and colonialism, slavery and servitude, and exploitation and oppression are recounted. Yet, Takaki never fails to reveal that however much they suffered, minorities and immigrant working people also resisted their oppressors and struggled to hold the Anglo-American powers that be accountable to their own professed ideals. Many times they failed. Still, at other times they succeeded and, in so doing, advanced their own and all Americans' prospects a bit further along.

The climactic moment of *A Different Mirror* is the Second World War. The contradictions at this time were glaring. The United States was committed to fighting fascism. It was a struggle defined as a democratic and antiracist mission. And yet, America itself was still divided by systems of apartheid and ethnic quotas. While American soldiers "of color" were serving their country abroad, their families continued to suffer discrimination and abuse at home. Even as the Japanese American young men of the 442d Regiment were liberating the survivors of Dachau, their own families were being held in "concentration camps" in America. These contradictions instigated a new political consciousness and renewed aspirations and, in the ensuing years, radical changes were accomplished, again, through social movement, organization, and struggle.

Following a decade and more in which the rich are being made richer and the poor poorer, and racial and ethnic differences are again being used by the politically powerful to turn working men and women against each other, Takaki performs a most valuable service in reminding us of how much has been accomplished and of those not so rare democratic moments when lines of accent, color, and custom were transcended in favor of broader working-class solidarities.

In the face of events last year like the riots in Los Angeles and the street-fighting in Brooklyn, New York, I hope we will see further works like *A Different Mirror.* Given the political, economic, and cultural challenges we face *as a nation,* and the foolish and dangerous rhetoric that passes for political commentary on radio and television talk shows, we need as many books like Takaki's as we can get.

9 Ideas Do Have Consequences: A Note on Rush, Newt, and the Culture Wars*

UNDERESTIMATING THE NEW RIGHT'S resources and determination to both recapture power and continue the fabrication of a new conservative political hegemony, many of us on the left had hoped that Bill Clinton's election to the presidency in 1992 would bring an end or, at least, a reduced level of hostilities to the seemingly interminable "culture wars." Obviously, that was just wishful thinking. On November 8, 1994—on the very evening I was delivering the Deutscher Memorial Lecture, "Why Do Ruling Classes Fear History?"—the Republicans were marching to victory in the midterm elections, eager to realize their political, economic, *and* cultural ambitions.

Indeed, by capturing both the Senate and the House of Representatives, the Republicans have been able to enact most of their promised "Contract with America."[1] Plus, it has afforded them new bully-pulpits from which to pursue their cultural combats. Actually, the "Contract" itself contained hardly a reference at all to questions of culture. What it emphasized were budget cuts, welfare reform, and tax reduction. However, in the months since November, the right has aggressively renewed the culture wars.

* This chapter first appeared in *The Times Higher Education Supplement,* July 28, 1995. I would like to thank the deputy editor, David Jobbins, for commissioning me to serve as a regular contributor to the newspaper's World View column.

Arguably, such battles have served merely to distract attention from more important political and economic developments. Most crucially, they have diverted public debate from the concurrent class war from above, by which the rich have gotten richer and working people and the poor have been made poorer at an unprecedented rate during the past twenty years.

And yet, the culture wars are not simply diversions. Whether we like it or not, for those of us working in the humanities and social studies they place on the public agenda the question of what it is that we are about: What is our social purpose—to serve as a bolster for the status quo *or* to serve as a critical force in contemporary America? And, beyond that, they pose the questions, What is the meaning of America? *and* Who is an American?

Therefore, at the heart of the culture wars we necessarily find the problem of history and historical education. For example, the National Standards in History project, commissioned by the Bush administration but released in late 1994 under Clinton, was pounced upon by conservatives in Congress and the media for its critical and multicultural approach to America's past. The standards are now being revised—how dramatically, we do not yet know.[2]

Also, the Smithsonian Institution's plans for the fiftieth anniversary of the dropping of the atomic bomb on Japan were forced to be cancelled because of congressional and, especially, conservative opposition to what many claimed was going to be "anti-American historical revisionism." The curators of the planned exhibit at the National Air and Space Museum in Washington apparently failed to highlight adequately atrocities committed by the Japanese military during the war and made the mistake of including questions about the decision to drop the bomb. At the same time, the Republican leadership announced their intentions to terminate both the National Endowment for the Arts and the National Endowment for the Humanities. (The latter is the major source of funding both for scholarship and for extra-academic public education in historical and cultural studies.[3])

Furthermore, conservatives reinvigorated their campaigns to portray teachers and scholars in history and the humanities as subversives (leading one to wonder when they'll propose resurrecting the House Un-American Activities Committee). The most persistent attack dog has been talk-radio figure, bestselling author, and proud college dropout Rush Limbaugh, who fulminates daily and nationally on his radio and late-night television shows about "the disease of poisonous liberalism," "commie-libs," "femi-Nazis," and how 1960s radicals have "bullied their way into power in academia" and are "distorting our history and indoctrinating our children and young people."[4]

Considering such assaults, the ascendance of Newt Gingrich to the post of Speaker of the House of Representatives and effective leader of the New Right Republicans is most intriguing for he holds a PhD in History and taught for several years at the college level (demonstrating that while the Republicans may be the stupid party, they are not uneducated).

Thus, I eagerly awaited the appearance of Gingrich's controversial book, *To Renew America* (controversial, because of the multi-million dollar advance on royalties that he was publicly forced to turn down from one of Rupert Murdoch's publishing houses for it seemed inappropriate in view of legislation pending in Congress affecting Murdoch's media holdings).[5] I wanted to know what this champion of the right had to say about history and historical teaching. What I have found just goes to show that a little bit of knowledge can be a dangerous thing. His attacks on academe simply repeat the (in most cases) absurd claims of others, and the historical arguments he makes are just plain silly. Unfortunately, given his official station, they cannot be ignored.

At the very outset of his book, Gingrich notes that his foremost childhood anxiety had to do with the question of the rise and fall of civilizations and, especially, the possibility of America's own demise. These worries led him as a boy to read Arnold Toynbee's *A Study of History* and science fiction writer Isaac Asimov's Foundation trilogy. Still plagued by the anxieties of his youth, Gingrich indicates that more recently the books that have inspired him are those by pop futurologists Alvin and Heidi Toffler, referring us specifically to *Future Shock*. Influenced by Toynbee, Asimov, and the Tofflers, Gingrich declares that we are on the verge of the "Third Wave Information Age," entailing a world-historical transformation comparable to the Agricultural and Industrial Revolutions.[6]

The challenge, according to Gingrich, is to prepare the United States to lead this new revolution. The problem is that "For the past thirty years, we have been influenced to abandon our culture and seem to have lost faith in the core values, traditions, and institutions of our civilization." And guess who is to blame? Predictably, Gingrich targets the 1960s generation as the culprits: "The intellectual nonsense propagated since 1965—in the media [and] on university campuses—now threatens to cripple our ability to teach the next generation to be Americans."

Talk about "nonsense"! Trying hard to give as much weight as he can to the current crisis, Gingrich asserts that "*From the arrival of English-speaking colonists in 1607 until 1965, there was one continuous civilization built around a set of commonly accepted legal and cultural principles. . . .* Since 1965, however, there has been a calculated effort by cultural elites to discredit this civilization and replace it with a culture of irresponsibility that is incompatible with American freedoms as we have known them" (my italics). This, from a PhD in History? For a start, what happened to slavery, racism, and segregation *and* the story of the hard-fought struggles from below waged against them?

Gingrich accuses the current cohort of college teachers of having "hijacked" higher education and of "brainwashing a generation with a distorted version of reality." He doesn't actually lay out his preferred curriculum, but his remarks, such as those just quoted, do give us a pretty good sense of what it would be like. In fact, Gingrich insists that American history must be told in "romantic terms," later adding that "America is a series of folktales that just happen to be true." Like Gingrich, I, too, am capable of getting romantic about American experience. But it is outrageous and dangerous to propose that historical education be reduced to legend, myth, and folklore.

Evidently, and tragically, the culture wars—and the class wars with which they are bound up—are far from over. Right now, however, I can do no better than close with a few more of Gingrich's own words: "All this would be laughable, if it weren't destructive of America's future . . . ideas do have consequences."

10 All That Is Solid Melts into Air . . . or Baseball and Capitalism, the View from Left Field*

> *To articulate the past historically does not mean to recognize it "the way it really was" (Ranke). It means to seize hold of a memory as it flashes up at a moment of danger. Historical materialism wishes to retain that image of the past which unexpectedly appears to man singled out by history at a moment of danger. The danger affects both the content of the tradition and its receivers. The same threat hangs over both: that of becoming a tool of the ruling classes.*
>
> —Walter Benjamin,
> *Theses on the Philosophy of History*

I AM NOT EXACTLY sure when I became a socialist, yet I know that it grew out of a critical and democratic spirit imbued in me by my grandparents and parents, and a sense that the things we hold most dear are constantly threatened by the workings of the market and those who wield power within it. But, especially, I believe it had something to do with our great national pastime, *baseball.*

* This chapter was first published in the *Elysian Fields Quarterly,* vol. 12, no. 1, 1993. I want to thank Stephen Lehman for his commitment to the magazine and his interest in my views on both times past and the national pastime. Also, I must acknowledge the curious fact that not long after publishing this cathartic memoir I made my first visits to California.

When I was a child growing up in the New York area in the 1950s, a good part of every spring and summer was taken up with playing ball, "for real" in a playground, field, or street setting and, on rainy days or when my mother called me to dinner too early, in the imagination in front of the hall mirror with glove on the hand and cap on the head, pretending that I was pitching to the top of the opposing team's lineup. The rest of the time was spent following the progress (or otherwise) of my absolutely favorite team, actually, the *only* team that mattered, the Brooklyn Dodgers.

My family, unlike most of the others that had moved out of "the city" and into the suburban New Jersey development where we had bought a house, came not from the Bronx but from Brooklyn and, thus, in contrast to my buddies who were avid followers of the Yankees, I was a devout fan of the Dodgers. Looking back, there is no doubt that although the 1950s were good years for the Dodgers, the Yankees were a phenomenon. But such commitments were not based on critical assessment, they had to do with family, tradition, sentiments, and roots—when we made bets we didn't check the odds, we just hoped and prayed that our team was better.

There was no question about my own family's attachments. Both of my parents were from Brooklyn (my dad had graduated from Thomas Jefferson High School, and my mom, from Tilden) and my grandfather was a close friend and associate of the then-manager of the team, Charlie Dressen. Indeed, when Grandpa Nat would take me to Ebbets Field I always got to meet the ballplayers and, presumably against the rules, I regularly got to sit in the Dodger dugout for part of the game. (I still have my collection of personally autographed baseballs and bats, and I carefully guard the photographs of me in a Dodger jacket, sitting on the laps of Duke Snyder and Gil Hodges.)

Of course, the Yankees versus Dodgers thing between my friends and me was played out in absurd arguments and acts by all concerned. But I committed the worst offense. One season Mickey Mantle himself came to live in our New Jersey town, renting a home in a neighboring housing tract. And—would you believe it?—that very same summer I actually won a Mickey Mantle baseball card in a game of "flip." Obviously, looking back, the smart thing to do would have been to hang out and wait at the local shopping center where Mickey and his family frequently stopped in order to get him to sign the card. But that was not for me, the Dodger fanatic. Instead, following an afternoon when my cohort and I ran into him at the candy and newspaper store, I stood before my friends, in a mean and foolish pose, and defiantly ripped the Mantle card into little pieces. Needless to say, my kids and my colleagues are forever astonished to hear this tale: "Do you know how much that card would be worth today—especially if you had gotten Mantle to sign it?"

All of my enthusiasm and fanaticism were undone, however, when I was not yet ten years old for, as we know, the owners of the Dodgers brutishly uprooted the team from Brooklyn and, having calculated their profitability as the Los Angeles Dodgers (it still hurts me to say it), transplanted them to southern California. I have never felt the same about "professional" sports since then (nor, to this day, have I ever visited California).

Yes, I admit to having enjoyed the Dodgers' 1959 World Series victory over the Chicago White Sox, but it really wasn't the same (better an uneven Brooklyn Bums than a triumphant *Los Angeles* Dodgers); and, naturally, living in Green Bay, Wisconsin as I now do, one organically becomes a Packer-backer—fortunately, this team's municipal, local, and dispersed stock ownership and "democratic" character make it safely bound to the town (though, by many accounts, the National Football League has tried on several occasions to encourage a Packers' move to a "larger market").

It wasn't merely a matter of growing up and realizing that things are not as simple as they always had seemed. More crucially, and long before I had ever heard of the Marx named Karl, I was introduced to the lessons of the *Communist Manifesto* regarding the progress of the capitalist market and its attendant alienation: "The bourgeoisie . . . has drowned the most heavenly ecstasies of religious fervor, of chivalrous enthusiasm, of philistine sentimentalism, in the icy waters of egotistical calculation. . . . All that is solid melts into air, all that is holy is profaned. . . ."

11 From Bases to Superstructures: The Great Transformation of Baseball*

BROOKLYN DODGERS THEME SONG

Oh, follow the Dodgers,
Follow the Dodgers around.
The infield, the outfield,
The catcher and that fellow on the mound.
Oh, the fans will come a running,
When the Dodgers go a gunning,
For the pennant we're fighting for today.
The Dodgers keep swinging,
And the fans will keep singing,
Follow the Dodgers, hooray.
There's a ballclub in Brooklyn,
The team they call "Dem Bums,"
But keep your eyes right on them
And watch for hits and runs. . . .

THE N.Y. GIANTS VICTORY MARCH

We're calling all fans,
All you Giant ball fans.
Come watch the home team,

---

* This chapter was first published in *Elysian Fields Quarterly,* vol. 12, no. 1, 1993, as a review of Neil J. Sullivan's *The Diamond Revolution: The Prospects for Baseball after the Collapse of Its Ruling Class* (New York, 1992).

Going places 'round those bases.
Cheer for your favorites,
Out at Coogan's Bluff.
Come watch those Polo Grounders,
Do their stuff.

AT THE SAME TIME that I am working on this essay, the story of the possible purchase of the San Francisco Giants by a group of Tampa Bay–area investors and the move of the team to St. Petersburg, Florida, is unfolding on sports, news, *and* business pages of the newspapers. This team really has traveled: from Atlantic to Pacific and—if all goes according to plan—down to the Gulf of Mexico! (And who knows where thereafter. My daughter has reminded me that on a recent episode of Mann & Machine, a cops-and-robbers TV series set in the not-too-distant future, the Giants were referred to as having been bought by a Japanese group and moved across the Pacific to Tokyo!) Once again, capital apparently commands; that is, money talks and—contrary to the usual rhyme—somebody walks.

Not surprisingly, the New York media have shown a special interest in the maneuvers and engagements under way in San Francisco and Tampa Bay, instigating recollections of emotionally rough times 35 years ago. For example, my mother has sent to me a piece titled "LOYALISTS: Fans Remember Dodgers and Giants" from *The Record* (August 16, 1992), the major newspaper from my northern New Jersey hometown area. The reporter had interviewed my mom for the article after learning from a sportswriter friend that our family had especially close ties to the Brooklyn Dodgers; indeed, my grandfather's friendships with Pee Wee Reese, Leo Durocher, Charlie Dressen, and others on the team meant "a steady stream of players would turn up" at my grandparents' home. As my mother recounts: "You've never seen anything like the way the fans and the players felt about each other. We really idolized them. . . . When they decided to leave, all hell broke loose. All of us could hardly believe they were leaving, but I remember my father being particularly devastated. He was heartbroken."

In fact, the reporter did a good job of conveying the surprise, the shock, and the sense of disappointment, betrayal, and loss felt by the fans. He also conveyed the nostalgia: "For most Giants and Dodgers fans, the loss of their team marked the end of a more innocent time."

Of course, for some writers and commentators nostalgia is *the* problem afflicting baseball. As Nicholas Dawidoff, author of a biography of Moe Berg, asks in his *New Republic* cover story: "Is nostalgia wrecking baseball?" (August 17, 1992). His own answer: *Yes, indeed!*

All I would say in response is that however persuasive a case Dawidoff and others seem to make regarding the ruination of baseball by "baseball nostalgia," they repeatedly fail to distinguish between nostalgia as recollections, memories, and a sincere missing of or longing for times past, and the commercial and corporate exploitation of nostalgia, with all the kitsch this entails. They never actually address the possibility that however artificial the recollections people have, the sense of loss and the desire for the restoration of a past time's pastime express their legitimate feelings and perceptions that something is missing from professional baseball and their current relationship to it.

One would imagine from the opening chapters of *The Diamond Revolution* that Neil J. Sullivan is merely yet another critic decrying our nostalgia for baseball's past. He commences his smartly and crisply written book with a deconstruction and debunking of the glory days of the game, the good old days of my generation's childhood, the 1950s (1946-57). And he forces us to acknowledge that those "good old days . . . were not nearly so simple as we would like to believe." Bluntly in the Preface and in detail in the ensuing chapters, Sullivan reminds us of the racism, labor strife, litigation, Congressional hearings, gambling, franchise moves, and expansion problems that characterized the pro baseball of years gone by.

The great value of this work is that it treats the game in *historical* perspective, providing a truly critical and timely consideration of baseball's past, present, *and* possible futures. And, thus, I must say that Neil Sullivan has produced a marvelous book, a book that can be and *should be read* and enjoyed by everyone interested in the progress of the game. Sullivan's project, however, is not simply the demystification, by way of recounting the political, cultural, and economic realities of earlier years, of "the pasts" engendered by our nostalgic recollections. Far beyond that, Sullivan's intention is to critically comprehend the dramatic transformation of baseball which we have been witnessing over the past few decades, to explain the making of this great transformation and, thereby, to increase our awareness of the changes and forces composing it in order that we ourselves might more effectively respond to them and, possibly, participate in shaping their continuing development. Moreover, appreciating that the emergence of nostalgia represents a popular desire to hold on to aspects of the baseball experience we have known, Sullivan seeks to recover and redeem the best traditions of the past in order to criticize contemporary developments and to inform our aspirations and visions for baseball's future: *"The Diamond Revolution* rests on the premise that how the past is understood will help to determine the history of baseball in the twenty-first century."

Neil Sullivan is an accomplished student of baseball's political economy and public history and, indeed, he wields the powers of the past most handily. An associate professor of public administration at Baruch College of the City University of New York, his first two books were *The Dodgers Move West* (1987) and *The Minors: The Struggles and the Triumph of Baseball's Poor Relations from 1876 to the Present* (1990). This new volume, in contrast to its forerunners, is more a work of synthesis and critical argument than primary scholarship (though such labors, including interviews and data gathering, were involved). It is, however, no less original and significant a contribution.

Sullivan proposes that we understand the "diamond revolution" that has transformed professional baseball since the Second World War in terms of a transition from one kind of social order to another. While he's no socialist or radical, Sullivan actually uses the language of Marxist historiography: The transformation of professional baseball is described as the game's transition from "feudalism to capitalism." Social historians might well quibble here, for baseball has always been a capitalist enterprise; nevertheless, to speak of a transition from one kind of political and economic structure (feudalism) to another (capitalism) makes for a good and even entertaining metaphor to capture and appreciate the changes which have been taking place. Consider the owners up to a few decades ago as feudal lords and/or plantation owners; the players as peasant-serfs or slaves; and, perhaps, the commissioner as absolute monarch trying both to secure his own authority and to protect the social system of the *ancien régime* in the face of new forces. That is, baseball's power structure had been practically medieval until the outbreak of the "diamond revolution," a revolution that has undermined and overturned the game's authoritarian order by way of the advance of the market economy, technological developments, *and* struggles from below demanding freedoms and social and economic improvements.

Speaking historically, Sullivan shows how the owners' feudal dynasties appeared to survive the threats of the postwar period: "they faced rebellions from players, foreign owners [the Pasquel brothers of Mexico], and minor leagues [the Pacific Coast League initiative to become a third major league], and they crushed each challenge." And yet, as he observes, looking back we can see that these were not deep and lasting triumphs for the baseball magnates; indeed, he contends, "the old order of baseball was [already] collapsing." He points out that the leading baseball families were beginning to depart the scene (for example, Comiskey and Mack) and newcomers were entering (the O'Malleys and Busches—the "rising bourgeoisie" we might call them). Concurrently, the business of baseball was being "industrialized" (my term) and "corporatized" as the growth of, and changes in, the front offices evidenced. Also, there was the elimination of the color barrier, a radical step—though much too long in coming—first taken by the Brooklyn Dodgers and Jackie Robinson in 1947, with other teams following in the course of the next decade. And, finally, there were the changes being motivated/propelled by new and spreading technologies of communication (television especially) and transportation (jet travel, but also cars, highways, and suburban road connections) that provided for a new "geography" of professional baseball.

The transition from feudalism to capitalism, as we well know, did not culminate in the "end of history" but, rather, gave rise to a whole new set of contradictions, problems, conflicts, *and* possibilities. Thus it has also been in baseball. The new class of owners brought a new dynamic to the game and responded to changing circumstances with, for example, franchise moves and, eventually, expansions entailing new stadium designs and construction, new broadcast agreements and commercial arrangements, and the restructuring of the relations between the major and minor leagues and of the patterns of recruitment and development of new talent.

Again, Sullivan writes critically, and most of his criticism is directed at the club owners for their persistent conservatism and greed. For example, he is sharp with the owners for their racist practices of the past, referring specifically to the injustice to African American ballplayers in excluding them from the "majors," to the club owners' failure to deal fairly with the owners of the Negro League before and after integration, and to what apartheid and racism sadly cost the game; and he also criticizes them for their continuing failure to move more deliberately and rapidly to integrate the ranks of management today. Indeed, Sullivan is persistently critical of the owners for their attempts to hold on to their power and money in the face of legitimate demands for change by players and fans alike.

Sullivan finds the "diamond revolution" progressive but, again, his task is to *critically* comprehend it and to make us aware of both the problems and, as the subtitle of his book declares, "the prospects for baseball after the collapse of its ruling class." The central issues he treats are: the problem of "portable franchises"; the political economy of new stadium construction and control; the question of expansion (Does it cheapen the game?); the politics and commerce of broadcasting; the relations between baseball and booze; and the game's "class struggle" (in a chapter titled "The Workers Arise"). Finally, he presents alternative scenarios of baseball's future and makes several specific recommendations to reform the game in favor of a brighter, broader, even more progressive future.

On the matter of moving franchises, Sullivan relates the myths and realities in a most objective fashion. In particular, he shows that relocation is not the commercial boon so often asserted and hoped for, and he chastises the team owners who blame their own failings on the particular communities where they find themselves. Rather than claim they are situated in a "bad baseball town," Sullivan says, owners should examine their own business and management practices for the respective causes of their declining attendance and profits. Related to the portability of franchises is the question of new stadia, though teams that stayed behind have also pursued the building of new facilities (the Chicago White Sox/Comiskey Park) or the renovation of old ones (the New York Yankees/Yankee Stadium). Sullivan discusses the architecture of the old and new "emerald cathedrals." Clearly preferring the former ones, he indicates a certain optimism that future stadia will combine the warmth of the old neighborhood-style ball parks with the safety and conveniences of the past generation's structures.

The real issue for Sullivan is not really design, but ownership. He is insistent that taxpayers should *not* bear the burden of new stadium construction. Admiring the development and success of Dodger Stadium—a private project with public support—he urges citizens to resist owners' threats to move unless their city builds a new palace to house them. Call the owners' bluffs, Sullivan says. If they move, it will not be the end of the world; if they are willing to stay, support them in building their own stadia. Other, more serious urban problems should take priority over keeping a pro baseball team in town. In any case, he argues (echoing the ideology of the New Right far more than anything of the left), the best stadium will be privately built and privately managed. Moreover, Sullivan proffers, stadium ownership will likely tie the team to the city! Perhaps he is right, but let's not forget that building ownership has not prevented all too many American manufacturers from abandoning factories and warehouses in favor of moving south and/or abroad. Which leads me to ask, contra Sullivan: Why not municipally owned stadia *and* municipally owned teams?

Sullivan is confident that baseball can afford still further expansion. Recommending that the major leagues expand to 32 teams in the not-too-distant future, he shows how, after each process of growth, baseball has been better off. In fact, he statistically demonstrates that there should be sufficient talent "out there" to eventually satisfy the needs of *60 high quality teams*—so long as the leagues invest in the means to develop it. It should be noted here that Sullivan's vision of baseball's growth and expansion sees a game that is not simply American or even North American, but *global* in the fashion of soccer, entailing a truly *World* Series. His optimism is also evident in the chapter on broadcasting, not only because the new satellite and cable media have provided major revenues, but also because they make games all the more accessible and the new production technologies will enable viewers to follow the game from their individually preferred vantage points (home plate? third base? the mound?).

I found Sullivan's chapter on "Baseball and Booze" the least intriguing. Here he looks at the entanglements between baseball and beer, sports and drugs, and baseball and tobacco. There was just too much territory to cover in a single chapter: alcohol abuse and the changing manner in which teams handle it; brewery ownership of ball clubs and its consequences (Busch ownership of the St. Louis Cardinals); baseball and beer advertising, and so on. In conclusion to the chapter, Sullivan meekly writes: "Alcohol and baseball will always be associated, and the owners who rake in so much money from beer have a special obligation to be responsible to their players and fans." To say the least.

The class struggle at the heart of baseball—owners vs. players—has changed dramatically since the 1950s. Most obvious here has been the aggressive unionization of the ballplayers and their successful campaigns to challenge the power and control of the owners. Sullivan reviews the struggles of the players and speaks admiringly of the leadership of their union, especially of Marvin Miller, whom he recognizes as having been hardworking, imaginative, risk-taking, and most articulate in his communication of the players' cause. By contrast, the owners and their commissioners (especially Bowie Kuhn) are portrayed as real reactionaries, possessed of a fortress mentality and regularly capable of committing radical, immoral, and illegal acts to hold on to their power and prerogatives. Nevertheless, after thirty years of organized class struggle—the fundamental political drama of the diamond revolution—the players' solidarity has broken the owners' monopoly of power and authority. This is best represented by the development of free agency and the decided improvement in players' salaries and benefits. As Sullivan sees it, though he is not confident that it will be resolved soon, the question that now presents itself is: Will the owners and players establish a real working relationship—better, a "partnership"—in which they share authority and jointly participate in the business decisions of the game?

In his final chapter, Sullivan observes that "The first phase of a revolution is the fun part. . . . The more difficult phase of a radical transition is establishing the new regime." He says there are two possible paths for the game to follow. One path involves growth in popularity, attendance, television viewing, and in the number of youngsters playing, and at the same time the major leagues going truly global. The other path entails contraction all around. The path taken, he writes, will depend in great part on baseball's leadership, in particular the commissioner's office. His first recommendation, therefore, is that the selection of future commissioners be done by a nominating committee composed of an equal number of owners and players, with their agreed-upon nominee being voted on by both the owners and the players at large, confirmation requiring a simple majority of both parties. Beyond that, Sullivan states that efforts to grow should be pursued slowly and patiently: "decisions should be biased in favor of tradition over innovation, because the heritage of the game is a great resource but one that could be squandered by fashion."

Sullivan goes on to make several specific recommendations that I cannot consider here. However, I would note that he calls for a prohibition on franchise moves: "If an owner wants to relocate to another community, he or she should sell the club and buy a new one. The record is clear that there have been bad owners but not bad baseball towns." Sounds good and right and I firmly support the proposed rule. Still, I hesitate to make it an *absolute* rule, for what if the Dodgers become so inspired by their longtime rivals' promised move from San Francisco to St. Petersburg that they too aspire to return to the East? Would we really say no to a *Brooklyn* Dodgers?

POSTSCRIPT, JULY 1995

The Giants have not left San Francisco for Florida. And on a sadder note, the Dodgers have not returned to Brooklyn. Nevertheless, the questions raised by Neil Sullivan in *The Diamond Revolution* remain on the public agenda.

The baseball players' strike in the face of the owners' intentions to impose a salary cap brought a sad halt to the 1994 season; and yet, however greedy one may think the players have been in these confrontations (and, admittedly, it is hard to feel otherwise when the sports media focus on the stars and their riches), the owners' recruitment of what they called "replacement players" to fill out their teams' rosters for the 1995 season must be seen for what it was—another instance in which corporate capital resorted to hiring "scab labor" in hopes of "busting the union." As I propose above, my own response to these events was to imagine and conversationally promote the idea of the return of the sport to the people, the fans, by way of public expropriations of the franchises and the establishment of municipally or cooperatively owned teams. Such fantasies have been further stimulated by the repeated threats by the owners of the Milwaukee Brewers to depart the city and Wisconsin if the state does not find a way to publicly finance the construction of a new baseball stadium for the team. Unfortunately, the current rage about the "inviolability of private property" prevents us from taking such democratic actions as the creation of municipally owned teams.

Still, there is a brighter side to professional sports. After many years of playing 3 of 8 games of their annual home season in Milwaukee, starting in 1995 the municipally owned Green Bay Packers football team will be playing all of their home games at Lambeau Field here in Green Bay. *The Pack is back . . . Go Pack!*

PART TWO

EDUCATION AND DEMOCRACY

12 Should the Fact That We Live in a Democratic Society Make a Difference in What Our Schools Are Like?*

THROUGH SCHOOLING AND EDUCATION a people expresses and cultivates its public values, identities, and aspirations, and prepares its newest generations to engage them. Thus, *a democratic society requires a democratic education.* Declaring ourselves a democracy, the proposition that America must provide a democratic education to its children and young people (at the least) is not really at issue. What has been and continues to be contested is the actual meaning of "democracy" and, in those terms, what a "democratic" education ought to entail. To appreciate the challenge we confront, we must see things historically.

The American experience, filled with paradox and contradiction and marked both by its record of economic growth and development and its chronicle of continental and imperial expansion, has been a long struggle to realize the democratic dream that *the people shall govern themselves.* The American Revolution and war for independence; the populism of Jacksonian politics; the Civil War and the ensuing abolition of slavery; the campaigns for women's suffrage and equality; the many generations of farmer and labor movements and Black struggles for survival, freedom, and justice: the first two hundred years and more of our history can be read as a narrative of continuous efforts *from the bottom up* to make real the aspiration that

---

* This chapter was first published as a contribution to Joe Kincheloe and Shirley Steinberg, eds., *Thirteen Questions: Reframing Education's Conversation* (New York, 1992).

"We, the people" shall rule. Comprehending our past in this way, the struggles throughout the long decade of the 1960s for the civil rights of racial and ethnic minorities, the social rights of the poor, and the equal rights of women, along with the movement against an imperial war in Southeast Asia and the less-celebrated but, perhaps, equally significant insurgency of working people, White and Black, male and female, in industry and the workplace, not to mention the environmental and consumer movements, are all recognizable as reassertions of the finest traditions of American life and history.[1]

Yet, for almost a generation now we have been subject to a persistent and, arguably, concerted "class war from above" resisting, opposing and, even, seeking to reverse the advances that had been accomplished in the spirit of liberty, equality, and democratic community. The powers that be mobilized against the achievements and reforms secured during the period that began with the New Deal of the 1930s and lasted through the Great Society of the 1960s and also against, most immediately, the threat they perceived from a possible coalescence of the several struggles of the day into a broader popular movement that would seek ever more extensive radical-democratic changes in the American social order. And, in the course of the 1970s, with the encouragement and manifold support of significant sectors of American business and corporate capital, there was formed under the banner of the New Right Republicans a political coalition of conservatives and neoconservatives that included Cold-warriors, free-marketeers, moral-majoritarians, and a host of other right-wing single-interest groups and organizations variably committed to undermining the post–Second World War liberal consensus and to halting the democratic struggles from below of labor and the "new social movements." The ascendance to power of this diverse coalition was registered in the 1980 and 1984 presidential election victories of Ronald Reagan and again in that of George Bush in 1988.[2]

From the start there were inherent contradictions in this New Right alliance—for example, those existing between the aspirations of the free-marketeers and those of the religious fundamentalists and, in another area, between the foreign-policy views of conservatives and those of neoconservatives—and, after a decade and more of Republican administrations, it is not only clear that the New Right has failed to accomplish its many enunciated goals but it would appear that the coalition itself is breaking up. There is, however, little reason to be joyful or optimistic, for there is no denying the consequences of a dozen years of New Right regimes. They have wrought confusion, disarray, and hardship. We have experienced a decade of greed and a politics of inequality in which the rich truly have gotten richer and the poor have been made poorer—a process by no means limited to the margins, that is, to the Donald Trumps at one end and the poor and homeless at the other, but, rather, one conditioning the lives of the vast majority of America's working people.[3] Moreover, if the New Right coalition does collapse, it will probably be due more to its own contradictions than to organized opposition from the left.

In fact, in one major respect the right has triumphed. That is, it has succeeded, to the decided benefit of the powers that be, in further fragmenting if not all but routing the struggles of working people and the oppressed. Evidently, the antagonisms of class, race, and gender not only persist but are intensified, and studies reveal that there is continuing popular commitment to the programs and priorities of New-Deal and postwar liberalism; nevertheless, the various movements for freedom and justice appear enervated and enfeebled, pursuing at best defensive actions. What we find is not merely increasing inequality, but political and cultural freedoms under attack and democratic activity becoming narrower and shallower, subordinated to the "freedom of the market," the imperatives of capital, and the manners of the media. In short, public culture and discourse is more and more subject to commercial norms and values and devoid of critical thought and debate about the future of American society. The New Right's legacy, therefore, would seem to be the "depoliticization" of public life and, thereby, the enhancement of the status quo and the position of the powers that be, especially that of the political and economic elites of corporate capital. Philip Mattera has described the current scene:

These days there is not much collective dreaming in America. The erosion of living standards and the increase in economic insecurity have brought about a climate of quiet frustration and cynicism. People have been caught between official pronouncements that these are the best of times and their personal realization that life is getting tougher every day. The contradictory evidence is having an immobilizing effect: most Americans do not see a way out of this dilemma and consequently have grown wary of any change at all. While people in other parts of the world, notably Eastern Europe, are boldly confronting their oppression, the U.S. feels like a political backwater.[4]

It is debatable whether or not the politics and ideas of the New Right have been actually *anti*-democratic. However, it is clearly the case both that their conception of democracy, of democratic life and practice, is a limited one and, stated in *historical* terms, that they conceive of it as already having been achieved. In other words, in their view *Democracy in America* (as Tocqueville composed it long ago) is accomplished. Indeed, they insist, not only does contemporary American liberal and capitalist democracy represent the high point of democratic development thus far, it represents the high point of democratic *possibilities,* the *culmination* of democracy's historical evolution. As one of their number, Francis Fukuyama, put it, we have arrived at the "end of history," beyond which the choice is either more of the same or political, economic, and cultural retrogression.[5] The New Right's program of "democratic education" indicates just such an understanding of history.

Now, at first sight it would seem that there have been actually two different and conflicting campaigns pursued by conservatives and neoconservatives (not necessarily respectively) for reforming and renewing American education in the 1980s and 1990s. Both point to the apparently poor performance by American schoolchildren on standardized objective tests in comparison to their European and Asian counterparts and regularly blame liberal and left educators for the problem; however, the respective campaigns proclaim different concerns and assert different priorities.

On the one hand, there are those who warn of the dangers of American economic and industrial decline and propose that education be reformed to address them. Looking toward the creation (or *re*-creation) and provision of a skilled, disciplined, and productive workforce for American industries and enterprises in their competition with German and Japanese corporations (or, as it is increasingly said, a workforce attractive to investments by the latter in the American economy), they stress a "back-to-basics," "teach the facts and nothing but the facts" approach to schooling, generally emphasizing training in math and science. The priorities of this campaign are vocational, industrial, and economic.

On the other hand, there are those who speak less of economic decline and far more of political and moral crisis, that is, of the fragmentation and disintegration of America's "common culture" and "shared values." They, too, call for a "return to the basics," but, emphasizing schooling in the humanities, especially literature and history, they stress the restoration of a core curriculum of ideas and ideals entailing, at the least, a common body of knowledge and information and, preferably, a canon of Great Books and personages representing "Western Civilization." The priorities enunciated here are civic, political, and cultural.[6]

Yet, however much they stress seemingly different concerns and priorities—respectively, the making of workers and the making of citizens—the two New Right campaigns for American education arise from the same vision and register the same understanding of America's past, present, and possible future—that we have arrived at the end of history—*and* express the same political project, that of assuring that we actually have. Both schemes for schooling delimit democratic education to a process of *transmission,* in the former that of skills and competencies and in the latter that of ideas and values. To be sure, schooling to develop skills and capacities for productive and valued employment and schooling to communicate knowledge and ideals for informed and active citizenship are, in principle, essential to any vision of democratic education. However, bound up with a version of history that conceives of contemporary America as the terminus of democratic development, the New Right vision of democratic education aspires (at best) to no more than the *reproduction* of the American economy and polity and culture as they are presently constituted. Bluntly stated, the New Right notion of democratic education reduces schooling to being a support of the world *as it is*.

For those of us who do not believe that we have come to the end of history, who do not believe that the contemporary American social order—however "progressive" it is, relatively speaking—represents the culmination of democratic development, such a state of affairs is obviously unacceptable. But our task is formidable. For a start, in the face of the triumphs of the New Right we need not only to make clear the inadequacies and limitations of their rendition of history and attendant conception of democracy but, also, to cultivate a popular awareness that the contemporary order of things, both the good and the bad, was not inevitable and that it need not remain this way. We must work toward the development of a popular comprehension that the present, too, is history and that nothing is gained without struggle. This entails both recovering and communicating the struggles for liberty, equality and democratic community that have contributed to the making of past and present (both the victories and the defeats), *and* revealing the possibilities which exist today for renewing that history.

Furthermore, along with our efforts to create a more critical and democratic historical memory, consciousness, and imagination—indeed, as part of such efforts—it is imperative that we articulate and proffer a conception of democratic education that supports the development of democratic life and actually enhances the likelihood of its realization. The political scientist Benjamin Barber expressed it well when he wrote that "all education ought to be radical—a reminder of the past, a challenge to the present, and a prod to the future."[7]

Unfortunately, all too often such aspirations have involved both a simplistic opposition to and a too hasty rejection of the educational initiatives enunciated by the New Right. I would argue that in certain crucial instances our response should not be that of opposing and disavowing their proposals but of critically appropriating, re-articulating, and turning them in a more truly democratic direction. For example, at the cost of being portrayed as unconcerned about not only "academic standards" but, also, about the needs of working people and the oppressed to become literate and skilled and, moreover, about the economic future of our country, we have in the past too readily denounced the campaign to reform education in support of economic and technological development. Instead, we should have been taking the lead in this area, seeking to make all the more effective the acquisition of basic skills, literacies, and competencies by America's schoolchildren for the sake both of improving their chances to secure and pursue productive livelihoods and of helping to assure continued American economic growth and development.

But that is not enough. And this is where our conception of democratic life and practice differs from that of the New Right. As Antonio Gramsci observed more than half of a century ago: "Democracy, by definition, cannot mean merely that an unskilled worker can become skilled. It must mean that every 'citizen' can 'govern' and that society places him, even if only abstractly, in a general condition to achieve this."[8]

In essence, we must develop a mode of education that not only does not predetermine or limit the "life chances" and livelihoods of young people but, beyond that, one that does not accept as natural or inevitable the socially created division between economy and polity, between our lives as workers and consumers and our lives as citizens. A democratic education must not only prepare upcoming generations to be both capable and effective workers and capable and effective citizens, but also prepare them to be capable of critically considering and effectively challenging the separation between these two roles and between the dictatorship characteristic of a capitalist economy and the democracy of a liberal polity and thus leading, hopefully, to the making of democratic changes and developments in both.

To accomplish such changes will also necessarily entail a different kind of response to the New Right's educational initiative regarding the crisis of the American polity and culture than those usually afforded by radical democrats. There *is* a crisis. And here, again, it is a mistake to simply reject the idea of a common culture, even when defined in terms of the "Western tradition." Rather, it is a question of critically appropriating—or, better, and more historically accurate, *re*-appropriating—Western traditions and American history and culture "from the bottom up," and of endeavoring to re-articulate them in a democratic and pluralistic fashion for ourselves and for future generations.

Moreover, a democratic education must involve not just a process of transmission and inculcation of ideas and ideals but, also, an experience of engaging, working through, and possibly even transforming them.[9] That is, not only the ideas and ideals of education, but the activity itself must be recognized as contributing (or not) to the making of active and critical democratic citizens. As Gramsci insisted, a democratic education should be "forming" of a young person as one who is "capable of thinking, studying and ruling—or controlling those who rule."[10]

Let us continue to insist that "We, the people" shall rule and, so inspired, create a democratic education whose purpose and promise is that of preparing ourselves and our children to do so.

13 A Radical Theology for Democratic Education[*]

THERE IS A GROWING recognition on the American left that we are becoming ever more estranged from public life and debate and that both public life and the left itself are suffering as a consequence. Thus, we find a variety of studies addressing the past and present state of public culture and the role of progressive intellectuals in the making of history. Such work includes consideration of the theory and practice of social, political, and cultural criticism and the question of how leftist intellectuals ought to situate themselves in relation to "power" and "the people." Moreover, evident in all these writings is a serious concern for how the intellectual left can transcend elitism, intellectualism, and academicism in order to reinvigorate the American polity in a *democratic* fashion and, thereby, extend, deepen, enrich, and possibly transform the meaning and experience of liberty, equality, and democracy.[1]

Sadly, it must be noted that although much attention is given to higher education in these studies, little or no consideration is given to elementary and secondary education. Yet, representing an original and critical extension to education (at all levels) of the intellectual left's project of renewal is Henry Giroux's *Schooling and the Struggle for Public Life*. In this work, Giroux offers an impassioned intellectual and moral confrontation with conservative, liberal, *and* radical theories of schooling from an explicitly *radical-democratic* perspective. Of course, he is not completely alone in his pursuit of the democracy-education problematic. There are Amy Gutmann's

---

[*] This chapter was first published in *Educational Theory*, vol. 39, no. 3, summer 1989, as a review of Henry A. Giroux's *Schooling and the Struggle for Public Life* (Minneapolis, 1988).

Democratic Education, which provides a principled and comprehensive argument for democratic control of education against both conservative and liberal models and policy directives, and Ira Katznelson and Margaret Weir's *Schooling for All,* which presents an outline history of the dialectical relationship between the social struggles of class, ethnicity, and race and the educational visions and practices pursued in urban America during the last hundred years and more.[2] Nevertheless, much more so than either Gutmann's theoretical and policy analyses and Katznelson and Weir's historical sociology, Giroux's book clearly reflects the project of reinvigorating American democracy and the presence and agency of the left within it.

Schooling and the Struggle for Public Life (hereafter, *Schooling*) is essentially about the making of democratic education for the sake of developing a critical citizenry, which, in case we have forgotten, has always been a central image of the classical republican vision. Before proceeding, I must admit that I was predisposed to liking this book. I have long admired Henry Giroux's work[3] and following the arguments that he has presented in articles these past few years, I looked forward with real eagerness to reading this volume. Though I continue to have certain reservations about his formulations, as I shall eventually note, I would strongly recommend that his book be read not only by teachers, those who teach teachers, and those who would be teachers, but by everyone concerned about education and the enhancement of democratic possibilities.

Critical and lively, Giroux's writings have always been characterized by passion and commitment and have revealed an intellect ever attentive to theoretical and scholarly developments in the cultural and social sciences. These characteristics are all the more evident in *Schooling*; indeed, the entire work resonates with energy and a sense of urgency, and even when treating dense theoretical issues and abstract concepts, Giroux's language still broadcasts an intensity of purpose (thus, the use of the word "theology" in my title).

Giroux's passion is signaled at the outset. In his prefatory remarks, he explains that the arrival of three baby boys in the course of his writing of this book inspired a renewed awareness of the "interplay of history, memory, and solidarity." He says that he found himself especially reconsidering his own sense of history: "The presence of children forces the issue of understanding and connecting one's own history with the history that one's children will both learn and experience." (He is thus led to recall the letter that Antonio Gramsci, not long before his death in one of Mussolini's prisons, wrote to his young son, Delio; "I think you must like history, as I liked it when I was your age, because it deals with living men, all the men in the world in so far as they unite together in society, and work and struggle and make a bid for a better life. All that can't fail to please you more than anything else. Isn't that right? I kiss you dearly.")

Through this experience, Giroux's own commitment to *historical* curricula and pedagogical practice was reaffirmed: "Schools are one of the few sites within public life in which students, both young and old, can experience and learn the language of community and democratic public life." But, of course, *the* history to be learned is not given or self-evident; a *critical* history must be recovered, having been marginalized or suppressed by the powers that be, past and present.[4] Giroux knows this and it informs every one of his chapters.

In his Introduction, "Schooling, Citizenship and the Struggle for Democracy," Giroux defines the political-ideological problem for radical democrats: "What is new in the 1980s is the absence of struggle over both redefining the meaning of patriotism and constructing a notion of citizenship that is consistent with the tenets of a critical democracy." The New Right, he argues, has mastered the discourse of the American nation-state and appropriated the concept of citizenship to its cause. The left has failed to combat this initiative: Liberals too readily accepted the anxiety-ridden portrait of post-1960s America advanced by the Trilateral Commission (this, sadly, can be seen as actually having enabled the even more anti-democratic right-wing propositions of the Heritage Foundation); and radicals, stuck in the rhetoric of critique and one-dimensional renditions of history, have persistently abandoned the idea of "citizenship" to the right, assuming it to be merely "bourgeois" ideology covering up the realities of "class."

Giroux proposes that the democratic left reclaim the past and present of citizenship, reconnecting it to and imbuing it with *democratic* meaning and purpose. This act of reclamation is to be realized as part of a broader effort "to develop a public philosophy that provides legitimation for developing counterpublic spheres in which a critical notion of citizenship can be given expression through a radical model of citizenship education." The definition of citizenship that Giroux offers is counterposed to those that subordinate the citizenry "to the narrow imperatives of the state"; that is, the citizenship envisioned by Giroux "becomes a process of dialogue and commitment rooted in a fundamental belief in the possibility of public life and the development of forms of solidarity that allow people to reflect and organize in order to criticize and constrain the power of the state and to 'overthrow relations [that is, race, gender, and class oppression] which inhibit and prevent the realization of humanity.'"

Functionalist models of education—right and left—portray schools as institutions "reproducing" the social order, that is, for example, the pattern of inequality, a workforce for American industry, and/or a common culture. Rejecting such models, with their attendant images of teachers as servants/pawns of the elites and inculcators of expectations, aspirations, and the "selective tradition," Giroux asks us to comprehend education as "cultural politics" and schools as "public spheres" potentially fostering critical citizens committed to democratic practices, aspirations, and development. Teachers in this view are to be understood as "transformative intellectuals" whose moral and political responsibilities are to engage and empower students through critical dialogue and experience and, at the same time, to link schools to their communities in support of movements for progressive social change. Again, Giroux not only confronts conservative and liberal educational thinkers but, also, challenges radical theorists whose critiques of American schooling fail to engender visions and strategies to transcend contemporary structures and practices.

Toward the elaboration of his vision of democratic education and appropriate strategies to bring it about, the chapters of

Giroux's *Schooling* treat certain fundamental problems: (a) the need for the development of a critical moral and ethical democratic discourse; (b) the problem of formulating an "emancipatory authority" coherent with such a democratic ethical discourse; (c) the imperative of devising conceptions of literacy and pedagogical practice that critically engage student and community voices and advance both their empowerment *and* the empowerment of teachers themselves; (d) the question of the future of teacher education in relation to the project of schooling for democracy; and (e) the challenge of anti-utopianism and the necessity of hope, and the assertion of radical truths within utopian aspirations.

To address these problems, Giroux draws upon—better, critically appropriates—the ideas of a variety of intellectual currents and figures. Correlated in the simplest fashion (on my part): Giroux's approach to developing a democratic ethical discourse is informed by postmodernist discourse theory; but, then, his formulation of emancipatory authority is created from a merging of the ideas of John Dewey and the "social reconstructionists," Antonio Gramsci, Walter Benjamin, and feminist liberation theology. Next, his conceptions of critical literacy and pedagogical practice draw upon the writings of Gramsci and his own close friend and spiritual mentor, the Brazilian intellectual Paulo Freire; and his proposals on teacher education depend upon recent developments in radical history, sociology, and cultural studies. Finally, his argument for hope and radical utopian thought based upon historical critique and remembrance refers again to Benjamin, and, most especially, to Ernst Bloch and Michel Foucault. It should be noted that Giroux's mobilization of "critical" theorists is never merely eclectic and, however often he directs us to other writers, what we gain from *Schooling* is not simply a survey of contemporary cultural thought, but an original and sustained argument and vision of education for democratic struggle.

Pivotal to Giroux's vision and project is the role of teachers as transformative intellectuals—a formulation of the relationship between "intellectuals and the people" intended to transcend in a democratic fashion the classical debate between Leninism and populism in which, respectively, intellectuals or the people are the "bearers of radical truth." A primary question in this regard is the ground upon which teachers as transformative intellectuals can stand; for, while Giroux accepts postmodernists' anti-foundationalism, he despairs of their refusal to link the "language of critique with a viable political project." Thus, he offers what he calls a "radical provisional morality" linked to the principles of "individual autonomy" and "democratic public life." These, of course, are essentially the political ideals of American liberal democracy. Does this mean that Giroux is ultimately merely pursuing the status quo? Hardly. Rather, we should recognize that he is seeking to act as a *connected* critic standing in the critical space between the social and the moral orders (that is, between what is and what ought, or is supposed, to be), for the latter is always potentially subversive of the former.[5]

Moreover, in contrast to conservatives who seek a return to a mythical nineteenth-century past and the restoration of "traditional" authorities, Giroux's transformative intellectuals are to ground their ethical discourse and agency in relations of solidarity with the oppressed, their experiences, aspirations, and struggles past and present. Thus, he calls for historical enquiry to recover the moral principles and visions of the oppressed created in the face of the tragedy that is history. This "remembrance" entails, he grants, a "frankly partisan" historiography, which, I would add, is best expressed by Walter Benjamin's notion of "rubbing history against the grain" or, as Benjamin also wrote: "Only that historian will have the gift of fanning the spark of hope in the past who is firmly convinced that *even the dead* will not be safe from the enemy [the ruling class] if he wins. And this enemy has not ceased to be victorious." In short: History from the bottom up.[6]

The task of the transformative intellectual is not simply to articulate these experiences and visions past and present—though this might well be the task of the critical historian—but to pursue a dialogical pedagogy that presumes that *both* educator and educatee are to be educated. Moreover, the teacher as transformative intellectual is to engage students in a process that entails the "interrogation" of "knowledges," both those of official and public cultures and of their own discourses of everyday life. Literacy in these terms is the development of student voice and empowerment:

> . . . critical literacy is both a narrative for agency as well as a referent for critique. As a narrative for agency, literacy becomes synonymous with an attempt to rescue history, experience and vision from conventional discourse and dominant social relations. It means developing the theoretical and practical conditions through which human beings can locate themselves in their own histories and in doing so make themselves present as actors in the struggle to expand the possibilities of human life and freedom.

In my own work I think of this as *historical* education based on the "powers of the past": perspective, critique, consciousness, remembrance, and imagination.

What of the preparation of teachers as intellectuals? Obviously, Giroux rejects conservative theories that view teachers as "technicians" whose responsibility it is to "transmit culture" or "train students for the labor market"; he, therefore, also finds inadequate or unacceptable their (derived) arguments that the way to improve teacher education is to simply increase academic requirements and/or abolish schools of education altogether. Indeed, schools of education become all the more essential in Giroux's model. While he argues against their abolition, he is insistent that they be drastically reformed. He then proceeds to outline, in some detail, the institutional structuring, curriculum content, and pedagogical practices that ought to characterize the reformed and revised "ed schools," drawing especially on work under way in historical, sociological, and, in particular, cultural studies. It would be marvelous to institute the proposals he advances; in fact, my thinking is that his vision for teacher education actually should be incorporated, at least in part, into liberal-arts programs.

Finally, Giroux concludes *Schooling* with a discussion of the pessimism and despair that he finds characteristic of most radical education theory, and he calls for a new "utopianism" against the "anti-utopianism" of the day. Again, his primary references here are to Bloch, feminist liberation theologians, and Foucault. Specifically, he urges a politics "emergent in everyday life," in which teachers as intellectuals articulate alternatives to the world as it is by drawing from ongoing struggles against oppression.

It should be quite evident that I find Giroux's arguments and vision most attractive and compelling. Yet, as I stated above, I do have real reservations regarding certain of his formulations. First, in the area of curriculum and its content—in other words, the issue of "the canon"—while Giroux's conception of "critical literacy" entails the "interrogation of knowledges," it is not made clear enough what place the canon is to have *as* knowledge. In view of his impressive familiarity with the work of Benjamin and Gramsci, I would have expected him to address this more directly than he does. In this regard he might have considered Gramsci's assertion that "the philosophy of praxis" (Marxism) does not involve a rejection of "Western civilization" but, rather, its incorporation; or Benjamin's dialectical criticism based on a social-history reading of "cultural treasures":

> Whoever has emerged victorious participates to this day in the triumphal procession in which the present rulers step over those who are lying prostrate. According to traditional practice, the spoils are carried along in the procession. They are called cultural treasures, and a historical materialist views them with cautious detachment. For without exception the cultural treasures he surveys have an origin which he cannot contemplate without horror. They owe their existence not only to the efforts of the great minds and talents who have created them, but also to the anonymous toil of their contemporaries. There is no document of civilization which is not at the same time a document of barbarism.[7]

Hostile to the view most recently associated with William J. Bennett and Allan Bloom[8] of education as "cultural transmission," Giroux—

who is too "Freireian" on this issue—too readily cedes "high culture" to the conservatives. Also, it should be registered that he does not distinguish adequately between the pedagogy desirable and possible in the humanities and social studies as opposed to that desirable in mathematics and science—a problem that has persistently plagued radical-education thought.

More problematic is Giroux's primary theoretical framework. Admittedly, he is presenting a work linking education and cultural studies, but it seems that he subscribes too much to the "discourse theory" of the latter, eschewing class and historical materialist analyses. There is a certain advantage in doing so, for discourse theorists have regularly been more sensitive to race and gender oppression than have Marxists. Yet there are problems with "radical pluralism." For example, although at one point in *Schooling* Giroux's terms effectively distinguish between "rac*ism*, sex*ism*, and class exploitation" (my italics), elsewhere his formulation drops the distinction and speaks of racism, sexism, and "class discrimination." It is not merely that the latter reads as if it were expressed by a liberal whose finest aspiration was "equal opportunity," but that it obscures the fact that whereas a radical-democratic transcendence of racism and sexism would be liberating of race and gender experiences and expressions, the transcendence of class entails its elimination and abolition as a structuring experience and identity. (In a related fashion, I find unhelpful his proposition that youth—in itself—be understood as an "oppressed social category" without reference to class, race, and gender.)

Giroux's eagerness to distance himself from historical materialism and class analyses also inhibits his development of a strategy for teachers as transformative intellectuals. For a start, why would teachers pursue the project Giroux offers? It strikes me that discourse theorists privilege intellectuals as "masters" of ideology and discourse,[9] and though Giroux would *not* subscribe to the "privileging" of teachers, his reliance on discourse theory allows for such a conclusion to be drawn. Of course, he would not argue that commitment to his project can simply be generated by the ideology of "professionalism" or the idea of teaching as a "calling," though the latter would be supportive.

Perhaps I am too "laborist," but Giroux's nomination of teachers as transformative intellectuals might have been more firmly grounded by recognizing teachers as, themselves, citizens and *working* people who have an *interest* in the democratic transformation of schools and the polity that they share with other working people. Giroux does not neglect the necessity of improving teachers' material lives and working conditions, including addressing the question of autonomy and control; however, these points remain underdeveloped and are not adequately linked to the larger project and vision he offers. This might have led him to a fuller consideration of Gramsci's idea of "organic intellectuals," and it might also have provided him with an *organizational* direction for the initiatives he calls for. The vehicle he offers seems not unlike a parent-teacher association, which is admirable, but teachers' unions are basically neglected in his discussion, which is unfortunate, for they have been effective mobilizers of teachers' material interests and might yet be better attuned to the questions of educational curricula and pedagogy and to the creation of alliances with other community and union organizations for progressive social change with-in schools and without.

In fact—again, I believe, because of his intention to distance himself from historical materialism and "traditional" radical and Marxist analyses—Giroux gives little consideration to the social order of corporate capitalism and the likelihood that the democratic struggles he imagines will have to articulate not only radical utopian visions but, quite possibly, a historically viable democratic-socialist program envisioning a *socialist* democracy that incorporates the historically progressive rights and freedoms engendered by *liberal* democracy.

It would seem that what I am in fact calling for is a second volume of *Schooling* in which Giroux moves on from the radical theology he provides to a discussion of the strategies—political and organizational—that ensue from his arguments and aspirations in the context of contemporary American political economy and political culture. Or, more important, we ourselves should carry out such work informed by the vision he has afforded us.

Reservations stated, I must reiterate that Giroux has succeeded in providing a stirring vision of schooling for democratic struggle and development. I expect—or, at least, hope—that *Schooling* will have the effect of revising the terms of discussion among radical and critical educators, enabling us, along with other members of the democratic intellectual left, to move beyond mere critique to the articulation of new visions for the making of American democratic history, ever attentive to the experience, agency, and aspirations of working people past and present.

14 Schooling for a Democratic America?*

HOWEVER MANY REASONS THERE were to long for and work toward bringing an end to the long decade of the 1980s and the Reagan-Bush regime, and however motivated I was by most of them, there was one that seemed to increasingly haunt my already anxious imagination regarding the possibility of "four more years," I still am not sure if it had to do with being an academic historian, a democratic socialist, a citizen, or (perhaps most importantly) a parent, but the issue that seemed to agitate me most intensely was education, that is, the future of American *public* education. I have come to believe that what we Americans make of public education is the fundamental test of our commitment to the ideals and practices of democracy.

To be clear, I had few illusions that a Democratic presidency would directly address my anxieties and concerns and no illusions that it would reflect my hopes and aspirations for public education. Our challenge was (and remains) a matter of, *first,* defending and securing public schooling against further assaults by the New Right forces mobilized and empowered by Reagan and Bush and, then, organizing and working to reinvigorate it. Indeed, contrary to the repeated assertions of commentators right and left—including prominent education figures—the problem was *not* George Bush's failure to live up to his promise of becoming the "education president," but the very political economies, public policies, and cultural initiatives

---

* This chapter was first published in *New Politics,* vol. 4, no. 3, summer 1993, as a review essay on Benjamin Barber's *An Aristocracy of Everyone: The Politics of Education and the Future of America* (New York, 1992) and Thomas Sowell's *Inside American Education: The Decline, the Deception, the Dogmas* (New York, 1993).

his administration was pursuing or licensing under the supervision of Secretary of Education Lamar Alexander.

The Bush administration and its attack dogs within and without government declared America's public schools beyond redemption and, depending on the particular source of the accusation, blamed: deferential school boards subject to well-organized special-interest groups; radical and/or incompetent teachers and their unions; professors and schools of education; and moral relativists of various persuasions (all of whom appear to have been college students in the late 1960s). Thus, they called for an "educational revolution" (from above), a revolution that was to involve: giving over responsibility for the reformation of America's schools to private and corporate initiative and enterprise (thereby effectively removing education from democratic control—not to mention serving as an effective union-busting strategy!); "empowering" parents with public funds or vouchers to be spent at the public, private, *or* religious schools of their choice (thereby subjecting the public schools to the "rigors" of the market, defining parents as consumers rather than citizens, *and* punching holes in the divide between church and state); and centralizing curricula via "national standards" and supposedly voluntary national exams (thereby determining local curricula and pedagogical practices as schools would gear up for the tests and teachers would train their students to pass the inevitable multiple-choice questions). Forget the rhetoric about the visionless presidency. As George Kaplan warned in *Education Week*: "Watch out for *America 2000* [the Bush education manifesto]; it really *is* a crusade."

It's not that all of these efforts and initiatives are suddenly undone by the arrival of a Clinton presidency; in fact, I expect various elements of America 2000 to be incorporated into the Democratic administration's own education program. It's that *alternative* possibilities and projects can now be revived and advanced—alternative, that is, to those that promised to further devastate public schooling and to construct "end-of-history" limits to democratic growth and development. If you have any doubts about the material and cultural damage wrought and the challenges we face, just read Jonathan Kozol's *Savage Inequalities.*[1]

I suppose that Thomas Sowell's *Inside American Education* was projected to be the next public-intellectual charge in support of America 2000 and the ambitions of corporate capital and cultural conservatism; but the New Right coalition was falling apart even as Sowell sat writing in his office at the Hoover Institution and, thus, in the end the book reads less like an exposé of "the decline, the deception, [and] the dogmas" of American public schooling and higher education today than a catalog or summation of the angst, the animosity, and the apoplexy of those richly funded neoconservative crusaders who marched before him, such as Allan Bloom *(The Closing of the American Mind)*, Roger Kimball *(Tenured Radicals)*, Charles J. Sykes *(Profscam)*, Dinesh D'Souza *(Illiberal Education)*, William J. Bennett *(Our Children and Our Country)*, Chester Finn *(We Must Take Charge)*, Rita Kramer *(Ed School Follies)*, and Martin Anderson *(Impostors in the Temple)*—talk about "nattering nabobs of negativity."[2]

Sowell's chapter titles register the shrill and hysterical tone and character of his work: "Impaired Faculties"; "Classroom Brainwashing"; "'New Racism' and Old Dogmas"; "Ideological Double Standards"; "Teaching and Preaching," and so on. Drawing from such reliable, critical, and scholarly sources *(sic!)* as the *Dartmouth Review* and the works of Phyllis Schlafly, Sowell parades before us incident upon incident in which knowledge, intellect, decency, and justice are denied or denigrated and children and young adults are exploited and corrupted by "radical" and "leftist" teachers and professors. He allows no room for doubt, and no opening for discussion or dialogue. Where I might have sought to engage him on common concerns—for example, the "psychologization" of elementary education and, in higher education, the subordination of teaching to research and "grantsmanship," the inadequacies of teacher education, and the elevation of athletics at the expense of learning—he leaves me, as did his predecessors, with no place from which to actually speak and attempt to pursue a real argument. It really is a "cultural war" for Sowell and his ilk.

Parroting his cronies, Sowell concludes that it is time to liberate public schooling from the "education establishment." This is to be accomplished by: closing down university schools of education; abolishing tenure for teachers; instituting a nationwide test of school performance; and submitting public education to marketplace competition via parental choice. At the college level Sowell calls for the abolition of professorial tenure and, also, for both a reduction in faculty governance and an increase in scrutiny, supervision, and control of the academy by external authorities such as "trustees, alumni and legislators." I hesitate to use such a term given the actual experience it recalls—and, to be clear, we have not been suffering such a regime—but *Inside American Education* is not just simplistic and nasty, it is neo-McCarthyite. At a lighter moment of the day, however, Sowell reminded me not so much of the Grand Inquisitor as of Groucho Marx in his role as President Wagstaff of Huxley College in the movie *Horsefeathers* where he sings: "Whatever it is, I'm against it!" Though I would not count on it, given the subsidies reportedly provided to publishers by such New Right benefactors as the Olin and Bradley foundations, perhaps the Clinton victory will at least lessen the attractiveness of such works to the major trade presses.

After reading Sowell, Benjamin Barber's collection of essays *An Aristocracy of Everyone* seems a model of reasonableness and moderation. In fact, a too quick perusal of Barber's chapter titles might lead you to think that all he is after is compromise and balance; consider those of two of his most pointed essays: "Radical Excesses and Post-Modernism" and "Conservative Excesses and Allan Bloom."

Yet, however "balanced" such work might at first appear, Barber's arguments are *not* moderate, nor are they intended to secure compromises and a truce in the contemporary "battle of ideas." The Walt Whitman Professor of Political Science at Rutgers University and author of such works as *Strong Democracy* and, with Patrick Watson, *The Struggle for Democracy,* Barber is one of our foremost democratic theorists.[3]

In *An Aristocracy of Everyone* he offers a discourse on the purpose and promise of education, *public* education, in and for democratic life and progress, and he proffers and outlines the curricular and pedagogical practices he believes essential to their realization. Actually, informed by and expressive of the ideals and aspirations of the long revolution and prophetic memory of *democracy,* Barber's arguments are far more critical and radical than those being shouted down from the bully-pulpits of the New Right or, for that matter, those being propagated by the deconstructionist left from its academic lecterns ("Nietzschean charlatans," Gramsci would have called them).

Barber opens the book with a dialectical vision of the relationship between democracy and public education wherein the purpose of the latter is the making of *citizens*—"women and men educated for excellence—by which term I mean the knowledge and competence to govern their own lives"—and the task for the educator is the "teaching of liberty." It is not a matter of accepting the inevitability of "elites," or of leveling *down*: "Democracy insists on levelling—that is the price of equality—but it aims always at levelling *up*" (my italics). He grants that Americans regularly celebrate just such a conception of the purpose of education; however, he observes, even as the nation proclaims its commitment to education, "it busies itself with other matters. It talks pedagogy but spends its resources elsewhere. It denigrates teachers as unprofessional but refuses them professional wages. . . ."

Barber does agree with Sowell et al. that American education is in crisis but, contra the New Right politicos and pundits who would sunder education and democracy in the name of "excellence" and/or "efficiency" and "competitiveness," he contends that to do so is to place democracy in peril. Indeed, he declaims, it is not simply public education that is problematic today, but American public life and democratic prospects more broadly. Thus, the renewal and reconstruction of public education must be articulated and pursued as part of a grander and more radical project of renewal and transformation of liberty, equality, *and* democratic community.

Additional resources dedicated to public education are, of course, essential, but they definitely will not be enough. There also must be a "revolution in how we understand our schools."

What should we make of all this talk of "revolution"? Actually, the revolution for which Barber calls would at the same time represent an act of restoration and redemption of a classical vision of schooling: "Historically, the meaning of *public* education was precisely education into what it meant to belong to a public: education in the *res publica*—in commonality, in community, in the common constitution that made plurality and difference possible." Clearly, Barber stands in opposition not only to the neoconservatives who would deny equality and multiculturalism but, equally, to the postmodernists who would deny the possibility of commonality and community in deference to and pursuit of "*over*-differentiation and *hyper*-pluralism" (my italics).

The goals of the curriculum and pedagogical practices that Barber proceeds to delineate are captured in the following words: "all education is or ought to be radical—a reminder of the past, a challenge to the present, and a prod to the future." Specifically, he urges that schooling for a democratic America entail the learning of *history, criticism,* and *service.* The teaching of history is not just to transmit the multi-cultural American story and identity (itself bound up in a larger Western *and* global experience), but also to develop an appreciation of the making of history—especially the struggle for democracy—and to foster imagination and hope about the future. The teaching of the skills of criticism is to enable Americans to investigate and check, to analyze and evaluate, *and* to contest and revise the story being taught and pursued. And the teaching of service is intended to cultivate and create active and participatory citizens experienced and engaged in the making and re-making of their democratic lives, communities, and history (not simply, as others have envisioned it, to encourage charity, alternative modes of repaying student loans, or the recognition of duty and obligations to the state).

I do not do justice to Barber's arguments and proposals—to most of which I find myself subscribing. Nevertheless, I am compelled to register a serious criticism: Barber fails to treat the works of those other scholars and intellectuals with whom he seems to share a commitment to democratic education. He writes as if he is alone—like Samson standing between and pushing against the pillars of the Philistines—with neocons to the right and postmods to the left. My complaint is not simply that he fails to critically and/or appreciatively acknowledge in the traditional academic fashion the efforts of those of us working along the same lines; but that by not doing so he also fails to mobilize, engage, or invoke the intellectual and political community so essential to the campaigns he envisions to reconstruct and reinvigorate public education and citizenship.

Having registered my complaint, I must not fail, first, to enthusiastically endorse Barber's three-dimensional curriculum and, second, to recommend his book to both the new secretary of education and the next chair of the National Endowment for the Humanities.

15 The Liberal Arts and Democracy*
(with Henry A. Giroux)

THE CURRENT PUBLIC DEBATE about humanities curricula and enlarging or restricting the literary canon is to be welcomed, for it represents an acknowledgement that schooling is about more than job training and preparation for careers. However, the terrain on which the debate is being pursued and the terms in which it is being conducted remain too narrowly drawn. Thus the debate has failed to articulate the critical promise of humanities education.

Both conservatives and liberals appeal to what appear to be admirable principles to support their respective arguments. In the name of "aesthetic and intellectual standards," conservatives claim that the current efforts to revise the literary canon should embody the classical ideal of the humanities curriculum which, in the words of Matthew Arnold, "represents the best that is known and thought in the world." Moreover, noting that American students are already woefully ignorant of or, at best, ill-acquainted with, the great works of Western civilization, they argue that to broaden the canon by replacing Western with non-Western writers or with writers who have been largely confined to subordinate traditions is to further undermine the transmission of our cultural heritage.

Liberals, inspired by more "democratic" aspirations, insist that behind the rhetoric about "standards" and "excellence" lie the

* This chapter is a somewhat shorter version of a "Point of View" originally titled "The Liberal Arts Must Be Reformed to Serve Democratic Ends," which appeared on the back page of the *Chronicle of Higher Education*, March 29, 1989.

faces of power, ethnocentrism, racism, and sexism. White males, they assert, have no monopoly on aesthetic and intellectual talent, and it is time to recognize this by incorporating literary works by Blacks, Latinos, Asians, and women into liberal-arts curricula. Indeed, they argue, since America is a pluralistic society situated in a global world order, it is only appropriate that students be made aware of and sensitive to the diversity of cultures and views of the world held by other groups.

What we seem to be confronted with is a debate over standards versus representation—a contest between elitism and democratic pluralism. And yet it is arguable that the voices being heard, in spite of their sharp differences, do actually share a common view of liberal-arts education. That is, they both seem to comprehend it as, first and foremost, the transmission of cultural treasures from one generation to the next, be those treasures singularly Western or not. Thus it has often seemed as though the debate were reducible to the question of the contents of course syllabi. This is unfortunate, for in the face of the great challenges we confront as a people, what is called for is a more critical and fundamental argument that transcends the limited focus on the canon.

What needs to be recognized and addressed in the current debate is that the crisis in liberal education is one of historical purpose and meaning, a crisis that challenges us to rethink in the most fundamental way the relationship between the role of the university and the imperatives of democracy in a mass society.

Historically, education in the humanities was conceived of as the essential preparation for governing—specifically, the preparation and outfitting of the governing elite. The humanities curriculum, composed of the "best" that had been said or written, was intended, as the social historian Elizabeth Fox-Genovese has observed in a 1986 article in *Salmagundi,* "to provide selected individuals with a collective history, culture, and epistemology so that they could run the world effectively."

In this context, the canon was considered to be a possession of dominant classes or groups; indeed, the canon was fashioned as a safeguard to ensure that the cultural property of such groups was passed on from generation to generation along with the family estates. Thus, it seems most appropriate that the literary canon should be subject to revision—as it has been before in the course of the expansion of democracy—so that it might incorporate and reflect the experience and aspirations of the women, members of minority groups, and children of the working class who have been entering the academy.

Nevertheless, by focusing on the literary canon as the "spoils" of democratic struggle, with integration and representation as their goals, liberals are failing to recognize the more radical vision of liberal-arts education to be found within its elite social origins and purpose. In other words, there ought to be a democratic appropriation and redemption of the historical conception of humanities education as preparation for governing. Conceived of this way, the fundamental question of the humanities curriculum ceases to be merely that of establishing the contents of the literary canon. Instead, the most important question becomes that of re-formulating the purpose and meaning of higher education in ways that contribute to the cultivation of an informed, critical *citizenry* capable of actively participating in shaping and governing a democratic society.

Such a view does not demand that the notion of a literary canon be rejected—though it likely commands a more historically grounded and critical reading of the concept. Such a view does propose that the way students engage and critically examine knowledge is just as important an issue as what texts are chosen for a class or program. It argues that treating texts as sacred sources undermines the possibility for dialogue, argument, and critical thinking, and ignores the way the texts of our cultural inheritance may have helped to create social relations that exploit, infantilize, and oppress. There are many canons in our history, and we need to look at how they have helped shape the major events of their time as well as of our own. For example, when analyzing works marginalized by the official canon, we need to ask how the texts have contributed to important struggles by women, racial and ethnic minorities, and other subordinate groups to lay claim to their own voices. In the briefest terms, we would urge a commitment to *historical* education and the development of humanities and liberal-arts curricula that cultivate perspective, critique, consciousness, remembrance, and imagination.

Let us formulate the debate over the canon to address what it means to educate students to be critical citizens. What kinds of knowledge and forms of pedagogy can be adopted that enable, rather than subvert, the formation of a democratic society? What knowledge can help create a democratic culture, form a new public language, and provide the basis for educating citizens about what it means to struggle for a real democracy? Those are the questions that need to be debated before the issues of content and pedagogy can be discussed within any meaningful context.

It seems almost fitting that in the Age of Reagan, questions regarding the purpose and meaning of the liberal arts disappeared from the discourse of public life and democracy. It is time to reconstruct a vision of the university that reasserts the connection between equity and excellence on the one hand and learning and the imperatives of democratic public life on the other. It is time to place the liberal arts once again in the center of the debate about what it means to educate students to participate in the democratic process.

16 The Ends of History? The Question of National Standards*

AS PART OF AMERICA 2000, and in conjunction with the Bush administration's plan to establish "national standards" in selected school subjects, the National Endowment for the Humanities (NEH) and the Department of Education have announced a $1.6-million project to develop the standards for history. In view of the many reports and horror stories about American students' ignorance of both United States and world history—referred to by teachers, professional historians, and the media alike as "the crisis of history"—such an undertaking seems in order. However, before such standards and guidelines are established there are certain fundamental questions that must be addressed regarding the purpose and the promise of historical education and, given the record of the Reagan and Bush administrations on matters "historical," we should be especially skeptical and wary of initiatives to determine "national standards"—potentially, a national curriculum—emanating from their offices.

The formation and ascendance in the 1970s of the curious coalition of Old Right, New Right, and neoconservative forces was made possible in part by the concerted use and abuse of the past, a practice pursued most astutely and incorrigibly by Ronald Reagan himself. Indeed, Reagan's mobilization and fabrication of history remained a defining feature of his campaigns and presidential speeches and statements, the crudest and most memorable examples

* This chapter was first published as a Commentary in *Education Week,* February 5, 1992.

of which were his references to the Nicaraguan *contras* as "freedom fighters . . . in the tradition of our Founding Fathers" and his remarks in 1985 regarding his visit to the military cemetery in Bitburg in which he stated that the Nazi SS officers buried there "were victims just as surely as the victims in the concentration camps."

Arguably, the Bush presidency lacked the color and rhetorical flourish of the Reagan years, but it was not oblivious to the possibilities of using and abusing the past. No great communicator, Bush nevertheless made it a point of recalling the errors of Munich 1938 and the ensuing horrors of Hitlerism to rally American and international public opinion in support of (what was to be an unfinished) war against Saddam Hussein. And let us not forget that his Policy Planning Staff at the State Department included Francis Fukuyama, who announced in a widely touted article that we had reached "the end of history."

Nor have the efforts to secure "the past" in support of the political goals and aspirations of the Republicans' conservative coalition been limited to political campaigns and speechmaking occasions. William J. Bennett, first as head of the National Endowment for the Humanities (NEH) and later as secretary of education, effectively harnessed academic and public concern about "the crisis of history" and, placing this issue on the political agenda, made it into a question of public policy. This in itself surely was to be welcomed. But the problem for Bennett and his successor at the NEH, Lynne V. Cheney, has never been simply a matter of reinvigorating historical education. First, their endeavors in this direction have entailed the persistent denigration of and attacks upon the more critical *and* democratic developments in historical scholarship and pedagogy of the past generation. Students and teachers of the experiences of working people, women, and racial and ethnic minorities have been subject over and over again to accusations of "ideological bias" and blamed for the decline in Americans' knowledge of their own history and the Western tradition that is supposedly undermining our "common culture" and "shared values" and threatening our national welfare and security. Thus, paralleling the campaigns against labor and the movements for gender and racial equality have been those against the recovery, interpretation, and teaching of labor, women's, and racial and ethnic minorities' histories.

At the same time, the reports and pronouncements issuing from Bennett's and Cheney's agencies have repeatedly advanced historical curricula that propose an acritical and one-dimensional narrative in which the United States is represented as sole heir to the "Western Heritage" and, following Fukuyama, its *final* fruition. Moreover, these curricula ignore the underside of Western civilization and American history and also our splendid traditions of dissent and struggle from below. Bennett himself referred to historical education as a means of "legitimiz[ing] the political system"; and he and his Assistant Secretary of Education Chester Finn, who has gone on to become the leading champion of national standards and curricula, wrote that such an education would help "foster social cohesion and a sense of national community and pride." Similarly, Cheney has referred to schooling in history as a "kind of civic glue" promoting nationalism and the sense that we are all part of a "common undertaking." Such sentiments and aspirations are alluring, especially in a period of national anxiety, social and cultural conflict, and economic distress. Yet let us not confuse the development of good and effective democratic citizenship with the making of an ideological consensus.

Of course, the most obvious question is: Whose values are to be defined as *the* values to be shared? But in the inevitable debate over multiculturalism versus a common culture, we must not fail to ask ourselves an even more fundamental question: What is the *purpose* of historical study and thought in a democratic polity? In other words, is the teaching and study of the past and the making of the present to be pursued for the sake of creating a consensus in favor of the status quo? *Or* is it to be pursued for the contributions it might render to the great public debates and arguments essential to a free and democratic life and the making of new history, perhaps, even *a* new history?

If our goal is the continued and further development of our democratic polity and culture, I would propose that historical education cultivate perspective, critique, consciousness, remembrance, and imagination—that is, *the powers of the past*. By *perspective* I mean the knowledge and recognition that the way things are is not the way they have always been nor the way they must necessarily be in the future. *Critique* involves a process of revealing and comprehending the social origins of the political, economic, and cultural orders in which we live and have lived. *Consciousness* refers to an appreciation of the making of history, an awareness of the "effort and sacrifice which the present has cost the past and which the future is costing the present." *Remembrance* entails an acknowledgement that while the past is not for living in, it is a reservoir of experience—both of tragedy and of hope—from which we draw in order to deliberate and to act. And *imagination* commands that we recognize the present as history and consider the structure, movement, and possibilities of the contemporary world and how we might act to develop the humanistic and prevent the barbaric.

I am not arguing necessarily against the creation of national standards or, even, a national curriculum for historical education (though I would warn and urge against the reduction of historical knowledge to multiple-choice exams!). Clearly, the teaching of history must be reinvigorated, and there is evidently broad support for the idea of establishing national education guidelines. However, we should be watchful and careful regarding how the national goals for historical study and thought are formulated. Critically conceived and smartly pursued, they could well contribute not only to the development of a generation of students who perform well on history tests but, also, to the development of a historically informed citizenry ready and eager to bring the lessons of the past to bear on the challenges of the present as we continue to extend and refine the ideas and practices of liberty, equality, and democracy. However, if they are subordinated to the politics of the day, we could well find ourselves at the end of history.

17 From *Lessons from History* to *National Standards*: Questions of Class, Labor, and American Radicalism *

INTRODUCTION

THE PUBLICATION OF THE three-volume *National Standards for History—United States History: Grades 5-12, World History: Grades 5-12,* and *History: Grades K-4*[1]—has generated right-wing rancor and accusation from the floors of Congress to op-ed pages and the studios of AM talk-radio shows. In the simplest of terms, the authors of the *National Standards* have been charged not just with having been "politically correct," but with being "thieves," "hijackers," and "balkanizers" of America's past.

Many of my fellow historians have been shocked and dismayed by the virulence of the conservatives' reaction. However, considering their original, clever, and effective politicization of the "crisis of history and historical education," and their continuing campaigns in the "culture wars," I was not at all surprised that New Right politicos and pundits would make the *National Standards for History*—commissioned by a Republican administration but released under a besieged Democratic one—a major public issue. But it is truly ironic, for the idea of enacting national standards in history originally had the politics of the New Right written all over it (as did

* This essay first appeared in the *Review of Education, Pedagogy and Cultural Studies*, vol. 17, no. 4, 1995. I want to thank the editor, Patrick Shannon, for commissioning the essay.

its counterpart in Britain, where Tory Prime Minister Margaret Thatcher had commissioned the creation of a "National Curriculum for History" with similar hopes of subordinating the teaching of history to the creation of a new conservative political consensus).[2]

Perhaps the best indicator of the irony of the situation is that the most vocal opponent of the now-published *National Standards*, Lynne Cheney, previously had been not only one of the project's most ardent advocates but, as head of the National Endowment for the Humanities (NEH) during the Bush administration, one of its chief benefactors. (Currently a fellow of the corporately funded neoconservative Washington think-tank the American Enterprise Institute, Cheney has been crusading not just for rejection of the *National Standards for History* but, also, for termination of the NEH itself.)[3]

It is not my task here to recount the story of the development of the *National Standards for History*, or to explain the brouhaha that the release of the three volumes has instigated; I have written at book-length on the making of the "crisis" leading to the creation of the National Standards project.[4] Rather, I will be looking specifically at the controversial *National Standards for United States History* volume. And, to be honest, my interest is both public and personal. As an early and outspoken critic of the Bush administration's intentions to institute national standards in history, I remain interested in what transpires in the process. Further, having served on one of the official task forces convened to consider a preliminary rendition of the National Standards, the volume *Lessons from History*,[5] I have been anxious and eager to examine the final version, for I was seriously concerned about what I found in it. Therefore, this essay begins by recalling the former efforts of the authors of the *National Standards for History* and then considers their final product in the light of my concerns about the earlier document.

LESSONS FROM HISTORY

I was recruited to the Organization of American Historians' (OAH) focus group on National Standards in the spring of 1992. My appointment to the OAH group was apparently due to my work on the politics of history and, most immediately, an editorial I had authored warning of the Republicans' political and hegemonic ambitions for historical education and, thus, of the dangerous implications of their scheme to create "national standards" for the discipline.[6] In fact, having foolishly underestimated my professional peers' commitments to the development of a critical telling of America's past and present, I remember being somewhat surprised when I actually was invited to be a member, considering my evident skepticism, if not outright hostility, toward the whole project. I was all the more surprised when—at the instigation of the chair of the OAH Educational Policy Committee—it was decided that in preparation for our deliberations all of the members of the group would be equipped with copies of my book *The Powers of the Past.*

The group's assigned task (the only phase of the process in which I was directly involved) was to examine and make recommendations on *Lessons from History,* the first stage in the development of the National Standards. With funding from the NEH and the U.S. Department of Education, the volume had been produced by the National Center for History in the Schools at UCLA under the direction of Charlotte Crabtree and Gary Nash, both of whom remained responsible for the project right through to the publication of the *National Standards* themselves. The actual initiative to establish national standards in core subjects such as history emanated from the Bush administration's broad program of educational reform, America 2000 (which was intended to secure for Bush himself the reputation of being the "education president"). Notably, while America 2000 was to be significantly revised by the new Clinton administration and retitled Goals 2000, the devising of national standards had strong bipartisan support from the nation's state governors and thus it continued without amendment.

From the very beginning, National Standards for History was a big project subjected to extensive and manifold professional scrutiny and input.[7] I well wondered, given the many and diverse voices being sought out, if the criticisms advanced would ever be addressed, for I figured they would all end up neutralizing one another. Here, too, my assumptions were eventually to be proven wrong.

   Lessons from History itself was a 300-page text consisting of four major chapters: (1) "The Case for History in Our Schools"; (2) "Determining What History to Teach"; (3) "Essential Understandings in United States History"; and (4) "Essential Understandings in World History." Our particular responsibility, Chapter 3, was divided into 14 units outlining American experience from "Three Worlds Meet (1450-1600)" to "The Recent United States (1961-Present)."

   Supplied with copies of *Lessons* ahead of time, we delivered our assessments to the chair of the group prior to our gathering together in Washington, D.C. (May 1992), enabling him to organize our discussions around four problem areas: Strategies; Broad Themes; Problems of Implementation; and Evaluation of Individual Sections.[8] There were approximately 20 of us in attendance—professors of history and education, junior– and senior– high school teachers from both public and private schools, and one foundation person. Men and women of different ages, we represented every region of the country and a pretty diverse set of American racial and ethnic groups. Space does not allow me to recount our deliberations in any detail, but they were lively and critical—and I learned a great deal about the teaching of history from my fellow members of the group, especially from the schoolteachers.

   At the "strategic" level, the generally shared concerns about *Lessons* had to with the absence of diversity of perspective, regarding both the voices of the past to be heard and the historiographical interpretations of the past to be accounted. Also, there was concern expressed about the text's failure to treat the differences between past and present, its tendency to offer simply a history of the "origins" of the modern world. Thematically speaking, members of the group noted a variety of weaknesses and omissions pertaining to: the global context of American history; social history (popular culture, family history, violence); religion; foreign policy; labor and working-class history; economics; and intellectual life.

Predictably, when we turned to "problems of implementation" the conversation was monopolized by the schoolteachers. Most important, they all seemed to agree that if there were to be national standards in the fashion of *Lessons,* then teachers would have to be properly trained and supported to deal with such sophisticated materials. Specific problems foreseen had to do with the need to expand teaching techniques; the difficulty in covering all of the proposed content areas and the responsibility and ability of teachers to select what to emphasize; and the need for additional resources such as documentary and supplementary materials.

Finally, and at some length, the group dealt with the individual chapters of *Lessons,* especially Chapter 3 covering American history. The criticisms were many, and they were pointed. Again, space does not suffice, but I should note that they included everything from issues of omission, emphasis, and priority, to questions of organization, presentation, and interpretation. Fully registered in the OAH focus group's report, my own concerns about *Lessons* had to do with the theory or understanding of history projected in its pages, the particular narrative of American history being advanced, and the treatments of the American working class, labor movement, and radical tradition.

I had assumed that *Lessons* would reflect conservatives' complaints about the contemporary historical profession, especially regarding the prominence in the discipline of *social* history, and their call for a return to a more traditional "political" approach to the past.[9] That was not the case, though it would have been preferable, for what was presented was an even more conservative view of history. That is, instead of emphasizing politics—which at least would have accorded a significant role to human agency—the text was shot through with techno-economic determinism.[10] As I wrote in my notes to the group: "Repeatedly, techno-economic developments are presented as causing, determining, and/or shaping social, political, and cultural changes, but they are not themselves comprehended as being caused, determined, and/or shaped by social, political, and cultural relations and developments." Strangely enough, as opposed to deferring to the demands of conservatives, the authors of *Lessons* had apparently gone in the completely opposite direction and rendered—surely, without ever intending it—a classically orthodox Marxist version of history in which the techno-economic "base" determines the political and cultural "superstructures."

Beyond the determinism, the actual narrative of American political life in *Lessons* did reflect a more traditionally conservative view of things. There was a persistent tendency to describe the development of American democracy as an "evolution." For all their talk about the "drama of history" in the preliminary chapters, I could not understand why *Lessons'* authors had failed to narrate the *making* of America in terms of the great arguments and struggles that have propelled it—not only a more challenging way of putting the nation's history, but, surely, a more inviting one, as well.

Although, as I have noted, a number of the group's members called for greater diversity of perspective, more voices from and on the past, my own reading of *Lessons* led me to conclude that experiences of race, ethnicity, and gender had been covered far more than was usually the case. However, it seemed to me that once again the great American political taboo against speaking of class had asserted itself. The class-structured character of American life and politics was not completely forgotten, but its treatment was spotty, weak, and mishandled. Consider the presentation of the labor movement. In my notes to the group, I wrote:

> First, early workingmen's politics, political parties, and campaigns are hardly mentioned. In fact, the "labor movement" is referred to as beginning in the late nineteenth century as a simple consequence of workplace-technological changes. Moreover, the movement disappears from American life after the New Deal except for reference to the United Farm Workers as a way of discussing Hispanic Americans. White-collar unionism is not mentioned at all—in spite of the fact that so many of the teachers who will be responsible for meeting "National Standards in History" will themselves be members of the NEA or AFT.

Not surprisingly, in view of the inadequate representation of labor (again, I quote from my notes to my colleagues):

> American socialism as a movement of immigrant and native-born workers, farmers, writers, and intellectuals is ignored— except as the eventual subject of "Red Scares" (which are supposedly due to the Bolshevik Revolution without any reference to the inequalities of property and class in America). One would think that the Socialist Party deserves some attention, at least in Unit IX on the Progressive Era! I find no mention of Eugene Debs—yet I would swear that even in my Cold-War high school social studies classes we learned about Debs. From what I can tell, "socialism" only gets a note in the very specific and problematic form of the Communist Party USA of the 1930s and there it gets lumped with the American Nazi Party. This kind of gross lumping mirrors Cold-War thinking about totalitarianism.

I had other qualms and reservations, but the feature of *Lessons* that agitated me the most was the merger of the Second World War and the Cold War in a single unit (XIII): "The war against Fascism," I wrote, "is neither a *prelude to* nor a *first phase* of the Cold War." I insisted that we demand separate units for each and, as the chair recorded it (in boldface type): "this complaint was seconded by all those present."

NATIONAL STANDARDS FOR UNITED STATES HISTORY

Having examined *Lessons from History,* I had good reason to remain hostile toward the National Standards for History project. I continued to assume the worst, and when the *National Standards* finally did appear I was definitely not inspired to optimism by the New Right's vituperations, for, given that the project had ceased to be subject to the controls of a Republican administration, I supposed that the likes of Rush Limbaugh would be upset no matter what the result. Moreover, the Republicans' victories in the recent midterm elections had set them to hungrily searching for further prey. So, I picked up the volume for U.S. history that bears the title *National Standards for United States History: Exploring the American Experience* possessed, to say the least, of great skepticism.[11] But, as I have already indicated, most of my assumptions were to be proven wrong.

What I have found is dramatically—dare I say, *radically*—different than *Lessons. National Standards* is an imposing document, truly reflective of contemporary historical scholarship and practice—and, presumably, for conservatives *that* is the problem. Indeed, the standards produced for American history should rile conservatives quite a bit given their intense hostility to the critical historiographies crafted since the 1960s—especially the socialization and democratization of the past *from the bottom up,* entailing the incorporation of previously excluded class, race, ethnic, and gender experiences and agencies.

Following a set of prefatory remarks, the *National Standards* volume is composed of four chapters plus an appendix listing contributors and participating organizations. In Chapter 1, "Developing Standards in United States History," the authors introduce the idea of standards in historical education; set out the rationale for developing them ("the education of the *public citizen*" and "the nurturing of the *private individual*"); explain the criteria (15 in number) used in formulating them; discuss briefly the periodization of American history provided (noting that it remains essentially political but adding that periods are overlapped in order to more effectively treat developments in social history); and review the definitions of the two types of standards, "historical understanding" and "historical thinking."

Regarding historical understanding, the authors note that the study of history must be integrative of the several "aspects" of human experience, referring specifically to the "social, political, scientific/technological, economic, and cultural," and must always set that experience in "historical time and geographic place." I remember that when I read *Lessons* I was worried that the five "aspects" were being represented as *trans*historical in character, that is, the categories were presented in a reified form as if they were not themselves historically and socially constituted. In other words, why not "political economy" instead of social, political, economic, and so on? This remains a problem in *National Standards,* but not as blatantly so as it was in the former text.

There are five types of "historical thinking" that teachers are to foster in their students: (1) chronological thinking—"a sense of historical time"; (2) historical comprehension—"the ability to [critically] read historical narratives . . . and to avoid 'present-mindedness'"; (3) historical analysis and interpretation—"the ability to compare and contrast . . . to consider multiple perspectives . . . and to compare and evaluate competing historical explanations of the past"; (4) historical research—"the ability to formulate historical questions from encounters with historical documents, artifacts, photos, visits to historical sites . . . and to construct a sound historical narrative or argument"; (5) historical issues–analysis and decision-making—"the ability to identify [and analyze] problems that confronted people in the past [and what they did about them] . . . and to bring historical perspectives to bear on informed decision-making in the present." These are laid out in greater detail in Chapter 2, "Standards in Historical Thinking," and translated into grade-specific competencies with grade-specific examples of how each might be achieved. (The grade-levels are logically grouped: 5-6, 7-8, 9-12.)

These "Historical Thinking Standards" are impressively developed and intellectually and pedagogically challenging, if not daunting. In view of the time regularly allowed and resources usually afforded to history teaching, all I can say is that, fortunately, it is competency that is called for, not mastery. And, with this in mind, the authors note three policy issues that will need to be addressed in the implementation of national standards: "ensuring equity for all students; providing adequate instructional time for history; and accommodating variability in state and local curriculum plans."

Chapter 3, "United States History Standards for Grades 5-12," periodizes American history into 10 "eras": (1) Three Worlds Meet (Beginnings to 1620); (2) Colonization and Settlement (1585-1763); (3) Revolution and the New Nation (1754-1820s); (4) Expansion and Reform (1801-1861); (5) Civil War and Reconstruction (1850-1877); (6) The Development of the Industrial United States (1870-1900); (7) The Emergence of Modern America (1890-1930); (8) The Great Depression and World War II (1929-1945); (9) Postwar United States (1945–early 1970s); (10) Contemporary United States (1968-present). Here, I will note simply that I was very pleased to see that in spite of reducing the number of eras from 14 to 10, the Second World War and the Cold War were no longer collapsed into each other.

Giving life to the historical thinking standards, these era-specific terms integrate historical thinking and historical understanding. In all, there are 31 main understandings to be cultivated and, again, each of these is translated into grade-specific competencies and accompanied by grade-specific examples of how students might achieve and demonstrate them. These, too, are very impressive and extremely challenging.

The authors of the *National Standards* had evidently paid attention to the proffered criticisms of *Lessons*. The Standards call not only for acquiring knowledge and understanding of America's multicultural history but, also, for recognizing the diversity of perspectives both in terms of the voices from the past to be heard and in terms of the historiographical interpretations of the past to be assayed. For example, in Era 3, Revolution and the New Nation, the authors state:

> In thinking about the causes and outcomes of the American Revolution, students need to confront the central issue of how revolutionary the Revolution actually was. In order to reach judgements about this, they necessarily will have to see the Revolution through different sets of eyes—enslaved and free Americans, Native Americans, white men and women of

different social classes, religions, ideological dispositions, regions and occupations.

At the same time (and somewhat evident in the lines cited), questions of historical interpretation are also posed throughout the Standards. For example, in Era 4, Expansion and Reform, one of the standards (Standard 2D) and competencies posed is to "Demonstrate understanding of the settlement of the West by: [Grades 9-12] Assessing the degree to which political democracy was a characteristic of the West, and evaluating the factors influencing political and social conditions on the frontier"; and an example provided of student achievement is:

> Analyze the debate among historians over the Frederick Jackson Turner thesis on "The Significance of the Frontier in American History." *Was political democracy characteristic of the West? What effect did frontier conditions have on Mexican Americans in New Mexico and California? How were gender roles defined in the West? If the West was a "crucible for democracy," why did so many Western states in the 1840s and 1850s initiate laws prohibiting the immigration of free blacks?*

The point is that in this fashion, even as it becomes more complex, American history also becomes more vibrant and—filled with voices, contests, hopes, tragedies, and possibilities—more engaging.

In similar ways, almost all of our group's concerns were met regarding such matters as the global context of American history and the handling of social experience, religion, intellectual life—and, also, most of my own having to do with determinism, the narrative of America, and the representation of the labor movement and American socialism. For a start, the determinism so prevalent in *Lessons* is greatly reduced in *National Standards* without ignoring or underestimating the significance of technological developments in the transformation of American life. Though I would have liked to see greater acknowledgement of the social and class determination of technological innovation itself, at least the one-dimensional story of technology determining social changes and relations is gone. History is much more fully portrayed as being made by people, struggling together and against each other in historically diverse and developing collectivities.

Moreover, class finds a much more central place in the *National Standards* narrative of the nation's history than in that presented in *Lessons.* I have pages of notes regarding the inscription of class *and* class conflict in *National Standards'* rendering of America's past, from the formation of labor systems in the Americas through the class-differential aspirations and responses to the Revolution and social and military combats of the Civil War to the class struggles of the making of the modern industrial-capitalist United States. The key thing is that along with questions of race, ethnicity, and gender, which are currently so prevalent not only in history and cultural studies but, also, in our public discourse, class, too, is apparently appreciated as a fundamental experience and determinant of American history.

My major complaint here is that the significance of class recedes somewhat in the standards of the last two eras, postwar and contemporary America, in favor, not unpredictably, of race, ethnicity, and gender. Thus, we seem to be presented with the liberal picture of America as a middle-class society whose material benefits and civil rights have yet to be granted equally to minorities and women. What is not adequately related about contemporary America is the class war from above that has been waged by capital and the powers that be against working people and the poor for at least a generation now.

Of course, I should not fail to note that teachers are not prohibited by the standards from developing this more critical understanding of contemporary history, and in places the door is actually left wide open to such considerations: For example, Standard 1B in Era 10, Contemporary United States, proposes that students should be able to "Demonstrate understanding of domestic policy issues in contemporary America by: [9-12] Analyzing why labor unionism declined in the Reagan-Bush era"; and examples of student achievement cited include questions such as "How supportive were the Reagan-Bush administrations of organized labor?" and "How has the public attitude toward labor unions changed in the latter half of the 20th century? What accounts for this change?"

In contrast to *Lessons, National Standards* does not limit the labor movement to the Industrial Revolution—and Eugene Debs does not fail to appear, along with Samuel Gompers of the American Federation of Labor (AFL) to his political right *and* "Big Bill" Haywood and the "Wobblies" of the Industrial Workers of the World (IWW) to his left. Moreover, labor action is not restricted to industrial and economic issues. Standard 3B of Era 6, The Development of the Industrial United States, calls for students to be able to "Demonstrate understanding of the rise of national labor unions and the role of state and federal governments in labor conflicts . . ."; and among the means by which they might show they have achieved this is the following: "Analyze the labor conflicts of 1894 and their impact on the development of American democracy. . . ." Similarly, in Era 8, The Great Depression and World War II, Standard 2B asks that students be able to "Demonstrate understanding of the impact of the New Deal on workers and the labor movement."

Unfortunately, in Era 9 on the postwar decades, the labor movement is still essentially absent, except for reference to César Chavez's United Farm Workers as a way of discussing the organizing efforts of Mexican Americans. There are references to changes in work, the workplace, and employments, but there is no acknowledgement of widespread worker insurgencies in the 1960s, the effect of which is to reproduce media images of (white-male) working-class complacency and conservatism in the face of struggles for race and gender justice and equality and against the war in Southeast Asia. It should not be forgotten that it was anxiety about widespread worker discontent and emerging demands for industrial democracy that instigated the creation of a government task force to look at "work in America" and eventually drove the corporate elite to commence its campaigns against liberalism and social democracy.[12] Still, as noted above, the labor movement is re-introduced in Era 10, in which the question of declining union membership is posed.

Finally, there is the matter of the treatment of the American radical tradition—what I call the *prophetic memory* of American democracy—and the even less publicly appreciated history of American socialism. The role of radicalism in the making of American democracy is accounted—arguably, how could it not be, given the nation's revolutionary foundations. And the making of democracy itself is appreciated as entailing not simply an evolution but *struggles*. What I especially like is that the authors saw fit to prescribe the pursuit of historical dialogues between past and present. In Era 3 on the American Revolution, Standard 1B says that students should be able to "Demonstrate understanding of the principles articulated in the Declaration of Independence by: [5-12] Explaining the major ideas . . . [7-12] Demonstrating the fundamental contradictions between the ideals of the Declaration and the realities of chattel slavery . . . [9-12] Comparing the Declaration to the French Declaration of the Rights of Man and Citizen and constructing an argument evaluating their importance to the spread of constitutional democracies in the 19th and 20th centuries." And in one of the examples of student achievement for grades 9-12 it is asked: "How have the ideas that inspired the American and French revolutions influenced the 20th-century revolutions in Mexico, Russia, China, Cuba, and Vietnam? How have Americans viewed these modern revolutions?"

Similarly, in Era 4, Expansion and Reform, Standard 4C requires students to "Demonstrate understanding of changing gender roles and the roles of different groups of women by: [9-12] Evaluating the links between the antebellum women's movement for equality and 20th-century feminism." In another direction, that is, the *suppression* of radicalism, there is significant reference to McCarthyism in Era 9, particularly in Standard 3A: "Demonstrate understanding of the origins and domestic consequences of the Cold War by: [7-12] Explaining the rise of McCarthyism and evaluating its effects on civil liberties . . . [9-12] Analyzing the reasons for the demise of

McCarthyism and explaining its overall significance and legacy." And among the examples of student achievement there is one that actually suggests a persistent pattern of oppression against radicals of the left: "Compare the 'red scare' in the post–World War I period with the 'second red scare' that emerged after World War II."

Though I firmly believe American socialism deserves even greater attention, *National Standards* does make far more of it than did *Lessons.* The Socialist Party of the Progressive decades is noted in several places (and as I have said, Eugene Debs and even the radical Wobblies of the IWW make appearances). More remarkable, perhaps, is that in Era 8 on the Depression of the 1930s, one of the examples of student achievement for Standard 2B on the New Deal and the labor movement, focusing on the growth of the Congress of Industrial Organizations (CIO) as an alternative to the AFL, includes reference to the role of union organizers from the American Communist Party in not unfavorable terms.

Lastly, Chapter 4, "Teaching Resources for United States History," is an annotated "bibliography" of media resources, printed sources and texts, and teaching materials that educators and students will find useful in addressing the subjects and questions posed in the previous chapters.

♦

I could continue to offer both praises and criticisms but, I repeat, *National Standards* is a dramatic improvement over *Lessons.* My reservations about the National Standards project were and still are warranted. However, if the popular and democratic will demands the creation of such programs for the nation's schools we would do well to adopt *National Standards for United States History*—so long as we remember that critical revision is in order, resources must be provided, and variability in its implementation must be allowed—for it does a fine job of representing current thinking among professional historians about the past and the making of the present.

Things, however, do not happen so easily. Humanities professors, historians included, are accused of undermining traditional values; museums are attacked for challenging popularly held beliefs; the primary support for historical scholarship, the NEH, is threatened with foreclosure; and, apparently due to political pressure from the Republican-dominated Congress, the authors of the *National Standards for History* have agreed to negotiate changes in the standards themselves. Let us hope the amendments to be made are not too repulsive—and, if necessary, raise our voices loudly in opposition to them.

18 Preparing the Next Generation of Public Intellectuals[*]

EDITORIALS AND COMMENTARIES FROM the political right, left, and center seem to agree on at least one point—that our civil society and public culture, the arenas in which we deliberate our collective priorities, policies, and projects, are in serious crisis and decline. Commentators decry the fact that only 50 percent of the American electorate votes in presidential elections. They lament the low quality of public debate and the lack of new answers and formulas to address the social problems, economic difficulties, and moral dilemmas we confront. They acknowledge that our foremost public institutions— political parties and organizations, labor unions and corporate enterprises, and social and public-interest movements—are failing to engender the kinds of public conversations and arguments that ought to characterize the public and political life of a great liberal-democratic nation. Right, left, and center there are calls for renewing social responsibility, civic duty, and active citizenship.

There is little agreement, however, on how to revitalize public debate in the United States. Some observers call for teaching students more about traditional values; others for teaching critical-thinking skills. Still others focus on reforming such parts of the political system as campaign finance and the primary-election caucuses.

[*] This chapter was first published on the back page of the *Chronicle of Higher Education,* June 12, 1991, as a "Point of View" titled "Colleges Must Prepare the Next Generation of Public Intellectuals." I must thank Karen Winkler for her editorial support in preparing the essay for publication in the paper.

I would argue that America's colleges and universities can be an important part of the solution—but not in the way many people think. Institutions of higher education cannot stand in for enfeebled institutions and organizations, nor provide a specific program or ideology to rescue or redeem our civil society, for there is no more of a consensus within academe regarding the particulars of what is to be done than there is in the larger polity—nor should there be. Nor will it be enough for academics to step in to fill the void in public debate. Commentators such as Russell Jacoby, Christopher Lasch, and Norman Birnbaum have challenged scholars to become "public intellectuals," speaking on public issues to a wide audience outside academe. This is appropriate, but I would also challenge my colleagues to teach their *students* to become the next generation of public intellectuals.

I would argue that along with the transmission of the knowledge and skills for and the commitment to critical thinking that, at least in principle, have long characterized our academic disciplines, we ought to be cultivating in our students the perspectives, voices, and practices that will enable them to pursue social and political criticism and to effectively engage extra-academic audiences in the process.

This is no simple project. For a start, it entails something of a revision or, at least, an addition to our prevalent conceptions of knowledge and its purposes. Our foremost intellectual traditions in the humanities and in the natural and social sciences have long stressed "objectivity," usually defined as a willingness to find ourselves "wrong," that is, to recognize through investigation and deliberation that the assumptions upon which we have built a position or thesis just do not hold up. Although objectivity recently has been besieged within the academy by proponents of "relativism," those who subscribe to the notion that "truth" is merely a matter of perspective, I believe it remains a most worthy and necessary ideal. Unfortunately, over time *objectivity* has become confused with *neutrality*, the assumption that we are not to become engaged in making value judgements and especially not in a public and committed fashion. It is this stance that has strongly contributed to the withdrawal of academic intellectuals from public debate.

I would insist that even as we impress upon our students the imperative and value of objectivity *and* its limits, we must reject the spurious equation of objectivity with neutrality and encourage students to apply their newly acquired scholarly skills, knowledge, and insights both to analyzing and to speaking out on public issues. We might call this the *democratic* conception of the purpose and promise of learning, the goal of which is the development of a citizenry not only capable of choosing among the alternatives provided by civic and political leaders, but also capable themselves of *formulating* alternative choices. Here I also have in mind that decidedly democratic vision of education in which the student is formed, in the words of the Italian Marxist and political theorist, Antonio Gramsci, "as a person capable of thinking, studying and ruling—or controlling those who rule."

Stated in the most preliminary and practical terms, we ought to assign exercises that require students to write not for us alone but also for the wider campus and, even better, for audiences locally and nationally. These assignments might take the form of articles, essays, or op-ed pieces. Indeed, in these years in which so many of us are attempting to institute "writing-across-the-curriculum programs," why shouldn't we organize, alongside the new technical and creative writing courses, still others specifically intended to develop the art of writing social, cultural, and political criticism?

In these courses students might begin by exploring the careers and works of selected American public intellectuals past and present such as Tom Paine, Frederick Douglass, Randolph Bourne, Charles and Mary Beard, Margaret Mead, and C. Wright Mills. In this way students would come to appreciate the personal and social costs of engaging in public debate, as well as different ways of meeting the challenge. Moreover, such biographical studies would acquaint students with the rich variety of intellectual and political traditions upon which they might draw and how these have been expressed in different ways in different historical moments. They could go on to discuss and debate both issues already present in the public media and concerns they believe ought to be questions of public debate; then they could develop their own perspectives and proposals on these questions in papers submitted both to the instructor *and* to a newspaper or other popular periodical.

The classroom experience itself should be organized as much as possible in the manner of an editorial board or workshop involving open consideration and criticism of each student's written piece, *not* for the purpose of securing consensus on the ideas expressed but, rather, to sharpen the words and arguments, thereby enhancing the student-author's ability to connect with his or her readers. Moreover, having the students themselves operate as a board or workshop should help to temper the professor's tendency to "scholasticism" with the more "popular" or "democratic" thinking of his or her students. Admittedly, this type of pedagogy is already under way in various quarters, for example, in journalism courses; however, it has not been widely applied in the humanities and social sciences because the teaching of the writing of social and cultural criticism especially directed to extra-academic audiences has not been considered a legitimate part of our curricula.

Not long ago (1989) I taught such a course as an experiment. Titled "History, Politics, and Criticism," it ranks among the most successful teaching experiences I have had and beginning next semester I will offer it on a regular basis. The class consists of lots of reading, writing, and talking—all in preparation for the creation of a 1000-word opinion piece to be submitted to a popular newspaper. In the coming semester the syllabus will begin with works dealing with being a social critic: Michael Walzer's *Interpretation and Social Criticism* and *The Company of Critics,* and Russell Jacoby's *The Last Intellectuals.* We will then move on to works representing conservatism (Robert Nisbet's *The Present Age*), neoconservatism (Peter Berger's *The Capitalist Revolution*), liberalism (Walter Russell Mead's *Mortal Splendor*), and social-democracy (Barbara Ehrenreich's *The Fear of Falling*). Also, along the way we will take in pieces from such magazines as the *National Review,* the *New Republic,* the *Nation,* and a variety of local publications. (It should also be noted that the first time I taught this course—as an experiment—it was limited to ten students; but, given the demands of a state university, I have had to raise the number allowed to enroll and, thus, the cap is now to be set at twenty.)

If last time was any indication, the experience will once again be emotionally demanding of students and teacher alike, for it requires persistent questioning, negotiation, and thinking aloud. Nevertheless, it was thrilling (whatever our personal viewpoints) to see our language, ideas, and arguments take finer and firmer shape after apparent demolitions and disasters. The issues and grievances that the students addressed—and on which they were, in fact, published in campus, city, and regional newspapers—included educational vouchers, the Iran-contra trials, the practices of temporary employment agencies, threatened changes to welfare programs, and the political potential of youth culture.

It was fascinating and encouraging to see the degree to which students, in one semester, learned to harness knowledge and discipline intellect without giving up passion, thereby enhancing their capacities to capture the imaginations of others. For their part, students voiced satisfaction in seeing their thoughts published and, in certain instances, having instigated responses, in sensing an active connection with public debate.

I am not suggesting that such teaching should inculcate a particular critical perspective. (Indeed, although I consider myself a democratic socialist, I most enjoy the times when my students and I take up the writings of the conservative and neoconservative thinkers for however mistaken, they are, unfortunately, all too often better composed for extra-academic audiences than are ours on the left.)

Nor should such courses be conceived of as sacrificing the pursuit of knowledge in favor of simply voicing one's opinion. It is important to stress that students ground their arguments in history and evidence. Moreover, training in the practice of criticism should not be restricted to students in the humanities and social sciences. Surely, in light of the technological possibilities and environmental challenges before us, it becomes all the more imperative that such skills and orientations also be possessed by students majoring in the sciences.

The attempt to develop a new generation of public intellectuals is very much in the spirit of our best academic traditions. As political scientist Benjamin Barber recently observed about the links between the university upheavals of the 1960s and classical pedagogical practice: "all education is and ought to be radical—a reminder of the past, a challenge to the present, and a prod to the future."

POSTCRIPT, JULY 1995

This chapter first appeared in 1991 as a "Point of View" in the *Chronicle of Higher Education.* Surprisingly, this short essay garnered more direct correspondence from fellow academics and, also, from administrators than any of the other short critical articles I have written. Most of the university teachers who contacted me were asking for copies of the syllabus in hopes of developing similar courses at their own schools, which ranged from community colleges to the more elite institutions. Others wrote to tell me about classes they were already offering that operated along similar lines and, thus, we exchanged experiences and observations. And the administrators I heard from were intrigued by the whole idea and wondered how they could possibly instigate such things on their own campuses.

There were two other letters. They were from quite different folk (though, notably, both were trained in American history). One was a humanities foundation administrator and the other a doctoral student in a prestigious graduate program, and yet they were both concerned about the same thing: that faculty who taught such courses and encouraged their students to become publicly engaged might themselves too readily shrink from public commitments, thinking, in an all too typical fashion, that teaching about such practices was engagement enough. In fact, the graduate student was convinced that his celebrated mentors "talked a good game," but when it came to actually pursuing public debate they regularly retreated to their studies. The point both letters made—and to which I fully subscribe—is that university professors themselves have to become more directly involved in public life and culture as "public intellectuals." We need to teach involvement not only in the class-room, but also by practice and example.

There was yet another response to the article, which I discovered somewhat accidentally. A student of the history and politics of the New Right, I do my best to keep up with the ideas and writings of conservative and neoconservative intellectuals (though it gets ever more difficult due both to the numbers involved and the repetitiveness of the arguments). A couple of years ago, I came upon Martin Anderson's *Impostors in the Temple: American Intellectuals Are Destroying Our Universities and Cheating Our Students of Their Future* (New York, 1992). A Senior Fellow at the most renowned of conservative think-tanks, the Hoover Institution on the campus of Stanford University, Anderson wrote the following:

> Many intellectuals seem to have a barely concealed lust for power, a lust which is rarely sated, a constant source of longing and frustration. It is as if the possession of superior intelligence somehow brings along with it the natural right to rule. Most of us think of education as thinking and studying and learning. But intellectuals often think about it in terms of power. Harvey Kaye, professor of social change and development at the University of Wisconsin, describes his "democratic vision of education" as one in which "the student is seen, in the words of Italian political theorist Antonio Gramsci 'as a person capable of thinking, studying and ruling—or controlling those who rule.'" (p. 127)

Fascinating. Just what does Anderson think democracy is about if it is not about *the people ruling?* And what does he believe education in a democracy should be about if not preparation to rule or, at the least, controlling those who do rule? In his attack on me, Anderson actually reveals his own and his fellow conservatives' persistent disdain for democratic life and politics.

Finally, I should note that I have taught the course a few times since the original publication of the essay and on the second occasion we generated a small, but not inconsequential, local media issue. In the wake of a long and tragic strike in one of the local papermills, one of the students wrote of the need for legislation to protect workers on strike from being laid off en masse and replaced by non-union workers. Published in the morning newspaper (remarkably, Green Bay, an urban center of about 150,000 people, has two papers, an independent morning paper and an afternoon Gannett-owned paper), it was, indeed, a passionately composed and beautifully written opinion piece that received a wide and critically appreciative response. Unfortunately, after it appeared, both newspapers announced that they would run locally authored opinion pieces (as opposed to nationally syndicated columns) only in the form of "letters to the editor." I immediately contacted the respective editors by letter and phone. The editor of the morning independent claimed that the paper instituted the policy to avoid becoming an outlet for class projects. "Students," he stated, "did not have the expertise for such writing." I countered with the argument that a democratic public culture and debate required not simply "expertise" but, just as much (if not more), "critically informed judgement." (And I added that, in fact, my students possessed more expertise than he realized, but even if they didn't—!) He rescinded the decision, and I promised, first, to let him know ahead of time when the course would be offered and, second, to make sure that the essays were not submitted to one newspaper alone (which had never been the case). The agreement was announced in an editorial statement in the paper.

The opinion-page editor at the Gannett-owned paper claimed that the decision to run locally authored pieces as 500-word letters had been made before the students began submitting to its pages. (Though I would just note that a few years previously, while I was chair of department, I had arranged for my colleagues and myself to write on a rotating basis a series of op-ed pieces for this paper in honor of the twentieth anniversary of our campus.) I kept up my letters and phone calls to the paper. Coincidentally, the Gannett corporation itself announced a fresh public initiative—NEWS 2000—promising a renewed commitment to the First Amendment and to the interests of the people of the regions and localities their papers served and, soon after, the newspaper began to recruit local voices for opinion columns.

PART THREE

INTELLECTUALS
AND POLITICS

19 Radicals and the Making of American Democracy: Toward a New Narrative of American History*

WHEN THE IDEA OF a roundtable session called "American Radicalism Reconsidered" first came up in 1993 it sounded, for quite selfish reasons, a splendid idea: Mari Jo Buhle, Paul Buhle, and I were in the process of completing the editorial labors on our book, *The American Radical,* and the book series on American radicalism that Elliott Gorn and I co-edit was starting to take real shape.[1] It definitely seemed the right time to be thinking aloud on the matter. However, the nearer these meetings drew, the less confident I felt about what I would have to say.

I may be naive, but my biggest concern wasn't radicalism; that subject has always been central to my work—in the 1970s in my graduate studies in Latin American history and in the 1980s in my work on E. P. Thompson and the British Marxist historians.[2] Moreover, wasn't it a *radical* vision of the purpose and promise of historical study and thought that originally attracted so many of us to the discipline—the vision of historians as "citizen-scholars," contributing to the democratic struggles and movements of the day by engaging and enlarging historical memory, consciousness, and imagination? Recall the 1974 draft of a MARHO (Mid-Atlantic Radical Historians Organization) "Statement of Principles":

* This chapter was first presented as a talk in the roundtable session, "Radicalism Reconsidered," chaired by Mari Jo Buhle at the 1994 Organization of American Historians' Meetings held in Atlanta, and then published in a revised version in *The History Teacher,* vol. 28, no. 2, February 1995.

History is practically the only academic discipline in which the possibilities of human experience, the creativeness of human action, is still a major object of study; and for which general literacy is the only prerequisite for accessibility. . . . The distinctiveness is decisive and should be cultivated. Historians are best situated to show not only that liberation is necessary, but also that it is possible.[3]

No, it wasn't radicalism; it was "America" I found daunting for, as I've just admitted, I am a recent arrival to American studies, coming to it only in the past several years while working on a book about Reaganism, Thatcherism, and the "crisis of history." In fact, what drove me to become an "Americanist" were the political and ideological campaigns of the New Right Republicans—most especially, their use and abuse of the past and their efforts to harness historical study and thought to the creation of a new conservative hegemony. I was convinced that historians were failing to appreciate and, as a consequence, failing to confront adequately these scoundrels and their projects.[4]

The point is that in spite of my best pretensions I am much more a student than a professor of American history and studies. Thus, I figured the best thing to do was talk about what had instigated me—*now,* of all times—to take up the history of *American* radicalism; what I have been learning, especially from working on the book projects, particularly *The American Radical*; and, finally, that grand old problem, "What is to be done?"[5]

In addition to the New Right's politics of history, there were two related problems that demanded a response—the crisis of the American left and the crisis of American history and narrative—both of which might be expressed as questions: "What does it mean to be a radical?" and "What does it mean to be an American?" Usually, these are discussed separately; occasionally, however, they are treated together, though, unfortunately, all too often the purpose of this treatment is to distance the terms "radical" and "American" from each other.

An example of this appeared not long ago on the Op-Ed page of the Sunday *New York Times*. Under the title "The Unpatriotic Academy," the celebrated philosopher Richard Rorty attacked the "academic left" for promoting multiculturalism rather than a singular national identity.[6] Shamelessly—like Arthur Schlesinger, Jr., in his book *The Disuniting of America*[7]—Rorty conflated the promoters of particularism with the contemporary academic Left as a whole, failing to distinguish separatists and ethnocentrists from multi-culturalists and critical historians. The argument against the former lot is not unreasonable and, to be honest, I am sympathetic when Rorty writes:

> If, in the interests of ideological purity, or out of the need to stay as angry as possible, the academic left insists on a "politics of difference," it will become increasingly isolated and ineffective. An unpatriotic left has never achieved anything. A left that refuses to take pride in its country will have no impact on the country's politics, and will eventually become an object of contempt.

However, in view of Rorty's rhetoric and the indiscriminate character of his attack (which is also characteristic of Schlesinger's work and reminiscent of earlier anti-radical crusades), it is quite reasonable to assume that his purposes included further alienating "radicalism" from "America"—or, better said, to once again define radicals as *un*-American. And, therefore, I find the piece unacceptable.

Still, this practice and the assumptions underlying it need to be addressed. Indeed, as I will argue, I think we are obliged to energetically proclaim the intimate and progressive relationship between the radical tradition and the making of American history—not simply or selfishly in defense of academic prerogatives, but because historical accuracy commands it.

After more than three decades of continuing class conflicts, new social movements, *and* new historical studies, *The American Radical* project was to serve, in part, as a stock-taking. Additionally, in view of the politics of the day and the related crises of the American left and American history and narrative, we hoped it would contribute to a renewed appreciation of the place of radicalism in American life.

We decided on a biographical approach because we imagined it the most effective way to reach students and, potentially, extra-academic audiences. It was not to be a reference- or a text-book (though it could be), but rather a "gathering" of representative figures. In short, we wanted to exhibit the historical breadth, cultural diversity, political and ideological pluralism, variety of struggles and movements, and manifold means of engagement and expression that have characterized radicalism in this country.

Actually, we did not at the outset foresee a big book; but the more we deliberated, the larger the volume grew. To keep it accessible we held to certain limits; and we remain painfully aware of the many people we left out. If nothing else, the sheer volume of figures warranting inclusion should serve to challenge our historical consciousness and imagination.

As Eric Foner suggests in his Foreword to our volume, one way of reminding ourselves about what the past 30 years have entailed is to consider *The American Radical* alongside previous works of its sort, for example, Charles A. Madison's study, *Critics and Crusaders* (1947), and Harvey Goldberg's edited collection, *American Radicals* (1957)[8]—both of which are valuable books regardless of the flaws we now find.

There are obvious and significant differences among the three volumes, surely determined to some extent by their respective historical moments. For a start, Madison included only 2 women (Margaret Fuller and Emma Goldman) among his 18 "critics and crusaders"; and, even worse, Goldberg's 16 radicals are all men. Moreover—and I know this further reveals my naiveté—I was surprised to find that there was not a single non-White figure in the ranks of either Madison's or Goldberg's rebels.

In contrast, our 46 American radicals include men and women of diverse backgrounds because, as Eric Foner observes in his Foreword to our volume, "radicals have been as diverse as the

American people themselves." Of course, conservative reviewers will refer to the multicultural composition of *The American Radical* as evidence of Buhle, Buhle, and Kaye's commitment to "political correctness."

The Contents pages of the three books register yet another important development. Madison divides his critics and crusaders into "Abolitionists," "Utopians," "Anarchists," "Dissident Economists," "Militant Liberals," and "Socialists." And Goldberg similarly arranges his by aspiration and practice: "Declarations of Independence," "Attacks on Privilege," "Toward the Equality of Rights," and an additional section, "Obstacles to Radicalism." However, the portraits in *The American Radical* are arranged chronologically without specific reference to cause or campaign.

I don't think we were being lazy in failing to group our chapters thematically. Rather, I think that here too the difference is a reflection of our respective historical moments and the readings of American history afforded. It's not just that the initiatives of the last 30 years have dictated a fuller, richer, and more pluralistic conception of American radicalism, one that encompasses independence fighters (e.g., Pontiac and Neolin, and Tom Paine), laborists (e.g., Eugene Debs, Mother Jones, and Ricardo Flores Magon), suffragists (e.g., Elizabeth Cady Stanton), abolitionists (e.g., Sojourner Truth, Abby Kelley, and Frederick Douglass), socialists (e.g., Elizabeth Gurley Flynn, W. E. B. Du Bois, Upton Sinclair, Vito Marcantonio, and Michael Harrington), feminists (e.g., Fanny Wright, Emma Goldman, and Isadora Duncan), pacifists (e.g., Dorothy Day, A. J. Muste, and Abbie Hoffman), environmentalists (e.g., John Muir and Rachel Carson), and campaigners for social justice and the civil rights of the oppressed (e.g., Walt Whitman, Ida B. Wells, Carlos Bulosan, Malcolm X, and Audre Lorde).[9]

It's also, I believe, that we have today a more critical understanding both of the radical tradition as a *tradition* and of its role in the making of America. The question that we will have to consider is: Have we effectively communicated and cultivated these understandings?

Written in the wake of the New Deal and the victory over Fascism, the narrative that frames Madison's *Critics and Crusaders* is one of progress towards Social Democracy, a continuous process enabled or, at the least, enhanced by the endeavors of radicals. To quote from his introductory and concluding remarks:

> The quest for freedom has been a basic characteristic of the American people from the very beginning. . . . There were always enough bold spirits ready to fight for the greater freedom of all. . . . This much is true: every battle for freedom has resulted in an expansion of human rights. . . . It was a continuous struggle because new wrongs always arose. [Yet] Notwithstanding their theoretical confusion and wide practical divergence, the various groups opposing the status quo have achieved notable success in their work to strengthen the democratic base of the American people. . . . The sum of social legislation enacted in recent years is of a truly revolutionary character. [And] It is at least partly due to the agitation of these critics and crusaders that the American people are at present enjoying a combination of political freedom and economic well-being which is the envy of the world. . . .

Furthermore, in response to the question "What of the future?" Madison declared that "The outcome is fairly obvious. . . . The doctrines of 'free enterprise' and 'rugged individualism' have gone the way of human slavery and the horse and buggy. . . . Social planning and control are both necessary and unavoidable. . . ." In Madison's view, the only issue that remained was just how "liberal" things would be.

A decade later—in the heyday of the postwar liberal consensus, Pax Americana and the suppression of radicalisms at home and abroad—Goldberg and his co-author of the Introduction, William Appleman Williams, advanced a quite different and far more somber view of things. As they saw it:

The United States has had its radicals, a fair number, at times acting alone and at times in concert; men who devoted themselves exceedingly well to the common weal. . . . But the truth must be faced, however disillusioning, that the richest tradition of American radicalism belongs to a small minority of courageous men and women; that their achievements, while outweighing their numbers, included neither a lasting mass movement nor a profound shift of power; that a greater number of radicals than these have failed to measure up to the standards of profundity and constancy required of them. . . .

In contrast to the progress, continuity, accomplishment, and optimism portrayed by Madison, Goldberg and Williams speak of tragedy and irony, discontinuity, defeat, and reasons to be pessimistic. In fact, they spend most of their time discussing the obstacles to, and failings of, American radicals, before closing with admonitions and an urgent call for renewal:

> To date radicalism . . . has failed to bring profound changes or to build a lasting movement. However comprehensible this is in the light of the American dream, the instruments of power, and the relentless demands on courage, it is tragic. But the failures themselves are meaningful instruction. . . . To borrow a bit of imagery . . . we might conclude that American radicalism stands at its last frontier. The expansionist philosophy of history has carried the United States to the last roundup where a nation confronts itself. . . . The issue is clear: who is to outline, plan, and direct America's effort to live at peace with itself and the world? . . . It remains the radical's present opportunity and responsibility to demonstrate and then substantiate his claim to power.

In the wake of the long 1980s, one might readily assume that the historical perspective framing Buhle, Buhle, and Kaye's *The*

American Radical would echo the views and sentiments of Goldberg and Williams rather than those of Madison. But that is not the case.

To be sure, after 20 years of concerted class war from above and political and cultural campaigns seeking to reverse the changes wrought in the 1930s or initiated in the struggles of the 1960s, there is no restoring a confident and progressive optimism about the advance of social democracy, justice, and civil rights. Nevertheless, our experience and our scholarship—however much recording discontinuities and defeats—also register persistence, accomplishment, and, even, reason for hope.

Our many contributors might not agree; but the lives and campaigns they present in their respective chapters of *The American Radical*—reflecting a generation of historical labors pursued from the bottom up—speak to the rearticulation of our national experience. As we state in our Afterword:

> The narrative of America emergent in these pages is the struggle for liberty, equality, and democracy. It is a narrative insisting that we recognize and appreciate the crucial role of the radical tradition as the prophetic memory of American experience—the tragic, the ironic, the progressive—and of the persistent and original possibilities to be found there. As these biographical portraits begin to account, in every generation men and women of diverse upbringings and identifications have stood to challenge oppression and exploitation and to reassert the fundamental proposition that "We, the People" shall rule. However varied their respective concerns and aspirations, America's radical activists, writers, and artists have conducted a long and continuing struggle to expand both the "we" in "We, the People" and the democratic process through which "the people" can genuinely govern.

Admittedly, American History can be told in many ways; but what I have learned is that the narrative we fashion—and we are fashioning one whether we intend it or not *and* whether postmodernists like it or not—must, without guaranteeing anything, testify to the central and dynamic role of the radical tradition in the making of American democracy.

Madison evidently exaggerates when he proclaims that "There were always enough bold spirits ready to fight for the greater freedom of all," for there have never been enough of such souls; and he is plainly "speechifying" when he writes that "This much is true: every battle for freedom has resulted in an expansion of human rights," for history has never been so wonderful. Yet, he is closer to the historical experience than are Goldberg and Williams when they portray American radicals as a rare breed of brave and, often, isolated and lonely men whose legacy is overwhelmingly more that of aspiration than accomplishment.

Undeniably, many an American dissenter has stood alone and suffered scorn and abuse; but—contra the myth of heroic alienation or marginality—not only have American radicals regularly been numerous (and even occasionally ubiquitous), their endeavors have often been bound up with the struggles of communities and popular movements, and their legacy, however marked by tragedy and defeat, is not merely visionary but equally inspiring for its history-making.

The radical tradition truly has been our "prophetic memory," recalling, refashioning, and extending in original and creative ways the promise and possibility of freedom, equality, and collective- and self-determination. In the face of multiple obstacles and oppositions, American radicalism itself has hardly been monolithic or uniform; and yet, in far more than the minds of historians it has been a tradition of remarkable continuity. As we denote in our Introduction—and I find this particularly fascinating: Succeeding generations of radicals have drawn inspiration and sustenance from the agency and ideas of their predecessors. Moreover, this process has repeatedly entailed remembrance and aspiration across lines of race, ethnicity, and gender.

What I have said may be obvious to most of you; but it is not so obvious to our fellow Americans—which brings us to the real challenge proposed by this roundtable reconsidering American radicalism. We have done well in critically recovering America's past and the place of the American radical tradition within it—and we are hardly finished. But have we done as much and as well in communicating and connecting our work to popular historical memory, consciousness, and imagination? As the great French historian and patriot Marc Bloch asked during the long night of German Occupation: "Most of us can say with some justice that we were good workmen [before the war]. Is it equally true to say that we were good citizens?"[10]

Recalling what originally drew us to history, I would argue, quite brashly—for, as in religion, there's nothing quite like a newcomer or convert to remind you of your commitments—that, along with recounting the experience of expansion, exploitation, and oppression, we remain obligated intellectually and politically to cultivate a popular understanding of the making of past, present, *and* future which appreciates that radicalism actually has been at the heart of what it means to be an American.

This becomes all the more imperative in the face of the apparent success by the powers that be to propagate cynicism, the sense that action—especially political action—is irrelevant. And, having served on the original Organization of American Historians' task force (1992) to review the project establishing national standards for history, I remain very worried about the "past and present" to be taught in our schools.[11]

I am not so naive or romantic as to believe that the historical redemption and popularization of the radical tradition will necessarily reinvigorate the prophetic memory of American democracy—which, though enervated and fragmented, persists in older and newer social movements alike. Yet, I would insist that we can contribute far more than we have to the reformation of historical memory, consciousness, and imagination. And, toward that end, the chapters of *The American Radical* do testify that campaigns for justice can succeed and struggles for liberty, equality, and democracy can prevail.

As my editorial predecessor, Harvey Goldberg, stated in his Foreword back in 1957—that is, on the eve of those most unexpected and startling 1960s:

> For very compelling reasons, the study of American radicals should be essential homework for this generation: because their record can give heart and stomach to Americans who are watching democracy weaken under the weight of conformism; and because their insights and errors, their accomplishments and failures can cast light, even many years later, on the problems of the present.

20 American Radicalism Past and Present: An Interview*

THE CONVERSATION HAS ALREADY BEGUN . . .

STEVE PAULSON: You speak of an American radical "tradition." Just how far back do you see this tradition extending?

HARVEY KAYE: Even the original Puritans were, in their day, radicals, if you think about the English Revolution of the seventeenth century and the kinds of changes that they were seeking to accomplish. And then there are the Native Americans' struggles which were so central to the American "frontier" experience—in spite of incessant efforts to marginalize them both geographically and historically. We see innumerable resistance campaigns by American Indians to block, prevent, and push back Anglo-American expansion. From the beginning, American experience was composed of radicalisms.

Moreover, even if we accept only the most traditional narrative of American history, this country was conceived in a revolution. Of course, a lot of people like to think of it as having been a less radical struggle than, say, the French Revolution, a political and social revolution in which they beheaded a king (but so had the English before them). Yet the more we look at the American Revolution, that is, the more historians have reexamined it over the past thirty years, the more we discover truly radical aspirations and moments.

* Occasioned by the publication of the book edited by Mari Jo Buhle, Paul Buhle, and myself, *The American Radical* (New York: Routledge, 1994), this chapter originated as a taped interview conducted by Steve Paulson for the Wisconsin Public Radio show *To the Best of Our Knowledge*. It was first broadcast on May 1, 1994, as part of an hour-long program on American radicalism.

SP: If you're saying that radicals are central to American history, that radical movements are not marginal, what are some of the great success stories of radicalism in this country?

HK: Well, we've already referred to the American Revolution . . .

SP: *The* great success story . . .

HK: Yes, *the* great success story. . . . But let's go on. Let's think in the narrowest of terms about what democracy is. Let's think about it just in terms of the right to vote—how's that? If we look at the period from 1776, to use the great date, all the way through the 1830s, we see repeated efforts to assure or, actually, to secure manhood suffrage, that is, in most states, White manhood suffrage. The point is that even White manhood suffrage was not guaranteed, not by the Constitution. It had to be struggled for, and we had state-by-state working-men's radicalisms associated with that.

Next, we have the struggles for the abolition of slavery and, eventually, the idea of general manhood suffrage. Now, admittedly, slavery came to an end in a bloody civil war, but the abolitionists were significant in making it a prominent political issue in early national American life. And, at the same time, there were the campaigns to secure the vote for women. We too often forget just how long that took but, finally, by the early twentieth century it's accomplished. So, we have these examples of success to start with—hard- and long-fought-for successes, but successes.

Continuing in the twentieth century, we can talk once again about the struggle for the vote, that is, to not just have the "right" to vote but to be *guaranteed* that right. I have in mind the successes of the second American Revolution, the Civil Rights struggles of the early 1960s. You know, we live in an age when people are ready to say that radicalisms are behind us, but in every generation radicalisms have arisen to assert a new version, a new reading of the original ideals, the original aspirations.

SP: The original ideals, meaning fairness and justice for all?

HK: Exactly, and how about "life, liberty, and the pursuit of happiness"? How about "all men are created equal" and, then, understanding that "men" means, or should mean, humanity as a whole? What I am talking about—and, to give proper credit, I've inherited the term from the British historian, Victor Kiernan—is a "prophetic memory." Radicals in American history have been *the prophetic memory* of what this country could yet be about. You know: looking back, seeking precedents, but then in the face of the problems of the day, the hurdles of the day, the oppressions of the day, reconceiving them anew and thereby reinvigorating the original ideals themselves. And, I should make clear, there's no guarantee of success here—I'm not writing some story of inevitable progress. The struggles were violent, they were bloody, there were defeats, there were tragedies. I think we've seen enough of that in the past 20 to 30 years to realize that there's nothing guaranteed in any of this.

SP: Do you think American radicalism is different from what you might find in Europe? Because, when I think about the impact of, say, people on the left, I can point to socialist leaders running countries in Europe, and you certainly don't have that in the United States.

HK: Right, right. Of course, there's that classic question posed by the German sociologist Werner Sombart: "Why is there no socialism in the United States?" And the issue of America being somehow "exceptional" is a good one to ask about. For generations, America presented itself as different in that it supposedly didn't require a socialism to create freedom, equality, and so on. . . . I should say here that I came to American history relatively late—I began at university in Latin American studies, and later I moved over to European and British studies—and I always tended to see those countries as somehow exemplary for their radicalisms and especially for their socialist traditions, most notably the West European cases. But now I've returned to American history and, from what I can see, I'm all the more convinced that what makes America exceptional is the very *diversity* of its radicalisms, in the sense that American radicalism is as diverse as the American people, thinking in terms of *who* have been radicals. And the struggles themselves have been remarkably popular. Only in the United States (and Britain) do we get mass-based women suffrage movements. Now, that says something very interesting about this country. And, to go back to Sombart's question, we shouldn't forget that there actually was a vibrant and sizable *American* socialist politics earlier in this century extending right across the country.

By the way, we often think of the struggles for "rights" narrowly, but these have been struggles for *democracy*. So, in its very diversity, American radicalism has been—I'm going to sound very patriotic here and I'm more than happy to do so—exceptional in its diversity *and* in its brashness, and radicals have suffered a lot along the way as well. In fact, I think that the real patriots in American history may well be the radicals.

SP: Hmm, that's an interesting twist . . .

HK: Yes, in other words, instead of thinking about patriotism as merely defending and conserving the ideals of the founders, it's the idea of reinvigorating and renewing the ideals of the founders. I find American radicalism not just persistent and diverse, but—however often replenished by immigrant generations—constantly *not* drawing its ideas from abroad. I mean, the House Un-American Activities Committee may have been eager to believe and pronounce that radicals were carriers of "alien" ideas and, of course, very early on we had the period of John Adams's Alien and Sedition Acts [1798]; but almost always the struggles are really home-grown, again, however much they were to be regularly renewed by immigrants.

And, I'll tell you, immigrants themselves catch on to American ideals very quickly. Think of Tom Paine. Here he is, he arrives in 1774 and in a short while, not much more than a year, people are approaching him to write what will eventually be *Common Sense.* Here's an immigrant to America and somehow he is able to articulate the very aspirations that are brewing in American life to declare its independence.

SP: I get the sense that you're especially fond of Tom Paine.

HK: Yes, very fond. He was my first childhood hero, which may sound rather silly but . . .

SP: Your first *childhood* hero?

HK: Yes, my first childhood hero, other than, say, Elvis Presley or someone like that. Yeah, really. . . . My grandfather had a little library in the back of the dining room where he kept the books he didn't need in his law office, and among them were the writings of Tom Paine. There was also a curious book that argued it was Thomas Paine and not Jefferson who really wrote the Declaration of Independence—and I remember being an obnoxious kid, and every time a teacher would ask "who wrote the Declaration of Independence?" I would raise my hand and say "Tom Paine." I even tried to make the argument, knowing I was wrong. I now realize the book itself was really questionable, but for a kid it was a fascinating kind of notion.

Yes, I've always admired Tom Paine. Maybe it was his life, the fact that he was an artisan in that great artisan age of the late eighteenth century, who came out of humble and impoverished beginnings in England and was given a second chance when he met Ben Franklin, who urged him to come to America. He then comes to what will eventually be the United States, which he, himself, will be very central to creating, and, arriving in Philadelphia, he begins to write about the problem of slavery and about the condition of women, and, in really no time at all, he is approached by Benjamin Rush and other radicals of the Continental Congress and asked to write something for the American cause (which, it should be noted, he originally wanted to call *Plain Truth,* but his publisher decided *Common Sense* would work all the more effectively).

SP: Well, if he was one of the great radicals of the eighteenth century, who are the great radicals today?

HK: I do think we've got some fascinating critics, if we think about radicals not only as crusaders but also as critics. Of course, I don't like everything they say and do, but there's Noam Chomsky, professor of linguistics at MIT, who is probably one of the most interesting of critical voices on American politics, foreign affairs and the media—always challenging. Then there's Edward Said, Palestinian American literary scholar at Columbia University, who also writes about American foreign policy and questions of imperialism; also, Cornel West, professor of African American studies at Harvard and co-chair of Democratic Socialists of America [DSA], who originally trained as a theologian and offers a very critical perspective on race and the possibilities of democratic socialism in America; Barbara Ehrenreich, who is a feminist writer and also a co-chair of DSA; Audre Lorde, the lesbian poet and gay activist who just passed away; César Chavez, organizer of the Mexican American farmworkers, who also just passed away. They are out there.

SP: What's interesting about some of those names you just mentioned, at least the first three, is that they're all professors, they're all in universities and I guess it raises the question of "Are intellectuals in universities likely to be people who have led mass movements?" as earlier radicals did.

HK: No, I don't think so. . . . As you know, this is an ongoing discussion on the left, a discussion about "public intellectuals" that you and I have had before and that other people have had for years now, and I plead guilty to being too long in the academy and, therefore, less able to name the radicals whose lives really are on the line as opposed to my fellow professors with tenure. It's just, admittedly, that they are the public names; they show up on the pages of the *New York Times,* in the progressive magazines, and on the Bill Moyers and William F. Buckley TV programs . . .

But I should add that I work with the Wisconsin labor movement through the Wisconsin Labor History Society and, while the unions are on the defensive today, there are some really dedicated and hard-working people out there in the trenches, trying to create bridges to movements beyond labor, you know, to the environmentalists, to women's groups. . . . I'm not an optimist—yes, I am an optimist—and I imagine great things coming in the future, not necessarily a repetition of the 1960s, we never repeat history, but there are possibilities and potentials out there.

SP: But I hear you hinting, although you haven't actually come out and said it, that we don't have radicals of the same stature that we've had in the past, we don't have a Martin Luther King today.

HK: I think we seem to be in a time when "particularisms" prevail. We used to talk about single-interest movements or special-interest movements . . . it's as if the radicals of the left, many of whom started out in "the new social movements," are reproducing that very problem in the form of "identity politics." Perhaps, the next great radical figure who will emerge, or is already emerging, is going to be that figure who is able to articulate a vision, a set of aspirations, that mobilizes and harnesses the aspirations of the different particularisms or movements. I don't imagine Cornel West will be that radical but he's got that kind of voice, say, in contrast to Chomsky who will always be a critic, not a movement person. Yes, Cornel West has that kind of voice.

SP: You haven't used the word Marxism much at all, in fact I'm not sure you've even mentioned that word. But I think if you're trying to look for an ideological framework in which radicals in recent decades have worked it would be the Marxist tradition, and yet obviously with the end of the Cold War, with the collapse of the Soviet Union and the fact that communism has become discredited, it would seem to throw into question the viability of that Marxist tradition. I guess the question is whether radicals need to work within that tradition?

HK: I remember someone saying that we're all Marxists today, we all now understand the kinds of issues, the kinds of questions, that the classical Marxist figures put on the table regarding class inequalities, but we've extended them, especially in the United States, to issues of race and to gender. But you know, I'm not so sure we should assume that we've left Marxism behind, that is, in "the past." I don't think we ever want to resurrect a particular version of Marxist ideology to be the unifying ideology, but I think we could learn a lot from Marxist arguments about class. I think we often forget that it's not just a question of culture, and it's not just a question of politics, and it's not even merely a question of "oppression," it is also a question of brutal material inequalities and exploitation and I think to that extent, at the least, there is still something to be drawn from the Marxist tradition—and in *that* sense I have no intention of throwing it out of my carriage.

SP: So, nothing's changed since the end of the Cold War?

HK: Nothing's changed . . . everything's always changing . . . no. . . . Clearly, things have changed, clearly. To the extent that communism is overthrown, I'm the first to celebrate, the very first. But, the abolition of communism does not mean that we're now in some grand liberal-democratic age representing "the end of history." I think that if you speak to a lot of people on the left you'll find that what we're aspiring to is "radical democracy," entailing a deeper and further democratization of our institutions.

In that sense we're talking about aspirations that for us go back to the 1960s, but which of course have deeper roots. Indeed, a lot of us who came through the 1960s—and I was just an undergraduate at the time—honestly believed that the future of America would involve a truly more democratic society. I don't even think many of us thought in terms of socialism—we thought in terms of "democracy," perhaps a *social* democracy, the extension of democracy from the political arena to the larger social, cultural, *and* economic arenas.

21 Tom Paine and the Making of the American Revolution[*]

LEAVING ENGLAND IN 1774 at the age of 37, Tom Paine came to America and became a radical. Invigorated by the society he discovered and inspired by the great possibilities he recognized within it, Paine's pamphlet *Common Sense* succeeded in redefining American struggles against British imperial rule as a war for national independence and a political revolution and, moreover, as the fundamental act of a world revolution against the tyranny and corruption of the old regimes of Europe. As Paine himself declaimed in words that fired the imagination of his fellow citizens-to-be: "We have it in our power to begin the world over again."

Born in 1737 at Thetford in Norfolk, Paine's life confirms that "only the past is predictable," for it is only with the hindsight of history that we can see in the years before his coming to America the making of a revolutionary and world-historical figure. His father, Joseph Paine, was a Quaker and staymaker, and his mother, Frances Cocke, was an Anglican and lawyer's daughter. Neither a happy nor an affluent couple, they nevertheless were extremely fond of their son and committed to his receiving a formal education. Thus, in addition to becoming well-versed in the Bible at home, from the age of 6 to 13 young Paine was enrolled in the village school, where his favorite subjects were science and poetry. At 14, however, he was apprenticed to his father, from whom he learned the craft of corsetmaking and also, no doubt, the dissenting and egalitarian spirit of the Quakers and the historical memory of "turning the world upside down" in the English Revolution of the 1640s and 1650s. It seems an artisan's life

* This chapter was first published in Mari Jo Buhle, Paul Buhle, and Harvey J. Kaye, eds., *The American Radical* (New York: Routledge, 1994).

promised too sedentary a future, for at 19 Paine ran away to serve aboard the privateer *King of Prussia.* Yet, whatever the adventure, the rigors and oppressions of life between the devil and the deep blue sea were too great and after a year he managed to get himself released, whereupon he went to London to work as a journeyman staymaker.

The next decade and a half were filled with tragic disappointments, mistakes, and failures. In 1759 Paine set up shop as a master craftsman on the southeast coast where he met and married his first love, Mary Lambert. Sadly, within a year he lost his wife in premature childbirth and soon after was forced to give up the business. He then prepared for and in 1764 secured appointment as an excise officer, but was expelled a year later for having stamped goods without inspecting them (a not unusual practice). During the next few years he kept alive by working as a staymaker, a teacher and, even, a preacher while he petitioned for reinstatement. Finally, in early 1768 Paine was posted to Lewes in Sussex. There he boarded with a tobacconist, whose daughter, Elizabeth Ollive, he married in 1771 on the shopkeeper's death. He also became active in local affairs and a "regular" in the Whiggish political debates at the White Hart Tavern, developing a friendly reputation as a man who enjoyed a few good drinks and who had a "skill with words." The biographer David Freeman Hawke describes Paine, now in his early thirties, as possessing "a long face dominated by a large, drooping nose and blue eyes so lively and piercing that few failed to remark upon them after a first meeting."

Recognizing his talents, Paine's fellow officers chose him to lead their campaign for higher salaries and, so commissioned, he penned his first pamphlet, *The Case of the Excise Officers* (1772), and moved to London to lobby Parliament. This stay in the capital increased his knowledge and resentment of aristocratic government and politics but, also, renewed his awareness of the popular radicalism of the middling and artisan classes. Additionally, it enabled him to advance his interest in natural philosophy through attendance at scientific lectures—occasions that placed him among circles of intellectuals and freethinkers which, fortuitously, included Benjamin

Franklin. Unfortunately, the campaign was defeated and in its wake Paine was discharged for ignoring his official duties, the tobacco shop failed, and he and his wife agreed to separate.

Penniless and without immediate prospects, but possessed of a seemingly indefatigable willingness to try again, Paine resolved to go to America, outfitted with a letter of introduction from the renowned Franklin. Little did either man suspect that the mix of historical and personal memories and skills that Paine carried with him would be so volatile when brought into contact with events in America. But, indeed, however British, America was another country, and the Philadelphia to which Paine was headed was its "capital."

Arriving in late 1774, Paine planned to open a school. However, following the publication of a few short newspaper articles, Paine was recruited to be editor of the *Pennsylvania Magazine,* which prospered under his direction. Paine himself wrote regularly and began to develop a public voice. Among the most pointed of his pieces were an essay on the oppression of women and another in which he called for the abolition of slavery and insisted upon Americans' responsibilities both to the liberated slaves and to the peoples of Africa. Although critical of British imperial practices, Paine originally favored reconciliation between Britain and the American colonies. Yet, following the events at Lexington and Concord in April 1775, he became an American "patriot" and published the poem "Liberty Tree," whose verses were enthusiastically received for their references to king and Parliament as "tyrannical powers."

In our all-too-cynical times, we should not assume Paine's commitment to the American cause to have been determined simply by his difficulties in England or, worse, mere opportunism. Whatever his grievances, we must not fail to appreciate the "America" he encountered. Life in the colonies was evidently structured by inequalities of class and status and Paine was well aware of the oppressions of slavery. Nevertheless, as an Englishman of some education and skill, he must have found America—an increasingly diverse society in the process of rapid growth and development—most attractive and, with Franklin's assistance, welcoming and accessible. Moreover, American resistance to British impositions, taxations, and restrictions already had been under way for a decade, politicizing not only the colonial elites but also the popular classes of artisans, shopkeepers, and farmers, and, particularly in Philadelphia, Paine could perceive the promise of an even more egalitarian and democratic order, for here was a polity being remade from the bottom up by an increasingly well-organized class of "mechanics"—the very sort of people from whence he had himself emerged. Perhaps it even reminded him of the hopes and possibilities suppressed in England over a century before. Surely, it cannot have been opportunism that propelled Paine into the struggle, for who actually knew what the rebellious colonists were pursuing—the restoration of "Englishmen's rights," reforms to the imperial system, or separation? In any case, what chance of success was there, whatever the goals, against the world's greatest power?

By late 1775 independence was being spoken of in various quarters and even among elements of the Continental Congress. But it was still the pronounced ambition of only a minority. Persuaded to write in support of separation by his friend Dr. Benjamin Rush, a younger radical and member of Congress who was himself still hesitant to do so, Paine published *Common Sense* in January 1776. Calling upon Americans to recognize their historic responsibilities and possibilities and make a true revolution of their struggles, Paine's arguments took hold of his new compatriots' shared but as-of-yet unarticulated sentiments and thoughts and expressed them in language bold and clear. As one historian has written: "The work literally exploded in the American consciousness." Within a few months as many as 150,000 copies of the pamphlet were sold (for which Paine refused any royalties), and independence became the declared aspiration of the majority.

Arguably, independence would eventually have become the Americans' cause even without the appearance of *Common Sense*. But Paine's writing brought that eventuality forward. Even more important, it declared the cause of American independence to be more than a question of separation from Britain—it proclaimed it a struggle *against* the tyranny of hereditary privilege both "monarchical and aristocratical" and *for* a democratic republic. Paine appealed directly to Americans' economic interests. Yet, in addition to accounting their commercial prospects, Paine's vision of independence asked them to see themselves as *"Americans,"* a people no longer subject to king and noble but—as was their "natural right"—*constituting themselves free and equal before God and "the law" and governing themselves through democratically elected representatives.*

Reflecting Paine's self-education in eighteenth-century liberalism and republicanism alike, the ideas expressed in *Common Sense* may not have been "philosophically" original but, mobilizing Biblical scripture, historical criticism, and the force of "reason" itself, Paine's arguments were radically original in appeal and consequence. It's not just that Paine addressed himself to Americans of all classes (of White society, that is), but that the very style and content of his words succeeded in articulating a more egalitarian and democratic conception of "the people" than had hitherto prevailed. In fact, as Eric Foner has shown, Paine's language captured the imagination of mechanics and farmers in an unprecedented fashion and, rhetorically incorporating them into the "political nation," it both engaged the working classes to the cause of independence and further empowered them in their own movements to restructure the political and social order.

Admittedly, Paine failed to directly incorporate into *Common Sense* either his abolitionist views or his concerns regarding the oppression of women. Nevertheless, his vision of a democratic republic was potentially unlimited—a point understood not only by Tories but, also, by elite-minded patriots such as John Adams, who grew anxious about the radical dreams which were bound to be engendered by so "popular a pamphlet." Paine himself projected the struggle into the future and well beyond American shores—"The cause of America is in a great measure the cause of all mankind"—*not* by way of an imperial America imposing its will upon the world but as a model of peaceful prosperity and democratic republicanism and, also, as a refuge:

> O ye that love mankind! Ye that dare oppose, not only the tyranny, but the tyrant, stand forth! Every spot of the world

is over-run with oppression. Freedom hath been hunted round the globe. Asia, and Africa have long expelled her. – Europe regards her like a stranger, and England hath given her warning to depart. O! receive the fugitive, and prepare in time an asylum for mankind.

Declared on July 4, 1776, independence was far from being secured. Paine himself enlisted in the Revolutionary army and was posted to forces near New York to serve as aide-de-camp to General Nathaniel Greene. But his major contribution was not to be as a combatant. The war had begun badly for the Americans and by late 1776 George Washington's army was in retreat across New Jersey. Was it to end so soon? Paine would not allow for such thinking. In December of the same year he wrote the first of his 16 *Crisis* papers, once again proffering words of inspiration that were to resound through generations:

> These are the times that try men's souls. The summer soldier and the sunshine patriot will, in this crisis, shrink from the service of their country; but he that stands it *now,* deserves the love and thanks of man and woman. Tyranny, like hell, is not easily conquered; yet we have this consolation with us, that the harder the conflict, the more glorious the triumph.

In 1777 Congress honored Paine with appointment as secretary to the Committee on Foreign Affairs, in which post he played an important role in negotiating the crucial alliance with France. But, always quick to act, Paine got himself entangled, and in trouble, in the "Silas Deane affair," when he publicly accused Deane of profiteering in his dealings with the French on behalf of Congress. The problem was neither in Paine's suspicions nor his principles, but that he indiscreetly had made use of secret diplomatic correspondence embarrassing to the French government. Harried by his political enemies, Paine was forced to resign in 1779. Still, he was "Common Sense" and it was not long before he was engaged as Clerk to the

Assembly of Pennsylvania, whose new constitution, the most radical and democratic of those of all the former colonies, was shaped by the ideas that Paine had himself sketched out in his famous revolutionary pamphlet.

Paine's writings of the 1780s treated subjects commercial—he supported the controversial Bank of North America because he felt such institutions to be essential for the economic development of the country—*and* constitutional—he favored a strong central government because he believed it imperative to secure the nation and enable the United States to assert a powerful republican presence internationally. But his energies were increasingly directed to scientific and technical matters and, with peace in 1783, he applied himself to the design and construction of an iron bridge, a project which was to instigate his return to Europe in pursuit of additional engineering expertise and capital. Fifty years of age, Paine departed America in 1787 expecting to be gone for only a short while. Yet he was not to return for 15 years.

If this biographical portrait were emanating from London or Paris, much of what has been said might well be treated merely as preface to Paine's revolutionary involvements back in England and France. The ensuing narrative would relate how he was irresistibly drawn into the politics of English radicalism and how, antagonized so by Edmund Burke's *Reflections on the Revolution in France* (1790), a fierce attack on the Revolution of 1789 that effectively launched modern Anglo-American conservatism, Paine was compelled to put aside his plans for the iron bridge and respond with *Rights of Man* (1791-92). In this treatise he once again directly and forcefully denied any legitimacy to monarchic and aristocratic government and advanced a defense not simply of French actions but of the right of all peoples, in every generation—including the Britons of his day!—to remake their political orders in directions libertarian, egalitarian, and democratic.

This narrative would go on to tell of the irony of Paine's escaping arrest for revolutionary incitements in England by being in Paris—having been honored with election to the French National

Convention—only later to be imprisoned for 10 months in France for having aligned himself with the moderate Girondins faction and speaking out against the execution of the king. It would also note that in the shadow of the guillotine Paine wrote *The Age of Reason,* a work proclaiming his deism and rendering a sustained critique of organized religion that was to become a primer for nineteenth-century free-thinkers. Finally, it would indicate how Paine's ideas developed beyond naive liberalism to the point where, in his final major work, *Agrarian Justice* (1797), he actually laid the groundwork for a social-democratic vision of the welfare state, apparently having recognized the threat posed to the progress of democratic republican-ism by growing extremes of wealth and poverty.

Truly, Paine was the first "international" revolutionary. But the narrative of Paine's career as prophet of the Age of Revolution should fully account how "America" continued to inform and inspire his arguments and imaginings. He himself registered it clearly at the outset of Part II of *Rights of Man.* Posing the question that still haunts philosophers today—"What Archimedes said of the mechanical powers, may be applied to Reason and Liberty: 'Had we,' said he, 'a place to stand upon, we might raise the world'"—Paine confidently answered with American experience: "The revolution of America presents in politics what was only theory in mechanics."

In 1802 he returned to the United States, spending his time between New York and his farm north of the city. However, he was disappointed—his appreciation of Americans' verve and audacity was no longer reciprocated. Once Paine had been celebrated as the champion of "Common Sense." Now, all but his truest friends, such as Thomas Jefferson, ignored him because of his denunciation of organized religion. He died in 1809 and, denied a place in the Quaker cemetery, was buried on his farm. In 1819, however, the coffin was dug up and loaded on a ship for reinterment in England. Curiously, but not inappropriately, it was lost in a storm somewhere in the mid-Atlantic.

Paine was excluded from the pantheon of America's Founders for many a generation; however, his historical memory was sustained by a variety of radical intellectuals and movements—democratic, socialist, and freethinking. In fact, my own introduction to Paine came not in school but from my grandfather, a brilliant trial lawyer who had come to this country as a Russian-Jewish boy in 1906. A socialist in his youth, he was eager to pass on to me a critical sense of history and a firm belief in the radical-democratic possibilities of America. Thus, among his gifts to me as a child, along with a volume of Old Testament Bible stories and personal recollections of growing up on the Lower East Side of New York, were the writings of Tom Paine.

SUGGESTED READINGS

Gregory Claeys, *Thomas Paine: Social and Political Thought* (London, 1989).

Howard Fast, *Citizen Tom Paine* (Orig. 1943; New York, 1983). A biographical novel.

Eric Foner, *Tom Paine and Revolutionary America* (New York, 1976).

Michael Foot and Isaac Kramnick, eds., *The Thomas Paine Reader* (New York, 1987).

David Freeman Hawke, *Paine* (New York, 1974).

David Powell, *Tom Paine: The Greatest Exile* (London, 1985).

22 Redeeming Reason and Freedom: The Challenge of C. Wright Mills*

THE ACADEMIC PROGRAM IN which I teach includes faculty trained in all of the major social sciences and even a couple from the humanities. Nevertheless, we regularly pronounce both to our students and to other faculty that the book which best defines our collective purpose is C. Wright Mills's *The Sociological Imagination.*[1] Indeed, it regularly appears on the syllabi of both our introductory and advanced required subjects and in my own courses I usually commence the semester's work with a review of the questions of totality, historicity, and social biography that Mills poses at the outset of the book.

And yet, when we have discussed among ourselves what the perennial value of the work is, we have discovered that each of us has our own ideas. Among the aspects we consider most significant are: Mills's critiques of the two dominant trends in social science of the 1950s, "abstracted empiricism" and "grand theory"; his perceptive commentary on the bureaucratic ethos and the slavishness of social scientists; the diagnosis of the crisis of

---

* This chapter was first published in the "Keyworks" series in *The Times Higher Education Supplement,* October 18, 1985, as a retrospective on C. Wright Mills's *The Sociological Imagination* (New York, 1959). I must thank Tony Galt for the many discussions we have had on Mills's classic work. I would just add that my colleagues and I remain equally committed to *The Sociological Imagination;* however, while I continue to find Mills's arguments on "the uses of history" of great value in my teaching, I now think the book's most important points are made in the chapters discussed toward the end of this essay.

reason and freedom; the arguments on the political responsibilities and tasks of social scientists as intellectuals; and even the appendix on intellectual craftsmanship.

For me, however, the central feature is the chapter on the "uses of history" and Mills's insistence on the necessity of historical perspective in social science, or, as he stated it: "All sociology worthy of the name is historical sociology."

Actually, I first read *The Sociological Imagination* quite late as a student, for like Mills, my BA and MA were not in sociology. In fact, it was not until 1974, while pursuing a Ph.D. in area studies and sociology at a large Southern state university, that I really had a look at it. Of course, I had heard of Mills before. I had attended high school in New Jersey not far from where he had lived, just outside New York City, and my social-studies teacher, who was fascinated by the American power structure, would often talk about Mills and even had a few of us read Mills's classic work of political sociology and social criticism, *The Power Elite.*[2] Then, at Rutgers University in the late 1960s, though a history student, I worked at *Transaction/Society* magazine for Irving Louis Horowitz, the editor and executor of Mills's collected essays and later his biographer.[3]

Yet it was not until I experienced the vacuousness of both methodologism and grand theory at firsthand that *The Sociological Imagination* really came to my attention. Not long after setting out on my doctoral studies, I started to have regrets about leaving the discipline of history; however, one of the newer faculty in the department insisted that I read Mills's discourse on the discipline in preparation for his social theory seminar.

He must have sensed what I was experiencing, for Mills's description of the Janus-faced development of sociology captured precisely the problems and failings of the social science that I seemed to be confronting. Moreover, Mills showed that what both empiricism and Parsonian structural-functionalism lacked was the "stuff of history." As I read on, Mills proceeded to resurrect the tradition of sociology that had originally attracted me; that is, the historical and critical approach of which he urged the renewal.

I soon discovered that Mills himself had contributed to its recovery by co-translating and editing *From Max Weber,* and by writing *The Marxists* not long before his death.[4] The former was crucial in providing an alternative reading of Weber in English to that presented by Talcott Parsons (that is, Weber the historical and political sociologist, as opposed to Weber, the grand-theoretical systematizer); and the latter, recovering the "plain Marxists" who worked in the finest critical spirit of the Grand Old Man, offered an alternative reading of the Marxist tradition in the shadows of the Cold War.

Since so many of the faculty subscribed to C. Wright Mills's arguments in *The Sociological Imagination,* even as they practiced otherwise, I found I could use Mills to validate my own area of the discipline, historical sociology. (My central text was Barrington Moore's *Social Origins of Dictatorship and Democracy,* which I had originally read as a masters degree student in London.)[5]

In time, it also became apparent that my experience was not uncommon. Indeed, historical social science was emerging all around in mushroom-like fashion, as indicated by the works of Immanuel Wallerstein, Eric Wolf, Perry Anderson, Charles Tilly, and so many others on a less grand scale.[6]

Now, a decade later, the rehistoricization of the social sciences is quite evident alongside, and in relation to, the "socialization" of historical studies. There are journals of historical social science; historical sociology textbooks like the late Philip Abrams's *Historical Sociology* and Theda Skocpol's collection *Vision and Method in Historical Sociology* (both of which refer to the influence of Mills);[7] and centers for such scholarship created by Wallerstein at the State University of New York–Binghamton, Charles Tilly at the University of Michigan, and Robert Brenner at UCLA.[8] Indeed, the leading formal theorist of the day, Anthony Giddens, has even called for the merger of sociology and history.[9]

Of course, for Mills, "historical" sociology did not mean merely the sociological study of the past, but most importantly "the present as history" (as the political economist Paul Sweezy put it). Yet we see this too in such works as Harry Braverman's *Labor and Monopoly Capital,* Christopher Lasch's *Haven in a Heartless World,* Russell Jacoby's *Social Amnesia,* Stuart Ewen's *Captains of Consciousness,* and David Noble's *America by Design* and *Forces of Production.*[10]

One cannot help but compare *The Sociological Imagination* to E. H. Carr's *What Is History?*,[11] not only because both books presciently called for the mutual development of historical sociology and social history, but also because both books spoke (and continue to speak) to a generation which believed that history meant more than "keeping the record straight" (though that alone is an arduous and disputatious task) and that social science meant more than providing information for public agencies and private corporations.

Both Mills and Carr envisioned their colleagues refashioning their respective disciplines to carry on a more critical participation in the realm of public discourse and thereby in the making of contemporary history. Mills wrote: "I believe that what may be called classic social analysis is a definable and usable set of traditions; that its essential feature is the concern with historical social structures; and that its problems are of direct relevance to urgent public issues and insistent human troubles"; and, in a similar fashion, Carr declaimed: "To enable man to understand the society of the past and to increase his mastery over the society of the present is the dual function of history."

Also, Mills and Carr similarly understood the historical period in which they were writing as one of transition, not merely in the sense that all of history is characterized by change, but transition in the epochal sense (and, though I am not among them, there are those who have seen premonitions of postmodernism in Mills's and Carr's words.) Mills stated that "We are at the ending of what is called The Modern Age. Just as Antiquity was followed by several centuries of Oriental ascendancy, which Westerners provincially called The Dark Ages, so now The Modern Age is being succeeded by a post-modern period. Perhaps we may call it The Fourth Epoch"; and Carr observed that "The middle years of the twentieth century find the world in a process of change probably more profound and more sweeping than any which has overtaken it since the medieval world broke up in ruins and the foundations of the modern world were laid in the fifteenth and sixteenth centuries."[12]

At the same time, however, this is the point at which these two stand in direct contrast to each other. Whereas Carr held an optimistic and progressive view of the future, involving the expansion of reason and freedom (though he was not oblivious to the dangers ahead), Mills was truly a pessimist and deeply imbued with Weberian thought: "The ideological mark of The Fourth Epoch—that which sets it off from The Modern Age—is that the ideas of freedom and of reason have become moot; that increased rationality may not be assumed to make for increased freedom." Unfortunately, in the brief light of one generation it often appears that Mills provided a more realistic appraisal of contemporary history than did Carr.

What, then, of Mills's political project for social scientists as intellectuals and his sincere concern for the rehabilitation and deepening of democracy? For a long time, the one aspect of Mills's thought that put me off was his subscription to an "elites and masses" conception of the social order, in contrast to a Marxian class analysis. This is especially apparent in *The Power Elite* and *The Causes of World War III*[13]—having outlined the existence and evils of the connections among the corporate, military, and bureaucratic elites in the former book, he then, in the later book, rejects the power elite's being dismantled for fear of the potential consequences due to the inertia of the masses. Rather, he calls for the formation of an intellectual elite that might influence the power elite and to which the latter would be held accountable. Thus, Peter Bachrach rightly called Mills a "democratic elitist."[14]

I still agree with Bachrach's appraisal, but having just reread *The Sociological Imagination* for the *n*th time, I see it standing somewhat apart from this line of argument, which gives it a special value in the current political circumstances. In the book we find Mills reasserting his commitment to the regeneration of a democratic polity, understood not in the limited form of liberal pluralism but in the sense of "publics" actively formulating and debating visions of the social order and its future development; and, at the same time, we find him struggling with the contradictions involved in combining committed intellectual work and political activism.

On the one hand, he rejects the proposition of intellectuals "standing in" for democratic publics or converting the masses in a Leninist fashion, because he recognizes that such means of rescuing democracy maximize the risk of ultimately subverting the ends being sought. On the other hand, he rejects the "simple democratic view that what men are interested in" is all that matters, for it neglects the fact that values held by people are often the product of inculcation—"often deliberately by vested interests."

Alternatively, in an effort to transcend the contradictions—which is especially difficult in the context of an elite/masses framework—Mills urges social scientists to address themselves to "public issues and private troubles." I may read too much into Mills's thinking, but I now believe he realized that although people often may not be able to express fully their shared concerns, or troubles, as grievances in public debate, nevertheless, they are quite sensitive to inhibitions, prohibitions, and threats to their freedom.

Thus, by addressing both issues and troubles (that is, potential issues), social scientists would be articulating popular grievances in the realm of public discourse and thus reinvigorating the formation of democratic publics. The promise of the sociological imagination, Mills said, is that it enables us to grasp "history and biography and the relations between the two within society." *The Sociological Imagination* remains essential reading.

23 A Tribute to E. P. Thompson, Marxist Historian and Radical Democrat (1924–1993)*

> *It is difficult to explain how memories affect one in middle life. For months, the past stretches behind one, as an inert record of events. Then, without forewarning, the past seems suddenly to open itself up inside one—with a more palpable emotional force than the vague present—in the gesture of a long-dead friend, or in the recall of some "spot of time" imbued with incommunicable significance. One is astonished to find oneself, while working in the garden or pottering about the kitchen, with tears on one's cheeks.*
>
> —E. P. Thompson, *Writing by Candlelight*

DOROTHY THOMPSON TELEPHONED TO let me know that her husband and lifelong comrade, Edward Thompson, had passed away on Saturday, August 28, 1993, at the age of 69. We spoke for a while, and of several matters, but there was one comment in particular that incited a whole chain of thoughts on my part. When I asked if Edward had been at home or in hospital at the time, she answered that he had died in the garden.

* First presented as the 1994 Lefler Lecture at Carleton College, Minnesota, this chapter was published in *New Politics,* no. 16, winter 1994. I want to thank Carl Weiner and his colleagues at Carleton College for inviting me to deliver the talk and Phyllis and Julius Jacobson for inviting its publication in the journal they edit.

During the days following the call, I kept thinking about Edward and Dorothy's garden at their home in Upper Wick, near Worcester, England. And my thoughts called forth memories of our very first meeting in 1983. I was in England, among other things to talk with Rodney Hilton, Christopher Hill, and Edward Thompson as part of my writing of *The British Marxist Historians*.[1] All were willing to be interviewed; Edward, much to my amazement, was not only prepared to meet, but also had immediately and most generously invited me to come and visit him and Dorothy at their home for a couple of days. He was deeply involved in peace campaigning and at that very moment preparing for a "debate" on BBC Radio with an American "defense analyst"; but he said that if I did come to the house we would not only have a chance to talk, it would also afford me a look at papers of which I might not be aware.

It was mid-January; chilly and damp as one would expect. I arrived late in the day with Dorothy, who had driven me down from the Midlands where she taught at Birmingham University. It was getting dark, but Edward was not to be found. I readily admit to having been very anxious, all the more so because Dorothy, herself a renowned historian of nineteenth-century British Labor and Chartism, had been grilling me in the car about my project and ideas;[2] presumably, it was in order to find out if I was just one more youngster about to write yet another "theoretical critique" of the work of E. P. Thompson and his historian comrades in the then-current structuralist fashion of the Birmingham University Center for Contemporary Cultural Studies.[3]

Wick Episcopi is a huge house and I figured that Edward was tucked away writing in his study upstairs. Nervous, I poked around in a groundfloor library-like room, hoping to discover some special insights into Edward Thompson's life and work. Then I heard the front door open, followed by the sound of a dog racing into the foyer and the voice of a man shouting "Dotty?" I meekly peered out of the library and saw before me a tall figure with a wild mop of almost-white hair, a pale, lined face with reddened cheeks, bright eyes, and the expression of someone who had just completed a fair day's labor—the supporting evidence for which was the mud and dirt covering him from his wellington boots up to his scratched jacket and gloves. This man had been clearing away dead bushes in preparation to plant new things.

A cultivator of history, democracy, and the land, Edward Thompson cleared away and planted more gardens and fields than the fruitful and pleasant ones behind Wick Episcopi. Truly, he ranks both as one of the great historians and as one of the great radical figures of our time. And yet, to put it that way—however much it must be put that way—is not sufficient, for it fails to capture the vibrant and dynamic connection *between* his historiography and his politics. Two sides of the same coin? That's too passive. Rather, we should say they were bound together in a critical and creative *dialectic* wherein his political commitments and involvements proposed questions to the past and his encounters and conversations with the past proposed arguments to the world in which he lived. And this Thompsonian dialectic between past and present engendered hopes and aspirations for the future. In this respect, Edward Thompson's career should be a model to us all.

Naturally, looking back over his career as historian and radical we can see periods when Thompson was more heavily engaged in one of his callings than the other—this seems to have been increasingly the case as he grew older. Yet, whatever the moment's engagement, it was charged by his hyperactive radical-democratic historical memory and imagination. Again, I am led to recall my first visit to Wick Episcopi: Returning to London by train, I was accompanied by Edward, now on his way to the BBC studios for the radio debate that evening. Driving down to the station he leaned over to me and, in a joking whisper, said it was now *his* turn to be nervous for he knew well that in contrast to his opponent, who made a living of such affairs, he was really just a citizen trying to confront and put a stop to the progress of "exterminism"—the dialectic to end all dialectics. Walking onto the station platform, he apologized for needing to smoke; I lied and said I could handle it (for I had no intention of giving up time with the man by sitting apart in a no-smoking carriage). Once on board, he threw himself into his notes, using me as his audience. I never really heard his arguments, for I wasn't so much listening as watching and studying him. He was undeniably a fascinating figure. Time and the countryside passed by. All of a sudden, he stopped and began to gaze out of the window of the moving train. The momentary silence and the look in his eyes alerted me to actually try to hear and mentally record what he would have to say. I expected a few lines on Thatcherism and Reaganism, or talk of war and peace, but instead he spoke of the eighteenth century. Pointing away to fields and a wooded rise in the distance, he told me about the area we were journeying through—of aristocrat and gentry and of the working people who had suffered and attempted to resist encroachment and depredation.

Later, on the plane back to the States, I thought about how his turning away from his notes to consider the historical landscape probably revealed a longing to return to the past and historical study, and no doubt that was part of it. In time, however, I realized that it was more than that. Indeed, I have come to believe that what I witnessed in that afternoon's act of remembrance was Edward Thompson reinvigorating his historical consciousness by resurrecting earlier episodes of "freeborn Englishmen" defending themselves and their liberties against the powers that be.

◆

Edward Palmer Thompson was born February 3, 1924, the second son of an English father, Edward John Thompson, and an American mother, Theodosia Jessup, who had been Methodist education missionaries in India. Both of his parents were ardent liberals and anti-imperialists, and Thompson himself remarked on several occasions that even before going up to university he had "cut his political teeth," first, on the cause of Indian independence, to which his father, a good friend of Nehru, was devoted,[4] and, then, on the Spanish Civil War, the first anti-Fascist struggle in Europe. Raised near Oxford, the younger Edward went to Cambridge University to read literature but later switched to history.

Arriving at university in 1942, Thompson joined the Communist Party. Of course, like most of his generation his studies were interrupted by the Second World War. Commissioned an officer in the British army and assigned command of a tank unit, he served in North Africa and Italy.[5] Preceding him into university, the Communist Party and, then, military service, Edward's older brother, Frank Thompson, a brilliant student of languages at Oxford and a promising poet, volunteered for service in Special Operations Executive (SOE) and was killed while fighting alongside partisans in the Balkans. In a letter home on Christmas Day 1943, Frank spoke of a democratic postwar Europe in words that firmly impressed themselves on Edward's memory and imagination:

> There is a spirit abroad in Europe which is finer and braver than anything that tired continent has known for centuries, and which cannot be withstood. You can if you like, think of it in terms of politics, but it is broader and more generous than any dogma. It is the confident will of whole peoples, who have known the utmost humiliation and suffering and have triumphed over it, to build their own life once and for all.[6]

Following the war, Edward returned to Cambridge where he met Dorothy Towers and, upon completing their degrees in 1946, they went together to Yugoslavia as members of a volunteer youth brigade that he himself led to aid in the construction of a railway.[7]

Returning to England, Edward and Dorothy were married in 1948 and in the same year he secured appointment as an adult education lecturer in the Extra-Mural Department of Leeds University. He said he went into adult education "because it seemed to me an area in which I would learn something about industrial England, and teach people who would teach me."[8] He and Dorothy remained active in the Communist Party and, also, in the Communist Party Historians' Group, which, he fondly recalled, helped make him a historian "more than anything . . . at Cambridge." Members of the group included the senior figures,

Maurice Dobb, A. L. Morton, and Dona Torr, and younger scholars like Christopher Hill, Rodney Hilton, Eric Hobsbawm, John Saville, Victor Kiernan, and George Rudé.

As my own work of the past 10 years has insistently contended, these remarkable Marxist intellectuals came to constitute a historiographical and theoretical tradition and, in addition to their outstanding individual contributions to British and European studies, they collectively have made profound contributions to historical study and thought *and* to the formation of a popular democratic historical consciousness. I would note three of their collective contributions in particular: their development of *class-struggle analysis,* derived from Marx and Engels's grand hypothesis that "the history of all hitherto existing society is the history of class struggle"; their development of the perspective known as *history from the bottom up,* entailing the historical recovery of the lives and struggles of the lower classes, the English common people, both peasants and workers; and their recovery and assemblage of an English *radical-democratic tradition* stretching from John Ball, Wat Tyler, and the Rising of 1381, through Gerrard Winstanley and the True Levellers of the English Revolution, to William Morris, Tom Mann, and the Labour Movement. A foremost example of this recovery and assemblage was Thompson's own first major work, *William Morris: Romantic to Revolutionary,*[9] in which he reunited the aesthetic, or cultural, and political aspirations of Morris's life and labors and, against the literary and academic grain of the times, revealed their powerful intimacy.

In 1956, Thompson left the Communist Party along with so many of his historian comrades. He had been an energetic and hard-working party activist, but increasingly he dissented from party positions and practices and, with fellow historian John Saville, he started up an internal journal of opposition, *The Reasoner.* His departure from the party was probably inevitable, but the final act was the Soviet invasion of Hungary and the failure of the British Communist Party to denounce and oppose it. On their leaving, Thompson and Saville renamed their journal *The New Reasoner,* which was later to be merged with the *Universities and Left Review* in favor of the *New Left Review* (1960).

No longer a party member, Thompson became a founding figure of the first British New Left and a prominent activist in the Campaign for Nuclear Disarmament (CND). Still, he remained a socialist and a Marxist—or, in his words, a "libertarian-communist" and "Morrisian-Marxist." Indeed, he even began writing of the possibilities for a truly *democratic*-socialist revolution in Britain. To some, such talk was outrageous and utopian, but Thompson felt himself informed far more by history than fantasy. As he wrote, in conclusion to the first New Left Book, *Out of Apathy*:

> It would be foolish to be sanguine. But foolish also to under-estimate the long and tenacious revolutionary tradition of the English commoner. It is a dogged, good-humored, responsible, tradition: yet a revolutionary tradition all the same. From the Leveller corporals ridden down by Cromwell's men at Burford to the weavers massed behind their banners at Peterloo, the struggle for democratic and for social rights has always been intertwined. From the Chartist camp meeting to the dockers' picket line it has expressed itself most naturally in the language of moral revolt. Its weaknesses, its carelessness of theory, we know too well; its strengths, its resilience and steady humanity, we too easily forget. It is a tradition which could leaven the socialist world.[10]

Thompson's historical imagination was already evident in *William Morris* and in his critical and political essays in the *New Reasoner* and *New Left Review*, but it became most apparent and was most beautifully expressed in the writing of his masterpiece, *The Making of the English Working Class*. Published thirty years ago, it stands as the most influential work of social history ever written. Indeed, one can only wonder at the number of dissertations and monographs—not only in Britain but, perhaps, especially here in North America—that open with the words Thompson offered in its Preface:

I am seeking to rescue the poor stockinger, the Luddite cropper, the "obsolete" hand-loom weaver, the "utopian" artisan, and even the deluded follower of Joanna Southcott, from the enormous condescension of posterity. Their crafts and traditions may have been dying. Their hostility to the new industrialism may have been backward-looking. Their communitarian ideals may have been fantasies. Their insurrectionary conspiracies may have been foolhardy. But they lived through these times of acute social disturbance and we did not. Their aspirations were valid in terms of their own experience; and if they were casualties, they remain, condemned in their own lives as casualties.[11]

Nine hundred pages in length, with all the essential academic accoutrements, *The Making of the English Working Class* is a most scholarly study. But we must not forget that its author was no traditional university don. In fact, the writing of the book appears to have been inspired primarily by Thompson's own experiences as a teacher and organizer of working-class adults in West Yorkshire, experiences that contradicted contemporary sociological and historical accounts—right, left, and center—of working-class culture and politics. Thompson's students had begun to teach him a great deal.

In light of a generation and more of history from the bottom up and the democratization of the historical past, we can too easily forget the state of historical study and thinking, and the ruling narrative it fortified, prior to the late 1960s. Political and academic thought of the postwar decades regularly ignored, denied, and/or misrepresented the contributions of the lower classes to the making of history. Moreover, the classic tale that the making of modern freedom was due to the "rise of the bourgeoisie" was reproduced in particular ways in the works of both liberals and Marxists.

Celebrating the liberal-democratic polity of the Cold-War West, liberal writers and political scientists equated its development with the formation and ascendance of the middle classes and its persistence with the capacity of competing pluralistic elites to govern effectively. Moreover, these publicists of the capitalist order regularly insisted that the survival of democracy—the extension and deepening of democratic life was unimaginable or too scary for them to entertain!—actually depended on the maintenance of popular political "apathy." From the perspective of these proponents of the "end of ideology," the intellectual fathers of Fukuyama's "end of history," laboring classes had been the primary supports for authoritarian and totalitarian movements and regimes and, thus, their active and direct participation in public and political life represented a perennial threat to democratic government.

Although orthodox Marxist writers had their own version of history and political development, it was actually quite similar to the liberal one. Democratic rights and freedoms were deemed to be merely "bourgeois" and, following Lenin's dictum that the working classes on their own are only capable of "trade unionism," it was assumed that the pursuit of socialism depended on the leadership of "the party" and the ideas of radicalized middle-class theorists and intellectuals. Neo-Marxist and New Left social theorists á la Herbert Marcuse and the Frankfurt School also wrote off working people, perceiving them to be co-opted by the technologies and consumerism of a booming postwar industrial-capitalism. Seeking alternatives, they went in search of new historical subjects and revolutionary agents among Third-World peasantries, racial minorities and the poor, and university intellectuals and students.

Mainstream historians and sociologists offered little challenge to these interpretations and polemics. Economic historians regularly treated the emergence of the working classes in narrowly economic and statistical terms, and social historians and historical sociologists, working from the dominant paradigm of modernization theory and structural-functionalism, viewed the class struggles of the nineteenth century as having been merely the immediate expressions of the social disruptions and economic crises resulting from rapid industrialization and urbanization and the difficult process of adapting to the exigencies and yet-to-be-realized opportunities of modern life.

Thompson's experience—along with the histories being recovered by his fellow British Marxist historians—denied those elitist renditions of past and present and led him to do battle with the narratives upon which they were based. He knew that his working-class students and comrades in the party and the peace movement were motivated not by authoritarian but by *democratic* values and ideals, and that, however much their lives were determined by forces and structures of power beyond their immediate grasp, their aspirations and continuing struggles threatened not democratic government but those who were eager to set limits to it.

Thus, *The Making of the English Working Class* was Thompson's response to the ideologists, historians, and social scientists. It is a book about class, but not in the sense that students of inequality and "stratification" had traditionally understood it. For Thompson class was not a static thing, not a structure or a category, but "something which in fact happens (and can be shown to have happened) in human relationships." To be more precise, *The Making*—so titled "because it is a study in an active process which owes as much to agency as conditioning"—is about the formation and coming to consciousness of the English working class from 1790 to the early 1830s culminating in Chartism and the first working-class political party.

Thompson faulted economic and social historians for their inadequate understandings of class experience and their blindness to the agency and creativity of the working class in struggle, and he chastised Old and New Lefts alike for their elitism. His own conception of class was truly innovative and refreshing, but, against assertions to the contrary, it remained quite Marxian. He wrote in the Preface: "The class experience is largely determined by the productive relations into which men [and women] are born—or enter involuntarily. Class consciousness is the way in which these experiences are handled in cultural terms: embodied in traditions, value-systems, ideas and institutional forms."

The Making of the English Working Class is not really a consecutive story but a set of related studies; yet, as readers of the work well know, its chapters render a moving narrative. From the tradition of Dissent to the tensions and contradictions of Method-ism; from the English Jacobin Corresponding Societies to the resurgent Radicalism of 1816-20s; and from the preindustrial crowd to Luddism: Thompson explores the making and *self*-making of the English working class through the experience of the intensification of exploitation and political oppression of the early Industrial Revolution. Thus, he makes us witness to the continuing assertion of the "rights of the freeborn Englishman" entailing particular notions of—and demands for—liberty, equality, and democracy and, also, to the development of an "ethos of mutuality" in the struggle to defend a besieged conception of community. In the end, although a second English Revolution failed to transpire, a revolution of sorts did take place, involving far more than a change in the mode of production.

As one would expect, following three decades of new scholarly work and thought—most of it empowered by *The Making of the English Working Class* itself—various criticisms have been directed at Thompson's book. At the outset, there were the theoretical and historical challenges advanced by Perry Anderson and Tom Nairn, who contended that Thompson had made far too much of working-class culture and agency.[12] However, in light of subsequent historiography, it is clear that *The Making of the English Working Class* has prevailed.

Thompson's conception of class and class formation, which he shared with his fellow British Marxist historians, was also subjected to attack—especially by the aforementioned structuralists at the Birmingham University Center for Contemporary Cultural Studies who, in the 1970s, were caught up in "Althusserian" thought. But, here too, ensuing work registers that Thompson's dialectical understanding of "determination"—entailing an appreciation of structure, experience, *and* agency/struggle—is historically and politically richer than one- or, even, two-dimensional determinisms.

Historians' criticisms have weighed in more heavily. Feminists have rightly contended that Thompson failed to address women's experience and agency and, thereby, failed to comprehend the gender dimensions of class and class formation. And many a social historian of nineteenth-century Britain has correctly questioned the degree to which the English working class can be said to have been "made" by the 1830s. Equipped with new questions, approaches, and methodologies, the recovery of the past continues and—as Marx and Engels themselves insisted—"all history must be studied afresh."

However fundamental and daunting the task of correcting and expanding the historical record, for Thompson it was not to be left at that. Neither was it sufficient to accomplish the reshaping of academic and intellectual discourse. *The Making of the English Working Class* was also intended to be a popular work, that is, it was written for the working people of England, whose own experience and agency had first compelled him to consider the past anew. As my fellow American historian Marcus Rediker has observed: "Thompson writes with continual human reference, affirming certain values over and against others, and he tries to make his readers [historians, the left and working people] active valuing agents as they think about history and politics." In the same vein, British education critic Fred Inglis explains how Thompson's historiography provides "a new past to live from; it changes the social memory so that, differently understanding how the present came about, the agent thinks forward to a new set of possibilities."[13] Deftly wielding the powers of the past, Thompson had the gift—of which Walter Benjamin had spoken—of "fanning the spark of hope in the past." The point is made, but we should give the last word here to the Romantic poet William Wordsworth, whose autobiographical poem, *The Prelude*, prefigures Edward Thompson's own experience of writing *The Making of the English Working Class*:

> *There I heard*
> *From mouths of men obscure and*
> *lowly, truths*
> *Replete with honour; sounds in unison*
> *With loftiest promises of good and fair.*

There was a truly prophetic element in Thompson's history but, sadly, it is not adequately heeded. In his concluding remarks,

Thompson observed that "both the Romantics and the Radical craftsmen opposed the annunciation of Acquisitive Man. In the failure of the two traditions to come to a point of junction, something was lost. How much we cannot be sure, for we are among the losers." Though I try to disabuse my students of the notion that history repeats itself, I must admit that it seems actually to have happened in the years immediately following the publication of *The Making of the English Working Class*. Accepting the media-reproduced myth of working-class authoritarianism, my own generation of radicalized university students and young people—in spite of all our calls for "participation" and "power to the people"—failed to articulate our democratic aspirations with those of the contemporary working class even as working people themselves were renewing their struggles for control of the workplace. Enter the New Right and renewed class war from above.

◆

The publication of *The Making of the English Working Class* led to Thompson joining the faculty of the newly established Warwick University in 1965 as reader in the Center for Social History. There, his scholarly investigations turned to eighteenth-century English society, especially aspects of popular culture, crime, and the law. In writings such as *Whigs and Hunters: The Origins of the Black Act* and the articles eventually brought together as *Customs in Common: Studies in Traditional Popular Culture*, Thompson explored the relations, antagonisms, and conflicts between "patricians and plebs," an order of struggle that he was to provocatively term "class struggle without class." Influenced by the ideas of Antonio Gramsci regarding hegemony and consciousness, the work of Thompson and his students—both British and North American—significantly revised our historical understandings of modes of "power and authority" and "rebellion and resistance."[14]

Installed as a full-time university teacher and scholar, Thompson continued to be energetically engaged as a public intellectual and, with Raymond Williams and Stuart Hall, he co-authored the *May Day Manifesto 1968,* which set out a new democratic-socialist political agenda for Britain. Still, academic garb ill suited him and, following a series of political confrontations with university authorities typical of the late-1960s,[15] he decided to leave Warwick and pursue a livelihood as an independent writer. Although he never returned to teaching in Britain, during the next 15 years the Thompsons together took up visiting professorships in North America at the University of Pittsburgh, Brown University, Rutgers University, and Queens University in Ontario.

Thompson's writings of the 1970s are many and varied. Yet, as diverse as his historical, theoretical, and political writings of the 1970s seem to be, they were all motivated by a growing historical interest in the State, crime, and the law, and by an intensifying concern that the democratic spirit of British working people was once again being overwhelmed by "apathy"—the sense that the structures of power cannot be challenged, that human agency, whether individual or collective, accomplishes little if anything. Alongside the studies of eighteenth-century English society, he produced several articles that revealed him to be a brilliant and most entertaining theorist, however much he (rather theatrically) insisted otherwise. Among these are his extended essays, "An Open Letter to Leszek Kolakowski" (1973) and "The Poverty of Theory or An Orrery of Errors" (1978), the latter being his counterattack against the anti-historical and anti-humanist claims of the French Marxist-structuralist philosopher Louis Althusser.[16] At the same time, Thompson composed a stream of shorter political and critical pieces for the pages of newspapers and magazines like the *New Statesman* and *New Society,* the connecting thread of which was the concentration and abuse of power by the British Establishment and the encroachment by the British State on the historically secured rights of "freeborn Britons." Repeatedly, Thompson warned his fellow citizens of historical amnesia and implored them to remember and renew their traditions of popular dissent from below.[17]

Thompson was no armchair critic. Steadily, his historical imagination and commitments propelled him into full-time political labors. Confronting the "Second Cold War" of the 1980s, he and Dorothy joined with other peace activists to found END (European Nuclear Disarmament). Mobilizing hundreds of thousands to the cause of nuclear disarmament, he penned the pamphlet *Protest and Survive* (1980), which called upon his fellow Britons and continentals—in the fashion of Tom Paine's revolutionary pamphlets, *Common Sense* and *Rights of Man*—to "act as if we are, already, citizens of Europe" and "throw whatever resources still exist in human culture across the path of this degenerative logic."[18] As Fred Inglis states in his memorial tribute, "Thompson Invictus":

> They came. They came by the millions from all over Europe, and not a few from North America. The missiles arrived and were reviled. The people stayed. Thompson spoke for them. In a few pages of pamphleteering, on a few hundred platforms, in the pages of the liberal press, tired, tirelessly, he wrote a different account of the history that had been and the history that might be. He summoned up the hideous nightmare of what he called "exterminism," and counterposed a vision of free peoples refusing to do what the hairy ogre Nobodaddy told them to do. And in the end—in Prague, Berlin, Bucharest and elsewhere—they didn't. It was even a sort of victory.[19]

Indeed, a victory. Frank Thompson's words—"There is a spirit abroad in Europe"—were redeemed and given new meaning by the agency of Edward and Dorothy Thompson and their comrades in the campaigns for European and global peace and freedom.

From the outset, Edward had persistently sought contacts and exchanges with East European and Soviet democrats and socialist humanists struggling under the weight of Stalinism.[20] Now, in the 1980s, he organized END working groups to serve as conduits of information about efforts under way to establish peace and human-rights organizations in the East. He went himself several times to Eastern Europe to meet with and deliver messages of support to dissident groups gathering clandestinely in homes and apartments.[21] Of course, there were frictions and differences of opinion between the campaigners East and West, but Thompson was convinced that the dialogues had to be pursued and maintained, if possible as conversations, if need be as continuing arguments. Pursuing "détente from below," Europeans might thus come to recognize each other as "fellow citizens"; their respective movements and shared struggles engendering an "ethos of mutuality" as had happened in the early nineteenth century among English workers of diverse trades and occupations. As was to be expected, American and European Cold-warriors rushed to claim the events of 1989 as a victory for the West, but, as Thompson did not fail to remind, the dictatorships were brought down by the East European peoples themselves.[22] As the experience becomes history and the democratic dreams are tragically subordinated to market priorities and/or nationalist fevers, we who work in the discipline charged with keeping the record straight have an obligation to make sure that the developing narrative registers the popular triumphs and, too, the prophetic agency of the man who spoke of a Europe "beyond the Cold War."

To the lament of many an academic, Thompson had found it necessary to put aside his historical scholarship for almost a decade; though he did eventually find time to complete a satiric work of science fiction, *The Sykaos Papers.*[23] Finally, with the end of the Cold War he was able to return to historical study and writing. Unfortunately, he now suffered a series of debilitating illnesses. And yet, in spite of his declining health, he continued to accomplish volumes. In addition to putting in order his classic collection of eighteenth-century chapters, *Customs in Common,* and writing a monograph on the work of his late father, *Alien Homage: Edward Thompson and Rabindranath Tagore,* Thompson finished his long-promised book on William Blake, *Witness against the Beast,* and revised and prepared another collection of his historical essays that he delivered to the publishers just weeks before his death.[24]

♦

I cannot avoid returning to the garden at Wick Episcopi but, before I do, there is a thought I must share. It is a silly one, perhaps, but one

I am entitled now to reveal. In December 1941, soon after America's entry into the Second World War, Winston Churchill addressed the United States Congress. Noting that his own mother was American, Churchill wondered aloud what might have been if, indeed, things had been reversed and it had been his father who was American. Well, I too have sometimes allowed myself to speculate about the "what ifs" of history and, recalling Churchill's remark, I have occasionally wondered what might have been if things had been turned around in Edward Thompson's case and, instead of his mother, it was his father who had been American.

Actually, for all his anger and criticism about the United States-as-superpower, Thompson really seemed to appreciate American exuberance, openness, and democratism. Among his dearest friends were many an American, most notably his fellow labor historians, David Montgomery and the late Herbert Gutman. Moreover, this devoté of English letters, especially Blake and the Romantics, readily proclaimed that his favorite contemporary poet was his friend and comrade from the American Midwest, Tom McGrath.[25] But his feelings for us were based on more than personal attachments. He was impressed by that which we too often take for granted and even allow to languish, that is, our popular constitutional traditions of free speech, public debate, open government and, when necessary, resistance of state authority. Occasionally, Thompson threw these American traditions at his fellow Britons as a challenge; occasionally, he threw them back at us as a wake-up call.

In this grain, I would also record that when Edward visited us in Green Bay in the spring of 1990 to speak to my students and colleagues, he delivered a talk not on English, but—composed as the Herbert Gutman Memorial Lecture—on *American*, specifically, *Native* American, history. It was a wonderful occasion. As I recollect him explaining, the subject was something he came upon when the wrong set of papers were placed before him at the London Library. The documents treated the origins of a group of Native Americans who came to be known as the Brotherton. Apparently "formed" in the late eighteenth century by English missionaries seeking to protect the remnants of various New England tribes, the Brotherton developed their own collective identity and later removed themselves to Wisconsin, establishing the town of Brotherton on the eastern shore of Lake Winnebago (about the same time in the early nineteenth century that a large segment of the Oneida Nation moved out here from New York).

Truly, I could not have asked for a better topic, for among my students were members of several tribes from this, the northeastern, part of the state (who, it should be noted, were afterwards the most vocally appreciative of Edward's talk). Although Edward was not in the greatest health, he fully rose to the occasion and spoke excitedly and passionately for more than an hour. Of course, since Green Bay is not so very far north of where the Brotherton had settled in Wisconsin (about an hour's drive), Edward was eager to make a fieldtrip to the area the next day with my family and me, and we were pleased to oblige. On the way, we popped into antique and second-hand shops, for Edward was hoping to find evidence of and references to the Brotherton settlement. More rewarding were our stops along the road to ask for spatial and temporal directions— Edward proceeded to amaze me by turning each stop into an oral history session, as the locals we met immediately sensed he was to be trusted. Also, with help, we found our way to the original Brotherton cemetery, barely marked, but not far off the main road. Edward was thrilled by the discovery and he and our two little girls, then 10 and 6 respectively, went from headstone to headstone surveying the names, dates, and other engraved bits of information still legible. On this, their first experience as historians, Rhiannon and Fiona that day apprenticed themselves to *the* master craftsman.

◆

To be honest, I have resisted this moment. I do not want to finish these notes, for it seems that as long I write, E. P. Thompson, the greatest living historian and radical, is not actually gone. But, having taken them as far as I can go at this time, I return to where my thoughts began, that is, to the telephone call from Dorothy. "He died in the garden," she said. Hearing that, I immediately recollected the words with which he concluded "The Poverty of Theory," his sparkling defense of the historical discipline, of Marxism as *historical* materialism, and of human agency in the making of history: "I may now with a better conscience, return to my proper work and to my own garden. I will watch how things grow."[26] Edward Thompson's proper work is done and his garden is cultivated. We have much to do.

24 Whither the American Left?*

A RECENTLY PUBLISHED COLLECTION of articles, *Unfinished Business: 20 Years of Socialist Review* (1992), will no doubt instigate historical and personal reflections among my colleagues and comrades regarding the experience and prospects of the contemporary American left. It did with me.

I confess that as an American undergraduate (1967-71) I had serious reservations about my own generation's "student movement." Opposed to the war in Vietnam and firmly committed to Civil Rights, I was, nevertheless, antagonized by many of my fellow students' elitism and hostility toward working-class people. Still, although I knew I was further left than liberalism, I do not recall thinking of myself as a socialist—more likely, I thought of myself in the American grain, as a radical democrat.

That changed, however, in the course of my year as a postgraduate student in London in the early 1970s, for in Britain I discovered a political culture in which socialism was neither exiled to the margins nor buried in scholarly monographs, but was, indeed, the proclaimed ideal of one of the two leading parties. Moreover, this party was linked to a labor movement apparently willing to confront the power structure in a public fashion (in fact, my love affair with the young woman whom I was to marry, and am married to still, began during those romantically dark winter nights afforded by the Miners' Strike of 1972 when the government imposed blackouts to conserve fuel supplies—and, thus, I have never stopped believing that there is an intimate connection between love and the class struggle);

---

* This chapter was first published in *The Times Higher Education Supplement,* May 15, 1992, as a review of and response to *Unfinished Business: 20 Years of Socialist Review* (London, 1991), edited by the *Socialist Review* Collective Staff.

and it was variably influenced and annoyed by a variety of left intellectual and political organizations whose arguments and aspirations were in many cases taken seriously enough to allow them a presence in the print and broadcast media.

It was a critical experience and in time I did come to identify myself as a socialist, believing not only that the making of socialist democracies was possible—a project in which intellectuals had a fundamental part to play—but, also (youthfully and foolishly), that the process could be well advanced by the time I reached middle age. This belief was further encouraged by the apparent progress of the British *and* American lefts and the crises of capitalism in the 1970s.

History, however, is filled with tragedies and disappointments, ironies and surprises. In the past two decades we have seen not the advance of democratic socialism but—preceding and paralleling the welcome collapse of Soviet communism—the retreat both of social democracy in Britain and Western Europe and of liberalism in North America in the face of a militant New Right declaiming "traditional" values and market principles. However ideological and foolish-sounding the "end-of-history" thesis may be, it starkly poses the question of the future of the left and the possibilities for radical-democratic change and socialism in sharp and urgent terms.

It might even be asked if, indeed, there remains an American left. Perhaps it survives merely as the paranoid delusion of a persistently hysterical American right, or as an invention on their part to maintain an enemy against whom to campaign (a new version of the "Red Scare"). This is not as silly as it sounds. Presently, the 1992 presidential and other electoral campaigns are dominated by candidates of the center through far-right. American labor unions continue to retreat in the face of class war from above and economic recession. And the African American and women's movements are struggling to protect victories of a generation ago against an increasingly conservative Supreme Court. Moreover—and contrary to the claims of press pundits and hacks, professions overpopulated by conservatives—the most immediate problems on university campuses seem to have to do less with the question of the literary canon, multiculturalist history or, even, "politically correct" ("PC") behavior, than with that of which departments will suffer the biggest cuts and/or mergers.

And yet, however much the politicos and columnists of the right exaggerate, their hysteria is due neither to simple paranoia nor to fantastic imaginations. There *is* an American left and, just possibly, its prospects are greater than its present circumstances and media presence—or *absence!*—imply. The most avowedly liberal presidential candidate of 1992, Tom Harkin of Iowa (who will likely drop out by the time this is in print), has run a mediocre campaign, and, on a most crucial and popular issue, the creation of a national healthcare system, he has been practically silent. In other words, the failure of a left-ish presidential campaign to "catch fire" may not be due so much to what pop sociologists are calling the "compassion fatigue" of the tax-paying citizenry as it is to the absence of a populist and social-democratic candidate to mobilize them.

Admittedly, the labor movement is in deep trouble, but, arguably, the situation can get no worse and, in fact, there are signs of democratic renewal commencing with recent developments in the long corrupt and reactionary Teamsters Union. At the same time, Black and other minority-group and feminist organizations may lose battles in the courts, but this might well challenge them to pursue more extensive public-political mobilizations and coalition-building targeted at state legislatures and Congress.

Finally, although American higher education is far from commanded by the left or, as one neoconservative attack dog has written, "tenured radicals," there can be no denying that at least in the humanities and social sciences the excitement, arguments, and debates of the past 20 years and more have been instigated by the questions, investigations, and publications of a generation of young—though now graying—academics whose enthusiasms and energies were originally engendered by their political and cultural commitments and engagements. Not only have there been established a vast array of critical political and academic journals—*Socialist Review, Radical America, Radical History Review, New Politics, Radical Review of Political Economy, Critical Sociology, Social Text, Cultural*

Critique (to name just a few)—but, as well, the mainstream disciplinary journals have become ever more critical due to the arrival of Marxian, feminist, and other "radical" scholars in their pages and on their editorial boards.

The problem of the American intellectual left is very much the ironic one highlighted by Russell Jacoby in *The Last Intellectuals:* We have worked so hard and smartly trying to both revise the scholarly agenda and secure ourselves in the academy that we have lost our capacity to engage publics, "the people."[1] In essence we have enclosed ourselves in an academic ghetto, making us all the more subject to accusation and attack by well-financed extra-academic "public intellectuals" of the right and their on-campus allies of the National Association of Scholars.[2]

Writing as an academic I can be accused of making too much of the role and responsibility of intellectuals in turning the situation around, that is, of reinvigorating the American left and, with it, public culture and political life in the United States. To be absolutely clear about it: Social change in America *will not—and should not*—be accomplished solely by intellectuals, left or right. To believe otherwise is both dangerous and elitist. However, political campaigns and struggles demand intellectual energies to make critical sense of the world and how it came to be this way *and* to bear witness to and articulate the hopes and aspirations of the people with whom one identifies and hopes to refashion the world. In these terms, left intellectuals have been failing themselves and the people whom they hope to engage and serve.

It should be recognized that we have done a respectable job in redeeming the experiences, agencies, and voices of the past "from the enormous condescension of posterity" (as E. P. Thompson once put it). And, arguably, we have developed insightful critiques of capitalism and patriarchal and racial and ethnic oppression. In this regard I do indeed recommend the many interesting and, yes, entertaining chapters to be found in *Unfinished Business.* However, we are now all well aware that we have not engaged—nor sufficiently sought to engage—contemporary popular experience and imagination.

Strangely, American conservatives have been ascendant for at least three presidential terms and yet they constantly bemoan their failure to develop the "vision thing." If anyone should be concerned about that it should be the American intellectual left. What we need to do is not just continue the recovery of the past from the bottom up and render challenging criticism of the powers that be, but, from these practices and out of public involvements and deliberations, commence the elaboration of a shared vision of past, present, and possible futures capable of speaking to and securing the critical commitment of working people, men and women, across the supposed racial and cultural divides.

Such a project confronts major, if not insurmountable, barriers. It's not just that many a good scholar has been seduced and led down a postmodern path to the land of *post-histoire* and, having taken refuge in some deconstructed hovel, has yet to be rescued. More problematic is that in the good name of pluralism and multiculturalism, left intellectuals too often have allowed themselves to be caught up merely in "identity politics" and particularisms of gender and sexuality, and race and ethnicity.

But let us suppose that there are still enough intellectual resources to go around. The problem remains that of connecting with public culture, of taking part in and shaping public debate and, in the process, fomenting a grander radical-democratic vision. The left is not without its public media: weeklies like the *Nation* and *In These Times;* monthlies like *Tikkun* and the *Progressive;* and quarterlies like the democratic-socialist *Dissent* and the liberal *American Prospect.*

Of course, a realist would ask, what are all these things next to the almost unlimited resources of the right—money, magazines, newspaper columns, radio and TV talk shows? My first inclination is to stand with Antonio Gramsci: "Pessimism of the intellect, optimism of the will." However, in this dramatic bicentennial of the first Age of Revolution, I also recall citizen Tom Paine's prophetic words in *The Rights of Man:* "What Archimedes said of the mechanical powers, may be applied to Reason and Liberty: '*Had we,*' said he, '*a place to stand upon, we might raise the world.*'"

25 The Last Intellectuals *or* Teachers for a Democratic Society?*

I MAY BE NAIVE, BUT I assume that most of us took up intellectual labors in the belief that we could thereby contribute to the advancement and enhancement of American culture *and* political life. Didn't we pursue graduate study in hopes that it would better enable us to engage as *citizen-scholars* in the public debates and struggles of the day? And didn't we believe that in alliance with working people and the oppressed we could participate in the making of history, expanding and deepening liberty, equality, and democracy? But, of course, the intervening years have not transpired as we had hoped.

Instigated by a shared apprehension about the struggles of Blacks, students, women, *and* labor, the defining feature of post-1960s American political history was the ascendance of a "New Right" coalition of free marketeers, old-time and neoconservatives, Cold-warriors, and moral majoritarians under the banner of Reagan Republicanism. Expressing the anxieties of the governing class—the fear that a broad alliance for social democracy and racial and gender justice and equality was in the making and promising of even more radical-democratic developments—neoconservative political scientist Samuel Huntington stated in the Trilateral Commission's 1975 report, *The Crisis of Democracy,* that "some of the problems of

* This chapter was first published in the *Review of Education, Pedagogy and Cultural Studies,* vol. 17, no. 1, 1995, as a review of Russell Jacoby's *Dogmatic Wisdom: How the Culture Wars Divert Education and Distract America* (New York, 1994). I have added portions of "The Last Intellectuals or Teachers for a New Society?," which appeared in *In These Times,* October 28, 1992.

governance in the United States today stem from an *'excess of democracy'"* (my italics).[1]

The most immediate threat, according to both the Trilateralists and the emergent leadership of the New Right, was the growing influence of the "adversary culture . . . of the media, foundations, *and universities"* (my italics). Thus, the corporate elites set about establishing new foundations to underwrite a predominantly extra-academic "counter-intelligentsia" to command media attention, reshape the public agenda, *and* marginalize the activities of "the value-oriented intellectuals who often devote themselves to the derogation of leadership, the challenging of authority, and the unmasking and delegitimation of established institutions."[2] The goal was not simply to enfeeble the political and intellectual left; it was to create a new conservative national consensus in favor of capital and the powers that be.

Admittedly, the forces of the New Right have failed to fully accomplish their goals and they may never do so, because for the meantime, at least, a neoliberal Clinton administration holds office. Nevertheless, there is little reason to be joyful. Their campaigns have wrought confusion, disarray, and hardship. By all accounts their policies provided for the rich to grow richer and working people poorer, and our material, social, and moral infrastructures have suffered steady decay.

Moreover, even if they have failed to create a new post-liberal consensus, in one important respect the New Right have succeeded. The (feared) radical-democratic coalition never transpired; in fact, the struggles of the 1960s are fragmented and enervated and political expectations and aspirations are dramatically reduced—not to mention that the political center has shifted to the right and the Clinton administration has yet to show the commitment to working people and the poor that it has shown to the ambitions of multinational capital.

At the same time, the anger and hostilities displayed in the Los Angeles riots/rising in the spring of 1992 and the alienation and dissatisfaction expressed in the course of the '92 election campaigns surely attest, in their respective ways, to a deep crisis in American social and political life.

What is sorely missing is a democratic politics to engage popular frustrations and the awareness of the increasing distance between American ideals and American realities. Sadly, as many of us are all too well aware, the past twenty years also have witnessed the undeniable retreat of the intellectual left. And all fingers seem to point to the academy, to the universities and the professoriate, especially to faculties in the humanities and social sciences, including education.

Commonly referred to as the "culture wars," the New Right's media-grabbing campaigns against higher education and the academic left have taken the form of assaults on teachers in the humanities and social studies, cleverly formulated as "the crisis of history," "the collapse of the canon," "the decline of cultural literacy," "the closing of the American mind," and, most recently, "PC" or "political correctness."[3]

Though not at all to the extent that our critics have asserted, it is true that a generation of New Left scholars has secured itself in colleges and universities with tenure and professorships. Furthermore, having done so according to the traditional rules of the game—arguably, with more verve and imagination than was usually called for—we have achieved positions of some import in our departments and professional associations, critically transforming our respective disciplines in the process by way of opening them to new approaches and subjects.

Unfortunately, whether it has been by necessity or desire, it must be acknowledged that in doing so we have all too often repressed the dream that originally motivated us, that is, of contributing to the popular and democratic struggles of the day. Instead, we have regularly directed our intellectual efforts and agencies to merely scholarly fora and academic politics. As the establishment not long ago of Teachers for a Democratic Culture (TDC) reveals, even when the academic left has aspired to overcome its isolation it often ends up recreating it anew.

The founding of Teachers for a Democratic Culture in the autumn of 1991 would appear to have been a most welcome and timely development.[4] Although the TDC organizers were overwhelmingly from literature departments, the placement of their "manifesto" in newsletters and campus mailboxes across the disciplines promised the making of a broad coalition and its very title (recalling Students for a Democratic Society/SDS) hinted at a new "cultural politics" on the part of the academic left.

The authors of the TDC manifesto commenced by celebrating the growing "diversity" and "democratization" of university classroom and curriculum alike. Acknowledging the outrageous and false accusations being leveled by the New Right and neoconservatives, TDC went on to proclaim that, contrary to the assertions of a "vociferous band of critics," recent "curricular reforms . . . have greatly enriched education rather than corrupted it" and that the controversies related to "admissions and hiring practices, the social functions of teaching and scholarship, and the status of such concepts as objectivity and ideology are signs of educational health, not decline."

The manifesto's authors then proceeded to reveal the "blatant hypocrisy" of the New Right critics in accusing the academic left of "politicizing" and "subverting" academic life even as they themselves have advanced and sought to impose an avowedly conservative political agenda on the humanities and social study. In fact, the authors specifically identified a few of these New Right hypocrites in order to fully reveal the character and extent of their campaigns. They referred first to the corporate-funded, on-campus activists of the National Association of Scholars (NAS) and, then, to the author of *Illiberal Education,* Dinesh D'Souza, as an example of the *extra*-academic "ideologues" recruited and retained by the likes of the neoconservative American Enterprise Institute and the John M. Olin Foundation for the purpose of popularizing the accusations against the academic left;[5] and, finally, illustrating the complicity of the Reagan-Bush administrations, the manifesto's authors highlighted the ambitions of Lynne V. Cheney who, as chair of the National Endowment for the Humanities (NEH), vigorously promoted the

New Right agenda for teaching and research and sought, contra the NEH's Congressional mandate, to pack the National Council on the Humanities with, excuse my putting it this way, "politically correct" conservatives.

The founders of Teachers for a Democratic Culture closed by declaring that the purpose of the organization was to be the defense of "democratic culture, and education" and called for others to join them in their efforts to "refute malicious distortions" and to "educate the interested public about matters that still too often remain shrouded in mystery—new literary theories and movements such as deconstruction, feminism, multi-culturalism, and the new historicism, and their actual effects in classroom practice."

In addressing the *political* character of our antagonists' attacks and calling for actions directed beyond the academic realm, the manifesto of Teachers for a Democratic Culture represented a critical advance beyond the beautifully crafted but academicist defense of the humanities offered in the American Council of Learned Societies' 1988 report, *Speaking for the Humanities.* However, the TDC document was most disappointing.

Although the authors of the TDC manifesto smartly denied that the academic realm stands outside of, and separate from, public culture, they did so not by insisting on the connections between them but, rather, by conflating academic culture with public culture as a whole. In effect, they reduced democratic culture and education to merely academic, indeed, *higher* academic, pursuits and practices: "In our view, a democratic culture . . . is a culture in which terms like 'canon,' 'literature,' 'artistic value,' 'common culture,' and even 'truth' are seen as disputed and not given. This means not that standards for judging art and scholarship must be discarded, but that standards should evolve out of democratic processes in which they can be thoughtfully challenged." Their equation of academic with public culture was also evident in their proposed program of action, which, again, was limited to combating distortions and misrepresentations and educating the interested public about the significance of recent higher academic and theoretical movements.

To be sure, Teachers for a Democratic Culture was to be supported for its commitment to defending the ongoing diversification and democratization of higher education. But, in the end, the organization's conception of democratic culture and education was too limited and too narrow, effectively abandoning the extra-academic public spheres to the New Right politicians and intellectuals. Where in the TDC manifesto was there an appreciation of the fact that the attacks on the humanities and social studies have been bound up with an even grander politics and project of the New Right, threatening not only intellectual and academic life but public culture and debate, indeed, democratic movements and possibilities, more broadly? And where in its program of action was there a recollection of the vision that first drew us to the humanities and social studies, a vision in which our labors were to contribute not simply to the transformation of our respective disciplines but, as part of the democratic struggles of the day, to the formation and re-formation of political and cultural thought and action?

The manifesto of Teachers for a Democratic Culture was an elitist document, not simply because its organizers were faculty from the upper-crust private and public institutions of higher education, but also because its "call to arms" seemed to boil down to protecting academic priorities and privileges. The TDC manifesto registered a narrowing of vision, a lowering of aspirations, and a continuing failure to grasp the challenges before us.

To be clear about it: We do need organizing, but not simply to secure our own academic accomplishments. We need it to work more effectively and more broadly for democratic culture, politics, and social change. To recall the words of the great Jewish sage Hillel: "If I am not for myself, who will be? But if I am only for myself, what am I? If not now, when?"

Of course, criticism of the academic left has emanated not only from the right. While neo- and paleo-conservatives alike have been bewailing the occupation of the academy by "tenured radicals," many of us on the left not only have been wondering what academy they are talking about, but also have been agonizing about our increasingly peripheral status in relation to politics and public life. Indeed, it sometimes seems as if the only evidence we really have of our extra-academic significance are the shots fired against us by the hired-guns of the right.

Whatever our criticisms of it, the work that actually "named" our experience and anxiety—the realization that for all of our radical rhetoric we find ourselves not just marginal to public debate but incapable of addressing the very people whose oppression we claim to understand—was Russell Jacoby's *The Last Intellectuals: American Culture in the Age of Academe.*[6] Previously known for writings in European intellectual history, Jacoby had been teaching part-time (mostly at UCLA) while trying to secure himself as a freelance scholar and writer.[7] Arguably, this experience afforded him a particular view of both higher education and his colleagues on the left (a view described by some as "critical perspective" and, by others, as "crankiness").

In *The Last Intellectuals* Jacoby argued that the decline, or crisis, of American culture was due to the absence of a "class" of public intellectuals contributing to and enriching public life and discourse. In particular, he contended that in contrast to previous generations of young intellects, the 1960s cohort—who had promised to radically reconstruct the American polity and society—had turned their backs on politics and public culture in favor of merely academic pursuits.

The book was not warmly received by its subjects; and, in fact, there were good reasons to be critical.[8] Historically speaking, it is arguable that Jacoby (nostalgically) exaggerated the public presence and influence of earlier generations of American intellectuals. Also, he did not fully appreciate what actually had been accomplished by the academic left. Furthermore, and I think this is crucial, Jacoby did not adequately account the ways in which the corporate-dominated media have actively excluded critical left voices, making our absence from public life seem to be solely of our own doing. Nevertheless, *The Last Intellectuals* was timely and important for, therein, Jacoby pointedly described how an imaginative and politically committed generation of young intellects had participated in its own alienation from public culture and debate. Again, it *named* the problematic of a generation.

Jacoby's new book, *Dogmatic Wisdom,* is also timely, but in a different sort of way. The "culture wars" are already named—indeed, whatever the original challenge, the whole thing is getting rather tiresome and boring (though apparently not to everyone).[9] It is my hope that the timeliness of Jacoby's new book will be that it has offered the *last* words on its subject!

In *Dogmatic Wisdom* Jacoby offers a historically informed and critical discussion of the culture wars in academe.[10] His basic argument is registered in the volume's subtitle, *How the Culture Wars Divert Education and Distract America.* As he explains: "Conservatives protest that education has lost its mind. Radicals respond that it is better than ever. The debate stays within the boundaries of curricula, books, and speech. Both sides suffer nearsightedness." Stated bluntly, the battles being waged are deflecting attention from the grander material and moral crises of American education and society.[11]

Jacoby soberly looks at several of the issues around which the culture wars are conducted, but especially he concerns himself with the battles over liberal arts curricula and canons, and "political correctness" and speech codes. On the former, he observes that the biggest and most publicized debates about courses and syllabi have been staged at the truly elite institutions (the Dukes and Stanfords) and are essentially irrelevant to most campuses because the over-whelming majority of college students are at schools where faculty-student ratios compel large lecture-hall teaching, text-book reading, and multiple-choice testing—that is, forget discussion, forget litera-ture and the classics past and present, and (most definitely) forget essay writing. Moreover, as Jacoby also points out, at most colleges and universities the so-called core curriculum or general education in the liberal arts has for some time been reduced simply to choosing from a "menu," that is, pick what you like from the set categories.

Conservative critics rightly condemn cafeteria-style educa-tion for its lack of intellectual coherence and integrity, but they ignore the real culprit. What is undermining liberal education, Jacoby writes, is not radicalism, but an "illiberal society. . . . An unbridled desire for practical knowledge and good money." In other words, *the market rules*. He adds that, sadly in contrast to contemporary conservatives, earlier conservatives who spoke in defense of the academy at least appreciated the threat to education of "grubby commercialism."

On the subject of "PC" and academic freedom, Jacoby rightly insists that the matter has been blown entirely out of proportion by the right and the media. Conservative claims that leftists are pursuing "McCarthyism" against "politically incorrect" profs are absurd. In the 1940s and 1950s, hundreds of academic leftists lost their jobs for political reasons; conservatives do not suffer so. Looking at the incidents reported by the right, Jacoby observes: "The loss of livelihood eviscerates freedom; and only the obtuse could miss the news that during the late forties and early fifties teachers were losing their jobs. . . . The recent cases belong in another category. . . . Those targeted do not become unemployed . . . cold shoulders, mortifying looks, and nasty comments do not constitute an infringement of academic freedom, much less fascism. . . ."

Noting that the besiegers of academe are richly sponsored by New Right foundations, Jacoby does not fail to make clear that the opposing sides in the academic culture wars are unevenly matched. Radicals may be tenured, but we are neither as well financed nor as well connected to the media as are the public intellectuals of the right. Nevertheless, as Jacoby goes on to illustrate, merely because the right finds the culture wars lucrative does not mean the academic left is innocent of all charges.

Here Jacoby returns to the theme of *The Last Intellectuals,* the retreat of the intellectual left from public life into academe. He repeats his criticisms of the academic left's convoluted and poor prose, especially characteristic of the writings of lit-crit postmodernists and poststructuralists. Such things, he says, were not true of the writings of those figures so admired by the left (Marx, Freud, and—it makes me nauseous to so include him—Nietzsche).

However, the problem is not just the language question, both the jargon and the "linguistic turn" of the postmodernists; the problem is also the "rank careerism," the "celebration of academic hierarchy, professions and success."

To be completely honest, I get a certain pleasure out of Jacoby's criticisms of the elite of the (so-called) academic left. I admit to envying the teaching loads of humanities and social science faculty at the "big-time" schools, their graduate seminars and assistants, high salaries (reportedly well into the six figures), and monopoly of research awards.[12] More important, I am regularly angered by the radical poses and self-serving rhetoric of my truly more affluent colleagues. If nothing else, consider that for all their talk about democracy and culture they fail to address—indeed, they actively avoid—matters of public education and schooling, the domain of public culture most energetically contested by the New Right. If they were sincerely interested in being *public* intellectuals they would start by tearing down the walls that separate them from education faculty and schoolteachers. Meanwhile, curricula and buildings alike disintegrate, public school funding is capped or cut, enrollments rise, and social antagonisms multiply. Enough is enough, it's time we overcame the "last intellectuals" syndrome. Jacoby's new book doesn't tell us what to do, but it should further remind us that we aren't doing what we set out to.

Circumstances demand that we reassert the vision of intellectual life and practice that first engaged our imaginations, aspirations, and commitments. We should begin by recalling the arguments of the late C. Wright Mills in *The Sociological Imagination,* arguments so crucial to the making of the American New Left and which inspired so many of us to social study. Confronting the political and cultural landscapes of the immediate postwar years and recognizing the bankruptcy of both classical liberalism and socialism, Mills challenged the limited conception of democratic public culture then being celebrated and promoted by politicians and pundits alike. For Mills, democratic life should not and must not be construed in terms of the marketplace, that is, reduced to merely "choosing between set alternatives." *Democracy*, he insisted, meant *participating in the formulation of the choices, arguing over them and, then, choosing.*[13] Mills further recognized that the revitalization and continued development of a vibrant democratic civil society and public culture required a vigorous "class" of intellectuals, public intellectuals, whose ambitions were not those of serving as philosopher-kings, nor as advisors to the king—the roles evidently aspired to by the ideologues of the New Right—but of working as citizen-scholars "directing their work *at* kings and *to* publics." And, he added, when such publics appear to be missing, portending the collapse of democracy itself, it becomes the task of the public intellectual to work toward their invigoration. This was the role that he called upon the professoriate to take up, recognizing that in a democracy "liberal education" could not be limited to matters of classroom and curricula: "It is the political task of . . . the liberal educator continually to translate personal troubles into public issues, and public issues into the terms of human meaning for a variety of individuals."

The situation we confront today is not that of three decades ago. Our present economic opportunities are evidently not those of the phenomenal postwar economic boom. Nevertheless, great social and material possibilities present themselves and we are endowed, by experience and scholarship, with the lessons of both the accomplishments and the defeats of our own and earlier struggles for civil, political, and social equality. Indeed, the problem of contemporary American public life is arguably not the absence of "publics" but their particularisms and incoherence, that is, the failure and seeming incapacity of existing movements for social justice and equality to engage each other in public "conversations" in favor of the development of a common agenda for democratic politics and social change. It is here that the critical and democratic intellectual should be working.

We should aspire to make real the possibilities that made our antagonists so anxious—especially, the formation of a broad radical-democratic coalition. Thus, in addition to directing our work ever more smartly and aggressively *at* the powers that be, we must renew our engagements *with* existing publics and agencies—the labor movement, women's and minorities' rights groups, and environmental, community, and religious organizations. We have particular knowledges and skills to proffer. As students of culture and society we are bearers of public histories and we are trained to recover and interpret experiences and texts and to communicate our findings and observations in public words and letters. Our scholarly labors have accomplished much and we have developed valuable understandings and critiques of capitalism and patriarchal and racial oppression. We are capable—or should strive to make ourselves capable—of speaking, writing, and teaching these knowledges and insights in the vernacular and by way of a variety of public media. Such endeavors represent a natural yet critical extension of what we already have been pursuing in our research and teaching.

At the same time, our task requires that we listen to, deliberate with, and learn from those with whom we hope to effect changes. Our ambition should be to articulate in publicly comprehensible terms the experiences and actions, the troubles and concerns, and the hopes and aspirations of the people with whom we are engaged. It is particularly imperative that our involvements be directed to the facilitation of conversations and the creation of solidarities among the respective publics and movements and that we endeavor to elaborate shared priorities, programs, and visions capable of speaking to and securing the commitments of working people, men and women, across the supposed racial and cultural divides.

There are deep fissures in American society, but our historical studies reveal that such divisions are not insurmountable. The most immediate issues and problems around which diverse groups might come together are: securing national health care, guaranteed family incomes, and productive and respectable jobs; increasing public investments in our cultural and material infrastructures, from public schooling and housing to parks, roads, and bridges; and extending and enhancing regional and environmental planning in favor of urban vitality and development.

Addressing the crisis of American public and political life will take more than the assuredly daunting project of seeking to foment the creation of a social-democratic coalition, a "new majority" as the late Michael Harrington put it. Reaffirming the ideals expressed 30 years ago in the Port Huron Statement and the foundation of Students for a Democratic Society (1962), we should strive to revive the American tradition of struggling to refashion and enlarge the concept and realm of democratic *citizenship*. This will entail both continuing the recovery and critical exploration of the varied meanings and makings of democracy past and present and, in light of those explorations, proposing and encouraging the development of new modes of popular political communication, participation, and governance that will extend democratic practices to long-excluded domains such as economic and industrial life. We can argue about the relationship between capitalism and democracy, but they are very much alike in one respect: The well-being of democracy, like that of capitalism, requires democracy's continual growth and development.

"Pessimism of the intellect, optimism of the will," Gramsci would remind us. As intellectuals we must afflict ourselves with the former, as radical democrats we must afflict the powers that be with the latter.

26 Whither America?*

SEEING JOHN SAYLES'S FILM *City of Hope* brought to mind an excursion my father and I had made a few years earlier along the New Jersey side of the Hudson River not far from where I had grown up. He was eager to show me the radical changes under way. And, indeed, replacing the old and deteriorating docks, warehouses, and working-class housing were snazzy high-rise buildings, townhouse developments, and shopping centers—as if a Riviera on the Hudson were being created. Of course, my father well knew the drive would bring out the social(ist) commentary in me and I obliged with remarks about capitalism, Reaganomics and the rich getting richer. He listened, not unappreciatively, but when I finished he observed how "a lot of money was being made . . . by the banks, the developers *and,*" with the emphasis added no doubt to fend off my predictable class analysis, "by the unions, too." I had no intention of fighting. In any case, I really was much too caught up in what I was seeing to offer a good argument, let alone an alternative. I also recall a sense of impotence in the face of the transformative powers of capital, and I wondered to myself, who knows what is to be done?

Knowing that *City of Hope* was set along the same stretch of riverside that my father and I had driven and believing that its theme was the corporate urban renewal that had so mystified me, I was hoping that Sayles had some answers or, at least, some critical insights—especially since he himself had lived in the area for some time (that is, on the Jersey side of the river, in Hoboken, I believe). His previous films had never

---

* This chapter was first published in the *American Historical Review,* vol. 98, no. 4, October 1993, as a review of John Sayles's film *City of Hope* (produced by Sarah Green and Maggie Renzi; written, directed, and edited by John Sayles, 1991). I must thank Robert Rosenstone for commissioning me to write the piece.

afforded easy or comforting conclusions, but a shared characteristic of such otherwise diverse movies as *Lianna* (1983), *Brother from Another Planet* (1984), *Matewan* (1987), and *Eight Men Out* (1988), was that however tragic their tales they had spoken of possibilities. In *Thinking in Pictures: The Making of the Movie "Matewan"* (1987), Sayles himself had written: "If storytelling has a positive function it's to put us in touch with other people's lives, to help us connect and draw strength or knowledge from people we'll never meet, to help us see beyond our own experience." However upset I was to be that it merely renewed my anxieties, *City of Hope* is a stunning film, challenging us to think hard about the long decade of greed.

My father's tour had attended to the new urban landscape and the vistas of Manhattan afforded from the comfort and security of our car. Sayles gets us out of our cars and into the streets of "Hudson City," a city in decline and decay but one already targeted by real estate developers for a revolution from above. *City of Hope* could easily have been conceived as yet another film about corporate ambitions and schemes, directing our attention across the river to the boardrooms and bedrooms of Wall Streeters—and, indeed, the propulsion for much of what transpires is a corporate syndicate's desire to secure a piece of land occupied by a run-down project in which are living poor Black and Hispanic families. But *City of Hope* is not immediately about corporate power and greed; in fact, except for a brief early scene in which the local assistant district attorney—having been promised a "campaign contribution"—assures them that the projects will "come down" on time, there are no Wall Street lawyers in sight. Rather, the film is about the power and accommodations to power of the "lower orders," the local elite and middle and working classes of the city, whose lives—however divided by class and, most especially, by race and ethnicity—are tightly bound up in a system whose most pervasive characteristics are corruption and dishonesty, a political order wherein the "common good" is arrived at when "the deal" is fixed.

City of Hope is actually a collection of deftly woven multi-character stories and entanglements far too numerous and complex to recount. More significant is Sayles's vision of contemporary urban America, which is dark and depressing and made all the more so by the fact that most of the "action"—a bungled robbery, police harassment of young Blacks, a racially motivated mugging, an attack on a Black community center, a torch-job, a protest march on the white politicos' campaign dinner, and a climactic shooting—transpires at night. Watching *City of Hope* I was actually reminded of Dante's *Inferno,* especially those circles of hell where the damned mete out their eternal punishments *to each other.* Sayles himself seems to allude to this at the outset, when he has us descending from the upper floors of a building under construction to the streets of Hudson City below. I can easily imagine a sign being posted at ground level: "Abandon All Hope Ye Who Enter Here" (Canto III).

Almost everyone in Hudson City is out to get something— more, ahead, or out—from you, for you, or on you; ambitions and aspirations made all the more urgent by the sense that you'd better move fast or you'll be swept under or aside when the developers take over. An arson fire takes the lives of a young mother and baby because no one knew they were squatting in the abandoned section of a building that was torched. As Baci, the mayor, explains to Joe Rinaldi, the owner of the apartments which had to "come down" (when confronted by Joe following the arson that Joe himself agreed to have carried out in order to get his son, Nick, off a robbery charge): "Accidents happen. . . . Those are the kinds of people accidents happen to. . . . Next couple of years this town is going to be one big yard sale and anyone with half a brain will make tracks and let the Blacks and Hispanics duke it out for whatever is left." Thus, Sayles captures the urban policies—nay, the entire culture and political economy—of the Reagan and Bush administrations (the consequences of which we now can recognize in South Central and Crown Heights).

No one stands fully outside the system. Even those who seek improvements and see themselves as battling the corruption discover that they are already implicated in it and must accept it, work the fix, and hope to accomplish something before it catches up with them.

Wynn, the Black city councilor pursuing reform, learns that, to effectively mobilize the anger of the Black and Hispanic "communities" against the Baci political machine, he has to compromise his own values and ideals. He is persuaded to do so by Errol, the Black former mayor forced to retire under threat of criminal prosecution. Errol, whose advice Wynn has sought, informs him that he himself had benefited from Errol's administrative "practices." Ultimately, Errol counsels—while lining up a shot on an otherwise "White" country club golf course—if you want to "help your people," the best you can do is "lie and hope for twelve good years."

Presenting us with a polity characterized by graft and demagoguery, a civil society reduced to tribalism, an economy in which the organization of the working class is bought off and racist, and a popular culture in which the rebelliousness of youth is vented in drugs, crime, and racially motivated assaults, does Sayles afford us any hope things could be made different? My father would have said that at least the developers were creating something new and surely preferable to the Hudson City revealed by Sayles—and, to be clear about it, there is no nostalgia, no lamenting the passing of the old in *City of Hope*. Perhaps I exaggerate, for once again Sayles grants us moments in which we can recognize possibilities, that there might yet be some way out of the inferno, not only individually but collectively. But such moments are few.

Consider what Sayles leaves us with: It is night again. Anxiously searching for his son, Joe Rinaldi finds Nick on one of the unenclosed upper floors of the original construction site. They talk, acknowledging their shared guilt for the fire at the apartments. Joe then sees that his son is seriously wounded. Promising not to leave him, he runs to the edge of the building and begins shouting for help. The only response comes from a deranged character in the street below shouting back up to him, "Help! Help! We need help!"

Being a romantic, I would have preferred a call for struggle, not aid. Nevertheless, *City of Hope* poses the essential historical question, Whither America?

27 The New American Crisis*

These are the times that try men's souls. The summer soldier and the sunshine patriot will, in this crisis, shrink from the service of their country; but he that stands it now, deserves the love and thanks of man and woman. Tyranny, like hell, is not easily conquered; yet we have this consolation with us, that the harder the conflict, the more glorious the triumph.

SO WROTE TOM PAINE in December 1776. Not even a year had passed since he had penned *Common Sense,* brashly announcing that "We have it in our power to begin the world over again" and effectively transforming the rambunctious and rebellious political sentiment of colonial America into a struggle for national independence. And it had been only several months since the democratic ideals he had begun to articulate were translated into the Declaration of Independence, the first modern revolutionary manifesto asserting the essential equality of humanity and a people's right to self-determination and "life, liberty, and the pursuit of happiness."

Now, however, with winter taking hold, the Revolution seemed to be in full retreat on the battlefield and doomed to collapse. Nevertheless, Paine would not surrender to despair. Hoping to re-energize the cause and further mobilize his fellow citizens-in-the-making against British imperialism and its Tory supporters, he set himself to producing a new series of pamphlets, to be known as *The*

---

* This chapter was originally written (in a somewhat longer version) as the Introduction to Greg Ruggiero and Stuart Sahulka, eds., *The New American Crisis: The Open Magazine Pamphlet Series Anthology, Volume 2* (New York: The New Press, 1996).

American Crisis. Seven years later, after many a campaign military, political, and ideological, independence was won.

But, of course, the struggle for freedom, equality and democracy in America had only begun. Generations of Americans were to find themselves confronting the power and ambitions of the propertied and the privileged, who have always been ready to declare the Revolution over and eager to get on with the business of the day. Yet, as much as the power elites past and present would attempt to declaim otherwise, the promise and possibility of America was neither inscribed nor to be comprehended in finite terms.

There is no evading the tragic character of the American experience: the genocidal treatment of native peoples; the slave trade and the slave regime; the repeated exploitation of immigrants young and old; the corporate devastation of working-class communities and the environment; imperial interventions and the suppression of popular revolutions abroad; persistent oppressions of class, race, ethnicity, and gender; and so on.

Yet, the exploitation, inequality, and injustice have not gone unchallenged. America's revolutionary foundations empowered a radical tradition that has made the nation's history—however contradictory, tragic or ironic the record—a narrative of the struggle, more often progressive than not, to expand both the "we" in "We, the People" and the process by which "the people" can genuinely govern.

From the outset, family farmers contested governments dominated by gentry landowners and urban financial and mercantile interests, and radical artisans and industrial mechanics—Tom Paine's own ilk—organized Workingmen's parties in efforts to control both their own labor and those who would govern them. These may read like experiences of defeat, but they clearly registered that America's working people were prepared to continue the fight to secure and defend their democratic rights—even if it now meant battling their fellow citizens.

In the southern states, African American men and women resisted and, occasionally, in the face of overwhelming odds, rebelled against a social order that sought to reduce them to being merely the property of their masters. In the process, they undermined the regime that held them in bondage and crafted cultural practices and institutions that have not only enabled them to endure and pursue a long and continuing struggle for justice and equality, but that also have deeply enriched other movements for freedom in America and the rest of the world.

In 1848 American women and a smaller number of men, many of whom were veterans of the ongoing anti-slavery movement (including the great African American orator and abolitionist Frederick Douglass), met in Seneca Falls, New York, for the first-ever women's rights convention. Composing their manifesto in the very language of the Declaration of Independence, the conventioneers proclaimed the equality of men and women and demanded that women be secured with the very same rights that male citizens possessed. The Women's Suffrage Amendment entered the Constitution seventy years later; though here, too, securing the franchise, however long the conflict and fundamental the right, was merely the first of many contests for gender equality.

The prophetic memory of America's promise and possibility and the struggle for liberty, equality, and democracy were refreshed again and again both by native-born and immigrant generations of radicals—agrarianists, populists, laborists, feminists, socialists, anarchists, pacifists, environmentalists, and campaigners for the civil and social rights of minorities.

The struggle continues and, once again, as so many times before, "These are the times that try men's [and women's] souls."

Reaganism, as the new political and economic regime of the 1980s came to be called, was pursued under the pretense of restoring America's greatness, industrial robustness, and military prowess, and redeeming the supposedly traditional values of family, law and order, and the work ethic. However, behind a rhetoric of patriotism and shared values, Reaganism inaugurated a period of blatant greed and profiteering in which the American economy was further deindustrialized and corporate capital was empowered to intensify its ongoing assault on organized labor. Also, it instituted a policy of "military Keynesianism" in which tax rates for the upper classes were cut and domestic programs were further defunded while billions of dollars more were spent on the military in pursuit of a second Cold War—thereby providing for the further decay of the country's infrastructure and for the streets and alleyways of America's cities to become home to hundreds of thousands of the nation's citizens young and old. As economists Samuel Bowles, David Gordon, and Thomas Weisskopf have accounted in the *Nation*, American life in the 1980s was increasingly shaped by a "garrison imperative"; within and without the workplace, Americans were to an ever greater degree being supervised and secured by "guard labor" and "threat labor."

If these acts, and the hardship and despoliation they wrought, were themselves not enough to warrant criminal charges, elements within and without the Reagan administration proceeded to aid state and guerrilla terrorism in Central America and to conspire against constitutional government in the Iran-contra affair.

At the same time, the New Right politicos were determined to drive from the public arena the surviving remnants of the New Left of the 1960s *and* to fabricate a new post-liberal conservative political hegemony. Cultural and ideological campaigns against liberals and progressives alike were enthusiastically pursued by Republican office-holders from their bully-pulpits, and their attacks were broadcast ever more widely by growing numbers of right-wing radio talk show hosts (the champion among them, Rush Limbaugh, even garnered a late-night television slot).

Portraying everyone from "unionized schoolteachers" and "leftist and feminist college professors" to "single-mothers on AFDC [Aid to Families with Dependent Children]" as somehow subversive of American life, the New Right has made public education and social welfare the major targets of its ideological "culture wars" and it has succeeded in shaping the public discourse on those subjects.

Sadly, the prominence of the right has been further enhanced by the apparent retreat of the political and intellectual left. The Democrats, the so-called "people's party," offered limited opposition and, even more often, deferred to the political-economic agenda of Reaganism. The more progressive segments of the political left, which, unfortunately, had failed to create the fearfully imagined radical-democratic coalition, have been marked by division and feebleness in the face of the conservatives' political juggernaut. And—to the extent that it was not completely due to decisions made by corporate media executives and producers—the intellectual left contributed to its own marginalization from public debate by transforming itself into an "academic left" and becoming self-absorbed in scholarly debates, debates made all the more incomprehensible, politically irrelevant, and (rightly) subject to ridicule by the importance given to the ideas and language of postmodernism and poststructuralism.

Moreover, the corporate news media regularly treated the Republican presidential victories as prime indicators that a conservative consensus was actually taking hold across the country, thereby reinforcing the New Right politicians' claims to possession of a mandate for their plans and projects.

The apparent defeat of the left in all its varieties *and* the concurrent dissolution of the Soviet empire and closing of the Cold War signaled the *global* triumph of capital. Thus, the intellectuals of the New Right proceeded to do what the agents of ruling classes have always been wont to do. They announced the "end of history," informing us that radical-democratic possibilities are finished, that the further progress and development of liberty and equality is foreclosed, forever. In fact, seeking to counter the widely held democratic assumption that progressive public action can decrease class and racial inequalities, certain elements of the New Right intelligentsia under the guise of social science have attempted to resurrect the old deterministic ideology of class, race and ethnicity-based "intelligence" differences. (I refer especially to the highly promoted 1994 book *The Bell Curve* by Charles Murray and Richard Herrnstein).

The powers that be may be keen to declare victory, but they are well aware—far more so, it often seems, than those of us constituting the intellectual left—that the struggle for liberty, equality, and democracy is not exhausted. The persistence of exploitation and oppression continues to generate social antagonisms and conflict, and America's radical traditions and historical ideals stand in inspiring contrast to the reality of contemporary experience. Indeed, however quiescent the people may seem, the majority of Americans are unpersuaded that the democratic promise and possibility of America is fulfilled. They remain anxious about the future, wary of their governing elites, committed to the values of social justice and equality and, even, prepared to support public action to address the nation's economic and social problems. The powerful realize these things.

Nevertheless, lacking a serious and organized opposition capable of presenting a truly alternative and comprehensive radical-democratic vision and project, the American people continue to be weighed down in cynicism and despair, expressing their anxieties and aspirations in ways ranging from the determined passivity of refusing to vote or get involved in any fashion whatsoever, to the willful naiveté supporting eccentric and demagogic populisms such as Ross Perot's 1992 presidential campaign and the Republican Party's 1994 "Contract with America."

For a brief moment it did seem that the politics of progressivism might be returned to the public political agenda. While "New Democrat" Bill Clinton never pretended to be a radical or, for that matter, even an old-style liberal, in the 1992 elections he did succeed in defeating the conservative Republican candidate and incumbent president, George Bush, by issuing a call for "change" and running on a platform that promised, for starters: a reduction in the military budget in favor of rebuilding the nation's infrastructure, from highways and bridges to housing and public schools; the establishment of a national, universal healthcare system; and the recommitment of the federal government to efforts to both ensure and extend the civil and social rights of all citizens. But, as we know, the only major changes legislated were the NAFTA (North American Free Trade Agreement) and GATT (General Agreement on Tariffs and Trade) pacts so ardently sought by multinational capital.

Admittedly, the Clinton administration did attempt the enactment of the more popularly aspired-to initiatives. However, in the absence of coherent and engaged political agencies pressuring from the left, retreat, compromise, and/or collapse became the orders of the day. Perhaps this was to be expected, for there was little chance that Clinton and his cohort were themselves going to mobilize the popular support necessary to confront the handsomely endowed forces of conservatism and reaction.

Undeniably, the struggle for liberty, equality, and democracy is in retreat and we face a crisis of dramatic proportions, for Clinton's failures have actually intensified the sense of disappointment and betrayal felt by those very social groups traditionally supportive of a progressive politics. Not only right-wing columnists are composing the obituaries for radical-democratic politics in America. In the wake of the 1994 congressional elections, there are also progressives writing of "The Death of the Left."

Nevertheless, I think we would do better to recall again the words of Tom Paine in the face of the revolutionary crisis of the winter of 1776—and, also, to remember and retell how, through the agency of generations of working men and women, American democracy has been extended and deepened and can be further still.

To be sure, there are no guarantees. However antithetical are capitalism and democracy—and however assured I am that struggles for the latter will continue to assert themselves against property, privilege, and the imperatives of the market—I make no assumptions about either immediate successes or ultimate triumphs. We have a long way to go, but we have so much on which to build. One thing I do know is that if we are to redeem the prophetic memory of America's promise and possibility and revive a truly progressive politics, we will need critical and radical voices, veteran and original, capable both of articulating the diverse needs and aspirations of working people and the oppressed and of cultivating visions and projects engaging of their consciousness and commitment.

NOTES

Chapter 1

1. Daniel Singer, "Armed with a Pen—Notes for a Political Portrait of Isaac Deutscher," in D. Horowitz, ed., *Isaac Deutscher, The Man and His Work* (London, 1971), 20.

2. E. H. Carr, Introduction to *Heretics and Renegades* (Orig. 1955; London, 1969 new ed.). Also, on Deutscher's life and work, see Tamara Deutscher, "Introduction: The Education of a Jewish Child," in Isaac Deutscher, *The Non-Jewish Jew and Other Essays* (New York, 1968), 1-24; and "On the Bibliography of Isaac Deutscher's Work" in *Isaac Deutscher, The Man and His Work*, 226-35.

3. Isaac Deutscher, *The Prophet Armed, Trotsky: 1879-1921* (New York, 1954); *The Prophet Unarmed, Trotsky: 1921-1929* (New York, 1959); and *The Prophet Outcast, Trotsky: 1929-1940* (New York, 1963). Also, we should note Deutscher's first book, *Stalin: A Political Biography* (New York, 1949); and his many other works and collections of essays and lectures, including, *Ironies of History: Essays on Contemporary Communism* (New York, 1996); *The Unfinished Revolution, Russia 1917-1967* (New York, 1967); *The Non-Jewish Jew and Other Essays*; *Russia, China and the West: A Contemporary Chronicle* (New York, 1970); and *Marxism, Wars and Revolution* (London, 1984).

4. Noted in David Horowitz's Introduction to *Isaac Deutscher, The Man and His Work*, 13-14.

5. C. Wright Mills, *The Marxists* (London, 1962), 97; Lee Baxandall, "New York Meets Oshkosh," in Paul Buhle, ed., *History and the New Left: Madison, Wisconsin, 1950-1970* (Philadelphia, 1990), 129.

6. We will not hold it against Deutscher's memory that among his leading admirers was the onetime American radical, David Horowitz, who— even as he offers apologetic reflections for his youthful leftist activism— proudly recalls that when he moved to London in the mid-1960s he made himself a devoted student of Isaac, "the perfect mentor, fully aware of the dark realities of the revolutionary past but still believing in the revolutionary idea." See D. Horowitz, "Letter to a Political Friend," Chapter 10 in Peter Collier and David Horowitz, *Destructive Generation: Second Thoughts About the '60s* (New York, 1989), 318.

7. Mervyn Jones, *Chances* (London, 1987), 206-7; Perry Anderson, "The Legacy of Isaac Deutscher," in *A Zone of Engagement* (London, 1992), 56-75.

8. Tariq Ali, *Street-Fighting Years* (London, 1987), 119-22.

9. Singer, "Armed with a Pen," 33.

Chapter 2

1. Francis Fukuyama, *The End of History and the Last Man* (New York, 1992). For a discussion of such notions see Lutz Niethammer, *Posthistoire: Has History Come to an End?*, translated by Patrick Camiller (London, 1992).

2. Edward Lutwak's remarks were in "Fascism As the Wave of the Future," *London Review of Books*, April 7, 1994.

3. Isaac Deutscher, *Heretics and Renegades* (New York, 1969), 7.

4. Howard Zinn, *Declarations of Independence: Cross-Examining American Ideology* (New York, 1990), 294.

5. Shim Jae Hoon, "A Rebel with a Cause Pays the Price for Dissent," *Far Eastern Economic Review*, July 10, 1986.

6. Jawaharlal Nehru, *Glimpses of World History* (Oxford, 1989 Centenary Edition); E. H. Carr, *What is History?* (New York, 1962).

7. Carr, *What is History?*, 207.

8. I should add here that the closing paragraphs of the magazine article indicate that while in prison Yu was expelled from the university once again and on his release he turned to translating and proofreading to make a living. He also became active in an organization for the families of political prisoners. Also, I must state clearly that in telling this particular story, I mean no disrespect to writers of fiction. The banning of their works and the attacks and imprisonments suffered by so many of their calling offer more than ample testimony to their ability to incite fear in the hearts of the powerful.

9. Plato, *Republic*, translated by Robin Waterfield (Oxford, 1994), 116.

10. J. H. Plumb, *The Death of the Past* (New York, 1969), 40.

11. Deborah Lipstadt, *Denying the Holocaust: The Growing Assault on Truth and Memory* (New York, 1993); Paul Hockenos, *Free to Hate: The Rise of the Right in Post-Communist Eastern Europe* (New York, 1993).

12. David Remnick, *Lenin's Tomb* (New York, 1993), 4.

13. Isaac Deutscher, *The Prophet Unarmed, Trotsky: 1921-1929* (New York, 1959), 155-160, and *The Prophet Outcast, Trotsky: 1929-1940* (New York, 1963), 168-171, 377ff; *The Unfinished Revolution, Russia 1917-1967* (New York, 1967), 102-115.

14. See Remnick, *Lenin's Tomb* and R. W. Davies, *Soviet History in the Gorbachev Revolution* (London, 1989).

15. On these developments see the double issue of *Across Frontiers*, nos. 4/5 (winter-spring 1989).

16. Milan Kundera, *The Book of Laughter and Forgetting* (New York, 1978), 3.

17. Jonathan Unger, Introduction to Unger, ed., *Using the Past to Serve the Present: Historiography and Politics in Contemporary China* (New York, 1993), 2-3.

18. See Ian Buruma, *The Wages of Guilt: Memories of War in Germany and Japan* (New York, 1994).

19. See Henry Rousso, *The Vichy Syndrome*, translated by Arthur Goldhammer (New York, 1991).

20. Frances Fitzgerald, *America Revised* (New York, 1980).

21. See Godfrey Hodgson, *America in Our Time* (New York, 1978), especially 67-99.

22. See Barbara Ehrenreich, *Fear of Falling* (New York, 1989), especially chapter 3, "The Discovery of the Working Class," 97-143.

23. Michael Crozier, Samuel P. Huntington, and Joji Watanuki, *Crisis of Democracy: Report on the Governability of Democracies to the Trilateral Commission* (New York, 1975), 6-7, 9, 113-15.

24. See Harvey J. Kaye, *The Powers of the Past: Reflections on the Crisis and the Promise of History* (Minneapolis, 1991).

25. Kundera, *The Book of Laughter and Forgetting*, 22.

26. Boris Kagarlitsky, *The Thinking Reed* (London, 1988), 105.

27. Raymond Williams, *The Long Revolution* (London, 1961).

28. Ronald Aronson, *The Dialectics of Disaster* (London, 1983), 301-2.

29. John Dunn, in Conclusion to Dunn, ed., *Democracy, The Unfinished Journey* (Oxford, 1992), 239.

30. Antonio Gramsci, *Letters from Prison*, translated by Lynne Lawner (New York, 1973), 273.

31. Howard Zinn, *Failure to Quit: Reflections of an Optimistic Historian* (Monroe, Maine, 1993), 157.

32. V. G. Kiernan, "Socialism, the Prophetic Memory," in H. J. Kaye, ed., *Poets, Politics and the People: Selected Writings of V. G. Kiernan* (London, 1989), 204-28.

33. Antonio Gramsci, *Selections from the Prison Notebooks*, edited and translated by Q. Hoare and G. Nowell Smith (New York, 1971), 34-35.

34. Joel Kovel, *Red Hunting in the Promised Land* (New York, 1993), 243.

35. Isaac Deutscher, *The Unfinished Revolution, Russia 1917-1967* (Oxford, 1967), 114.

Chapter 6

1. John Berger, *Ways of Seeing* (London, 1972), 33.

2. Walter Benjamin, "The Storyteller," in *Illuminations,* edited and introduced by Hannah Arendt (New York, 1969), 83-110.

3. Walter Benjamin, "Theses on the Philosophy of History," in *Illuminations,* 255-66.

4. John Berger, "Uses of Photography" (1978) in *About Looking* (New York, 1980), 48-63; and, with Jean Mohr, *Another Way of Telling* (New York, 1982). Also, see Harvey J. Kaye, *The Education of Desire: Marxists and the Writing of History* (New York, 1992), Chapter 7, "John Berger and the Question of History."

5. Berger, "Uses of Photography," 56, 58-63.

6. Hermione Harris, "Nicaragua: Two Years of Revolution," *Race and Class,* vol. 23, no. 1 (1981), 4.

7. Harald Jung, "The Fall of Somoza: Behind the Nicaraguan Revolution," *New Left Review,* no. 117 (September/October 1979), 69-89.

8. John Berger, *Art and Revolution* (New York, 1969), 131.

9. Ibid., 131.

10. Alejo Carpentier, *Reasons of State,* translated by Frances Patridge (London, 1976), 85.

11. Jung, "The Fall of Somoza," 84-89.

12. Diego Arenas Guzman, *La Revolución Mexicana—eslabones de un tiempo histórico* (Mexico, 1969).

Chapter 8

1. Frances Fitzgerald, *Fire in the Lake* (New York, 1973), 9. Compare her early 1970s observation with her remarks in *America Revised* (New York, 1980).

2. I have discussed this in a book-length work, *The Powers of the Past: Reflections on The Crisis and the Promise of History* (Minneapolis, 1991).

3. See Eric Foner, ed., *The New American History* (Philadelphia, 1990).

4. On the crisis of history and the use and abuse of the past in the politics of Reaganism and the New Right, see Kaye, *The Powers of the Past.* For rather different views of the crisis and "what is to be done," see Arthur M. Schlesinger, *The Disuniting of America: Reflections on a Multicultural Society* (New York, 1992—originally a Whittle book!) and Peter

Stearns, *Meaning Over Memory: Recasting the Teaching of Culture and History* (Chapel Hill, 1993).

5. For outstanding examples of such work see Susan Porter Benson, Stephen Brier and Roy Rosenzweig, eds., *Presenting the Past* (Philadelphia, 1986); Warren Leon and Roy Rosenzweig, eds., *History Museums in the United States: A Critical Assessment* (Urbana, 1989); the special issue of the *Journal of American History* 75 (March 1989), on *Memory and American History*; David Glassberg, *American Historical Pageantry: The Uses of Tradition in the Early Twentieth Century* (Chapel Hill, 1990); and John Bodnar, *Remaking America: Public Memory, Commemoration and Patriotism in the Twentieth Century* (Princeton, 1992).

6. Note should also be made of Michael Kammen's related volume, *Meadows of Memory: Images of Time and Tradition in American Art and Culture* (Austin, 1992). Kammen's many important contributions to American cultural history are well known through books such as: the Pulitzer Prize winner *People of Paradox* (New York, 1972); *A Season of Youth: The American Revolution and the Historical Imagination* (New York, 1978); *A Machine That Would Go of Itself* (New York, 1986); and *Selvages and Biases: The Fabric of History in American Culture* (New York, 1987).

7. Kammen's interest in American "difference" was recently expressed in the essay, "The Problem of American Exceptionalism," *American Quarterly* 45 (March 1993), 1-43.

8. Antonio Gramsci, *Selections from the Prison Notebooks,* edited and translated by Q. Hoare and G. Nowell Smith (London, 1971), 161.

Chapter 9

1. See the book version of "the Contract" with additional remarks by Newt Gingrich: Ed Gillespie and Bob Schellhas, eds., *Contract with America* (New York, 1994). Also, see the ensuing "contract" put out by the right-wing Christian Coalition under the leadership of Ralph Reed: *Contract with the American Family* (New York, 1995).

2. See the discussions of the National Standards in History project in chapters 16 and 17. For a comprehensive examination of the "crisis of history and historical education," see my earlier book, *The Powers of the Past* (Minneapolis, 1991).

3. On the controversy, see Mike Wallace, "The Battle of the Enola Gay," *Radical Historians Newsletter*, no. 72 (May 1995), 1-32.

4. See Rush Limbaugh, *The Way Things Ought To Be* (New York, 1992) and *See, I Told You So* (New York, 1994 edition).

5. Newt Gingrich, *To Renew America* (New York, 1995). Also, with William R. Forstchen, Gingrich has co-authored a novel of "alternative history," that is, "what if?" history, titled *1945* (New York, 1995).

6. Arnold Toynbee, *A Study of History* (originally 12 vols., London, 1934-61); Isaac Asimov, *Foundation, Foundation and Empire,* and *Second Foundation* (New York, 1951-53); and Alvin Toffler, *Future Shock* (New York, 1970).

Chapter 12

1. See Paul Buhle and Alan Dawley, eds., *Working for Democracy* (Urbana, IL, 1985) and Mari Jo Buhle, Paul Buhle, and Harvey J. Kaye, eds., *The American Radical* (New York, 1994).

2. See Sidney Blumenthal, *The Rise of the Counter-Establishment* (New York, 1986) and Jerome Himmelstein, *To the Right: The Transformation of American Conservatism* (Berkeley, CA, 1990).

3. See Kevin Phillips, *The Politics of Rich and Poor* (New York, 1990) and Philip Mattera, *Prosperity Lost* (New York, 1990).

4. Mattera, *Prosperity Lost,* 187.

5. Francis Fukuyama, "The End of History?," *The National Interest,* no. 16 (summer 1989), 3-18.

6. See William J. Bennett, *Our Children and Our Country* (New York, 1988), Alan Bloom, *The Closing of the American Mind* (New York, 1987), and E. D. Hirsch, *Cultural Literacy* (Boston, 1987).

7. Benjamin Barber, "Cultural Conservatism and Democratic Education: Lessons from the Sixties," *Salmagundi*, no. 81 (winter 1989), 159-73.
8. Antonio Gramsci, *Selections from the Prison Notebooks*, edited and translated by Q. Hoare and G. Novell Smith (New York, 1971), 40.
9. See the closing chapter of Harvey J. Kaye, *The Powers of the Past: Reflections on the Crisis and Promise of History* (Minneapolis, 1991).
10. Antonio Gramsci, *Selections from the Prison Notebooks*, 40.

Chapter 13

1. For example, see Russell Jacoby, *The Last Intellectuals* (New York, 1987); Jim Merod, *The Political Responsibility of the Intellectual* (Ithaca, N.Y., 1987); Michael Walzer, *Interpretation and Social Criticism* (Cambridge, Mass., 1987) and *The Company of Critics* (New York, 1988); and Norman Birnbaum, *Radical Renewal* (New York, 1988).
2. Amy Gutmann, *Democratic Education* (Princeton, 1987); Ira Katznelson and Margaret Weir, *Schooling for All*, rev. ed. (Berkeley, 1985).
3. Henry A. Giroux, *Ideology, Culture and the Process of Schooling* (Philadelphia, 1981); *Theory and Resistance in Education* (South Hadley, Mass., 1984); with Stanley Aronowitz, *Education Under Siege* (South Hadley, Mass., 1985); and *Teachers as Intellectuals* (South Hadley, Mass., 1988).
4. See Harvey J. Kaye, *The Powers of the Past: Reflections on the Crisis and Promise of History* (Minneapolis, 1991).
5. Michael Walzer, *Interpretation and Social Criticism*, 22.
6. Walter Benjamin, "Theses on the Philosophy of History" in *Illuminations* (New York, 1968), 257. On "history from the bottom up," see Harvey J. Kaye, *The British Marxist Historians* (New York, 1995) and *The Education of Desire: Marxists and the Writing of History* (New York, 1992).
7. Benjamin, "Theses on the Philosophy of History," 256. It may be unorthodox to have done so, but in reading *Schooling* I was compelled to contact Giroux on this point and out of our argument/dialogue

arose a co-authored essay, "The Liberal Arts Must Be Reformed to Serve Democratic Ends" which appeared in the *Chronicle of Higher Education,* March 29, 1989 (and is included in this volume, chapter 15). I make no apologies, for I believe serious intellectual and political development requires such contact.

8. William J. Bennett, *Our Children and Our Country* (New York, 1988); Allan Bloom, *The Closing of the American Mind* (Chicago, 1987).
9. See Ellen Meiksins Wood, *The Retreat from Class* (London, 1985).

Chapter 14

1. Jonathan Kozol, *Savage Inequalities* (New York, 1991).
2. Allan Bloom, *The Closing of the American Mind* (New York, 1987); Roger Kimball, *Tenured Radicals* (New York, 1990); Charles J. Sykes, *Profscam* (New York, 1990); Dinesh D'Souza, *Illiberal Education* (New York, 1987); William J. Bennett, *Our Children and Our Country* (New York, 1988); Chester Finn, *We Must Take Charge* (New York, 1991); Rita Kramer, *Ed School Follies* (New York, 1991); and Martin Anderson, *Impostors in the Temple* (New York, 1992).
3. Benjamin R. Barber, *Strong Democracy* (New York, 1984) and, with Patrick Watson, *The Struggle for Democracy* (New York, 1989—a coffeetable-sized book to accompany the public-television series also titled *The Struggle for Democracy*).

Chapter 17

1. *National Standards for History* (UCLA National Center for History in the Schools, 1994).
2. In the same ironic vein, the British National Curriculum for History also turned out to be not exactly what Thatcher and the Tories had

hoped to implement. See the *National Curriculum History Working Group: Final Report* (London, April 1990).

3. For example, see Lynne Cheney's op-ed piece, "Mocking America at U.S. Expense," *New York Times*, March 10, 1995, A15.

4. See Harvey J. Kaye, *The Powers of the Past: Reflections on the Crisis and the Promise of History* (Minneapolis, 1991).

5. The National Center for History in the Schools at UCLA, *Lessons from History: Essential Understandings and Historical Perspectives Students Should Acquire*, edited by Charlotte Crabtree, et al. (University of California–Los Angeles and the National Endowment for the Humanities, 1992).

6. See chapter 16, "The Ends of History?," in this work, for my commentary addressing the establishment of the National Standards for History project that originally appeared in *Education Week*, February 5, 1992.

7. Numerous and diverse organizations in addition to the NEH contributed to the project, and along with those of the OAH (Organization of American Historians) and AHA (American Historical Association), focus groups were convened by the Council of Chief State School Officers, the Association for Supervision and Curriculum Development, the National Council for Social Studies, the Council of State Social Studies Specialists, the National Council for History Education, and the Organization of History Teachers. For a list of "Contributors and Participating Organizations," see the Appendix to *National Standards for United States History* (261-71).

8. My comments throughout this section draw on the *OAH Focus Group Report* (May 14, 1992) prepared by the Chair of the OAH Educational Policy Committee, Professor Bertram Wyatt-Brown, and submitted to the OAH. The report included the notes of the respective members of the group. Nevertheless, the interpretations offered are strictly my own.

9. In particular, see Gertrude Himmelfarb, *The New History and the Old* (Cambridge, 1987).

10. For example, in *Lessons from History* (UCLA National Center for History in the Schools, 1992) see 90, 117, 124.

11. Hereafter, I will refer to the volume, *National Standards for United States History*, as *National Standards*.

12. *Work in America: Report of a Special Task Force to the Secretary of Health, Education, and Welfare* (Cambridge, 1973). Also, see Barbara Ehrenreich, *Fear of Falling* (New York, 1989), 120-21.

· **Chapter 19**

1. Mari Jo Buhle, Paul Buhle, and Harvey J. Kaye, eds., *The American Radical* (New York, 1994); the book series I am editing with Elliott J. Gorn is *American Radicals* (New York, Routledge). The first two volumes—on democratic socialist Michael Harrington and radical historian William Appleman Williams, respectively—were published in the fall of 1995.

2. For example, see Harvey J. Kaye, *The British Marxist Historians* (New York, 1995) and *The Education of Desire: Marxists and the Writing of History* (New York, 1993).

3. MARHO (Mid-Atlantic Radical Historians Organization), "A Draft Statement of Principles" (1974), reprinted in the *Journal of American History*, vol. 76, no. 2 (September 1989), 487-88.

4. Harvey J. Kaye, *The Powers of the Past: Reflections on the Crisis and Promise of History* (Minneapolis, 1991).

5. For the record, although Mari Jo Buhle, Paul Buhle and, separately, Elliott Gorn may be responsible for a lot of my thinking, they are not to be held accountable for anything I say.

6. Richard Rorty, "The Unpatriotic Academy," the *Sunday New York Times*, February 13, 1994, E15.

7. Arthur M. Schlesinger, Jr., *The Disuniting of America: Reflections on a Multicultural Society* (New York, 1992).

8. Charles A. Madison, *Critics and Crusaders: A Century of American Protest* (New York, 1947); Harvey Goldberg, ed., *American Radicals: Some Problems and Personalities* (New York, 1957).

9. Obviously, the figures noted in the parentheses do not represent the full contents of the book. Also, it should be recognized that the struggles of these radicals were by no means limited to the "causes"

alongside which their names are cited (for example, Emma Goldman's politics were not only feminist, but also anarchist; W. E. B. Du Bois was a socialist *and* a campaigner for racial justice and equality; Abbie Hoffman's radical career included anti-war *and* environmental activism, and so on).

10. Marc Bloch, *Strange Defeat: A Statement of Evidence Written in 1940,* translated by Gerard Hopkins (Oxford, 1949), 173.

11. The National Center for History in the Schools at UCLA, *Lessons From History: Essential Understandings and Historical Perspectives Students Should Acquire,* edited by Charlotte Crabtree, et al. (University of California–Los Angeles and the National Endowment for the Humanities, 1992).

Chapter 22

1. C. Wright Mills, *The Sociological Imagination* (New York, 1959).

2. C. Wright Mills, *The Power Elite* (New York, 1956). Also, see C. Wright Mills, *Power, Politics and the People: The Collected Essays of C. Wright Mills,* edited with an introduction by Irving Louis Horowitz (New York, 1963); *The New Men of Power* (New York, 1948); and *White Collar: The American Middle Classes* (New York, 1951).

3. See note 2 for reference to the essay collection, and Irving Louis Horowitz, *C. Wright Mills: An American Utopian* (New York, 1983).

4. Hans Gerth and C. Wright Mills, eds., *From Max Weber: Essays in Sociology* (New York, 1946); C. Wright Mills, *The Marxists* (New York, 1962).

5. Barrington Moore, Jr., *Social Origins of Dictatorship and Democracy: Lord and Peasant in the Making of the Modern World* (Boston, 1966).

6. See Immanuel Wallerstein, *The Modern World System* (New York, 1974); Eric Wolf, *Peasant Wars of the Twentieth Century* (New York, 1969) and *Europe and the People without History* (Berkeley, 1982); Perry Anderson, *Lineages of the Absolutist State* (London, 1974) and *Passages from Antiquity to Feudalism* (London, 1974); and Charles Tilly, ed., *The Formation of National States in Western Europe* (Princeton, 1975).

7. Philip Abrams, *Historical Sociology* (New York, 1982); Theda Skocpol, ed., *Vision and Method in Historical Sociology* (Cambridge, 1984).

8. Wallerstein's center is the Braudel Center, named in honor of the great French historian of the *Annales* school, Fernand Braudel. Tilly left Michigan in the mid-1980s and, with his partner, Louise Tilly, established the graduate program in historical studies at the New School for Social Research in New York. Brenner's center at UCLA is the Center for History and Social Theory.

9. Anthony Giddens, *Central Problems in Social Theory* (London, 1979).

10. Harry Braverman, *Labor and Monopoly Capital* (New York, 1974); Stuart Ewen, *Captains of Consciousness* (New York, 1976); Christopher Lasch, *Haven in a Heartless World* (New York, 1977); Russell Jacoby, *Social Amnesia* (Boston, 1975); and David Noble, *America by Design* (New York, 1977) and *Forces of Production* (New York, 1984). In fact, these works represented what was a developing school of American historical sociology and criticism.

11. E. H. Carr, *What Is History?* (New York, 1961).

12. Also, see E. H. Carr's earlier set of lectures for the BBC (British Broadcasting Corporation), *The New Society* (London, 1951).

13. C. Wright Mills, *The Causes of World War III* (New York, 1958).

14. Peter Bachrach, *The Theory of Democratic Elitism: A Critique* (Boston, 1967). I would also recommend Jim Miller, "Democracy and the Intellectual: C. Wright Mills Reconsidered," *Salmagundi*, nos. 70-71, spring-summer 1986, 82-107.

Chapter 23

1. Harvey J. Kaye, *The British Marxist Historians* (New York, 1995). Also, see H. J. Kaye and K. McClelland, eds., *E. P. Thompson: Critical Perspectives* (Philadelphia, 1990) and H. J. Kaye, *The Education of Desire: Marxists and the Writing of History* (New York, 1992). And, specifically on Edward Thompson, see Bryan Palmer, *E. P. Thompson: Objections and Oppositions* (London, 1994).

2. See, for example, Dorothy Thompson, *The Chartists* (New York, 1984), and *Outsiders* (London, 1993).

3. See J. Clarke, et al., eds., *Working Class Culture* (London, 1979).

4. See E. P. Thompson, "The Nehru Tradition," in Thompson, *Writing by Candlelight* (London, 1980). Also, see E. P. Thompson, *Alien Homage: Edward Thompson and Rabindranath Tagore* (New Delhi, 1993).

5. See E. P. Thompson, "The Liberation of Perugia," in *The Heavy Dancers* (London, 1985).

6. Theodosia Jessup Thompson and E. P. Thompson, eds., *There Is a Spirit in Europe: A Memoir of Frank Thompson* (London, 1947). Also forthcoming are Edward Thompson's lectures on Frank's wartime experience.

7. See E. P. Thompson, ed., *The Railway* (London, 1948).

8. See "Interview with E. P. Thompson," MARHO (Mid-Atlantic Radical Historians Organization), *Visions of History* (New York, 1983).

9. E. P. Thompson, *William Morris, Romantic to Revolutionary* (London, 1955; rev. ed. New York, 1977).

10. E. P. Thompson, *Out of Apathy* (London, 1960), 308.

11. E. P. Thompson, *The Making of the English Working Class* (London, 1963), 12.

12. For Perry Anderson's most developed critique of Thompson's work and politics see his book *Arguments within English Marxism* (London, 1980).

13. Marcus Rediker, "Getting Out of the Graveyard: Perry Anderson, Edward Thompson, and the Arguments of English Marxism," *Radical History Review,* no. 26 (1982), 125, and Fred Inglis, *Radical Earnestness* (Oxford, 1982), 199.

14. E. P. Thompson, *Whigs and Hunters: The Origins of the Black Act* (New York, 1975), and *Customs in Common: Studies in Traditional Popular Culture* (New York, 1992). Also, see Douglas Hay, Peter Linebaugh, and E. P. Thompson, eds., *Albion's Fatal Tree* (New York, 1975).

15. E. P. Thompson, Raymond Williams, and S. Hall, eds., *May Day Manifesto 1968* (London, 1968). On the Warwick events, see E. P. Thompson, ed., *Warwick University Ltd* (London, 1970).

16. E. P. Thompson, *The Poverty of Theory and Other Essays* (London, 1978).

17. See Thompson's *Writing by Candlelight.*

18. The pamphlet was reprinted in the book *Protest and Survive* (London, 1980). Also, see Thompson's authored and edited works: *Beyond the Cold War* (London, 1982); *Exterminism and Cold War* (London, 1982); *The Heavy Dancers* (1985); *Star Wars* (London, 1985); *Mad Dogs* (London, 1986); and *Prospectus for a Habitable Planet* (London, 1987).

19. Fred Inglis, "Thompson Invictus," the *Nation,* September 20, 1993.

20. See, for example, *Détente and Socialist Democracy—A Discussion with Roy Medvedev* (Nottingham, 1975).

21. For example, see the END (European Nuclear Disarmament) Special Report, *The New Hungarian Peace Movement* (1982).

22. E. P. Thompson, "History Turns on a New Hinge," the *Nation,* January 29, 1990.

23. E. P. Thompson, *The Sykaos Papers* (London, 1988).

24. E. P. Thompson, *Witness against the Beast* (New York, 1993) and *Persons and Polemics* (London, 1994).

25. See Thompson's "Homage to Tom McGrath," in *The Heavy Dancers.*

26. E. P. Thompson, *The Poverty of Theory and Other Essays,* 192.

Chapter 24

1. Russell Jacoby, *The Last Intellectuals: American Culture in the Age of Academe* (New York, 1987).

2. See Jon Wiener, *Professors, Politics and Pop* (New York, 1992).

Chapter 25

1. See Michael Crozier, Samuel P. Huntington, and Joji Watanuki, *The Crisis of Democracy: Report on the Governability of Democracies to the Trilateral Commission* (New York, 1975), 79.

2. Ibid., 6-7.

3. The best known books in this genre are: Allan Bloom, *The Closing of the American Mind* (New York, 1987); Roger Kimball, *Tenured*

Radicals (New York, 1990); Charles Sykes, *Profscam* (New York, 1990); Dinesh D'Souza, *Illiberal Education* (New York, 1991); and Martin Anderson, *Impostors in the Temple* (New York, 1992). On the making of the New Right and their originating the culture wars in the "crisis of history" discourse, see Harvey J. Kaye, *The Powers of the Past* (Minneapolis, 1991).

4. For a copy of the TDC (Teachers for a Democratic Culture) manifesto, see Patricia Aufderheide, ed., *Beyond PC: Towards a Politics of Understanding* (St Paul, Minn, 1992), 67-70. For essays in the "culture wars" by one of the founding figures of the TDC, see Gerald Graff, *Beyond the Culture Wars: How Teaching the Conflicts Can Revitalize American Education* (New York, 1992).

5. See Ellen Messer-Davidow, "Manufacturing the Attack on Liberalized Higher Education," *Social Text*, no. 36, Fall 1993, 40-81.

6. Russell Jacoby, *The Last Intellectuals: American Culture in the Age of Academe* (New York, 1987).

7. For example, see Jacoby's *Social Amnesia* (Boston, 1975) and *Dialectic of Defeat: Contours of Western Marxism* (New York, 1981).

8. See Lynn Garafola, "The Last Intellectuals," *New Left Review*, no. 169, May/June 1988, 122-28.

9. Perhaps, the right is too well funded to give it up; but there are also those on the left who seem to like wallowing in the PC discourse. On the right see the special issue of *Partisan Review*, "The Politics of Political Correctness," vol. 60, no. 4 (1993); and, on the left, see "A Symposium on Political Correctness," *Social Text*, no. 36, fall 1993, 1-39.

10. I recollect an early newspaper review of *Dogmatic Wisdom*—which I have lost—rightly, and favorably, comparing it with Robert Hughes's *Culture of Complaint: The Fraying of America* (New York, 1993).

11. Here, I must recommend Jonathan Kozol, *Savage Inequalities* (New York, 1992).

12. Without assistants, I teach seven classes a year, including, each semester, an introductory course with up to 200 predominantly first-generation students; and, while I admit to being endowed with a "named professorship," my salary is a very far cry from six figures.

13. C. Wright Mills, *The Sociological Imagination* (New York, 1959).

INDEX